MW00856907

ARCHIVAL BASICS

**AMERICAN ASSOCIATION
FOR STATE AND LOCAL HISTORY
BOOK SERIES**

SERIES EDITOR
Rebecca K. Shrum, Indiana University–Purdue University Indianapolis

MANAGING EDITOR
John Garrison Marks, AASLH

EDITORIAL BOARD
Anne W. Ackerson, Leading by Design
William Bomar, University of Alabama Museums
Jonathan Cain, University of Oregon Libraries
Jessica Dorman, The Historic New Orleans Collection
Laura Koloski, Pew Center for Arts & Heritage
Russell Lewis, Chicago History Museum
Jane Lindsay, Juneau-Douglas City Museum
Ann E. McCleary, University of West Georgia
Maria Montalvo, Emory University
Porchia Moore, Johns Hopkins University
Debra Reid, The Henry Ford
Laura Roberts, Roberts Consulting
Kimberly Springle, Charles Sumner School Museum and Archives
William S. Walker, Cooperstown Graduate Program, SUNT Oneonta

ABOUT THE SERIES
The American Association for State and Local History Book Series addresses issues critical to the field of state and local history through interpretive, intellectual, scholarly, and educational texts. To submit a proposal or manuscript to the series, please request proposal guidelines from AASLH headquarters: AASLH Editorial Board, 2021 21st Ave. South, Suite 320, Nashville, Tennessee 37212. Telephone: (615) 320-3203. Website: www.aaslh.org.

ABOUT THE ORGANIZATION
The American Association for State and Local History (AASLH) is a national history membership association headquartered in Nashville, Tennessee, that provides leadership and support for its members who preserve and interpret state and local history in order to make the past more meaningful to all people. AASLH members are leaders in preserving, researching, and interpreting traces of the American past to connect the people, thoughts, and events of yesterday with the creative memories and abiding concerns of people, communities, and our nation today. In addition to sponsorship of this book series, AASLH publishes *History News* magazine, a newsletter, technical leaflets and reports, and other materials; confers prizes and awards in recognition of outstanding achievement in the field; supports a broad education program and other activities designed to help members work more effectively; and advocates on behalf of the discipline of history. To join AASLH, go to www.aaslh.org or contact Membership Services, AASLH, 2021 21st Ave. South, Suite 320, Nashville, TN 37212.

The Council of State Archivists (CoSA) is a nonprofit membership organization of the state and territorial government archives in the fifty states, five territories, and District of Columbia. Through collaborative research, education, and advocacy, CoSA provides leadership that strengthens and supports state and territorial archives in their work to preserve and provide access to government records. CoSA facilitates networking, information sharing, and project collaboration among its member organizations to help state and territorial government archives with their responsibilities for protecting the rights and historical documents of the American people. Read more at www.statearchivists.org

ARCHIVAL BASICS

A Practical Manual for Working with Historical Collections

Charlie Arp

Rowman & Littlefield
Lanham • Boulder • New York • London

Credits and acknowledgments of sources for material or information used with permission appear on the appropriate page within the text.

Published by Rowman & Littlefield
An imprint of The Rowman & Littlefield Publishing Group, Inc.
4501 Forbes Boulevard, Suite 200, Lanham, Maryland 20706
www.rowman.com

6 Tinworth Street, London, SE11 5AL, United Kingdom

Copyright © 2019 by The Rowman & Littlefield Publishing Group, Inc.

All rights reserved. No part of this book may be reproduced in any form or by any electronic or mechanical means, including information storage and retrieval systems, without written permission from the publisher, except by a reviewer who may quote passages in a review.

British Library Cataloguing in Publication Information Available

Library of Congress Cataloging-in-Publication Data

Names: Arp, Charlie, 1954– author.
Title: Archival basics : a practical manual for working with historical
  collections / Charlie Arp.
Description: Lanham : Rowman & Littlefield, 2019. | Series: American
  Association for State and Local History book series | Includes
  bibliographical references and index.
Identifiers: LCCN 2018052706 (print) | LCCN 2018053112 (ebook) | ISBN
  9781538104569 (Electronic) | ISBN 9781538104545 (cloth : alk. paper) |
  ISBN 9781538104552 (pbk. : alk. paper)
Subjects: LCSH: Archives—Handbooks, manuals, etc. | Archival
  materials—Handbooks, manuals, etc.
Classification: LCC CD950 (ebook) | LCC CD950 .A77 2019 (print) | DDC
  027—dc23
LC record available at https://lccn.loc.gov/2018052706

∞™ The paper used in this publication meets the minimum requirements of American National Standard for Information Sciences—Permanence of Paper for Printed Library Materials, ANSI/NISO Z39.48-1992.

Printed in the United States of America

Contents

There are templates and documents referenced at different points in the book for you to use and modify as needed to fit your circumstances. Examples of these templates and documents include a collections policy worksheet, an appraisal scorecard, a blank deposit agreement, a facilities assessment questionnaire, and a reference policy among others. The templates and documents are available free to you via download from the AASLH website at https://learn.aaslh.org/archivalbasics as Word and/or PDF documents.

List of Illustrations

Figures

Tables

Preface

Archival Basics: A Practical Manual for Working with Historical Collections was written to give people who are responsible for the care of historical records but who have not been formally trained in archival work an introduction to managing and protecting historical record collections. It focuses on the fundamental concepts needed to collect, preserve, and provide access to archival records. It is based on the Basics of Archival Continuing Education (BACE) course, created with funding provided by a 2001 National Leadership grant from the Institute of Museum and Library Services (IMLS).

This book is intended for anyone who works with historical records who has not been formally trained as an archivist. If you are a museum curator who needs archival skills, a librarian in charge of archival special collections, a volunteer for a historical society, or a town employee who oversees historical government records, this book is for you. The archival concepts, strategies, and skills taught in this book are the same for nonprofit, for-profit, public, or private organizations.

Purpose

Archival Basics: A Practical Manual for Working with Historical Collections introduces the basic archival concepts and gives practical advice on implementing those concepts. It focuses on the policies, procedures, and assessments every archival institution needs to use to function legally and effectively. I explain these policies, procedures, and assessments to you and provide you with the templates so you can create your own version of these documents based on your organization's specific circumstances and needs.

In some cases, I give advice described as good, better, or best. This organizational scheme enables you to pick the level of implementation advice best suited to your needs. Good implementation advice is defined as the minimum steps an archival organization needs to take in whatever topic is being discussed. Better implementation advice goes beyond that and best implementation advice defines how a mature archival organization handles an archival task or responsibility. The book also provides additional resources on archival topics so if you want more information on specific topics you know where to find it. This is not the only reference book someone working in an archives should have, but it may be the first book they should have.

There are two themes running throughout the book. The first is that the answer to most archival questions depends on circumstances. The circumstances of the collection or item you are working with and/or institutional circumstances including the resources available to you will determine the right course of action for you to take. What is right for one institution or for one collection may not be correct for another.

The second theme is what I call the underlying philosophical theme of archival work—*as archivists we need to preserve the collections in our care while providing access to them.* There is an on-going struggle, a tension in archival work between preserving and protecting the records we collect and making those records available for research. If we do not protect the records in our care, we fail history. If we do not let researchers use the records we collect, there is no reason for us to collect records. Most archivists will agree that preservation trumps access. Balancing access and preservation is the essence of archival work.

Organization

The book is organized in thirteen chapters and concluding remarks.

Chapter 1—Introduction to Archives and Archivists
Chapter 2—Collections Policy
Chapter 3—Appraisal
Chapter 4—Accessioning
Chapter 5—Arrangement
Chapter 6—Preservation
Chapter 7—Description
Chapter 8—Housing Collections
Chapter 9—Security and Disaster Planning
Chapter 10—Reference
Chapter 11—Outreach
Chapter 12—Digital Records
Chapter 13—Digitization
Conclusion

The chapters are comprised of sections and most chapters end with a quiz and a summary. The quizzes test your understanding of the major points covered in the chapter. Definitions, implementation tips, and exercises are highlighted in boxes throughout the book. Many definitions are included in the quiz questions.

There are templates and documents referenced at different points in the book for you to use and modify as needed to fit your circumstances. Examples of these templates and documents include a collections policy worksheet, an appraisal scorecard, a blank deposit agreement, a facilities assessment questionnaire, and a reference policy among others. The templates and documents are available free to you via download from the AASLH website at https://learn.aaslh.org/archivalbasics as Word and/or PDF documents.

Acknowledgments

This book uses the content of the Basics of Archival Continuing Education (BACE) course funded by a 2001 Institute of Museums and Library Services (IMLS) National Leadership grant. The BACE course was designed to give organizations and individuals responsible for the care of historical records who lacked formal archival training an introduction to the core functions of managing and protecting historical records collections. The content of the BACE course was created by myself, Kathleen Roe, and Raymond LaFever of the New York State Archives, and Sandra Clark and Phillip Kwiatkowski from the Michigan Historical Center. Two consultants, Grace Lessner and Judy Cobb, also contributed to the BACE content as editors.

I have augmented the BACE course content based on experience and the comments from those taking the online BACE course sponsored by the American Association of State and Local History (AASLH), which I have proctored since 2003. I have also added chapters on digital records and digitization to the book due to the changing needs of those working with historical records. These topics were not covered in the BACE course because they were considered out of scope at that time. I asked for help creating this new content from the Council of State Archivists (CoSA), who along with AASLH have been involved with the BACE project from the beginning. While I am confident in my knowledge and experience, I wanted others knowledgeable on these issues to edit and comment on this new content before presenting it. Anne Ackerson, then executive director of CoSA, asked for volunteers, and Veronica Martzahl from the Massachusetts State Archives, Nick Connizzo of the Vermont State Archives, and Allen Ramsey from the Connecticut State Archives, offered to work with me. The chapters on digital records and digitization would not be possible without their gracious assistance.

As the book neared completion, Charles Harmon of Rowman & Littlefield and I decided to ask CoSA to review the entire book. Barbara Teague, executive director of CoSA, graciously agreed to ask for other reviewers, and Beth Golding, Florida State archivist, and Christian Skipper, appraisal and outreach archivist at the Maryland State Archives, agreed to review the book. Anne W. Ackerson of Creative Leadership & Management Solutions and former executive director of CoSA, facilitated their review. John Marks, senior manager of strategic initiatives for AASLH, also had two anonymous individuals review the book. I thank all the reviewers, Barbara and CoSA, and Mark and AASLH for all their kind assistance in writing this book.

Like every author, I need to thank those who influenced my career. I would not have become an archivist without the help of George Bain, the soft-spoken Virginia gentleman who was the University Archivist at Ohio University, and my mentor. John Stewart, my first archival supervisor at the Ohio Historical Society (OHS) helped me understand the realities of working in archives. George Parkinson, then director of the Archives Library Division of OHS forced me to write clearer and justify my decisions. George and I didn't always see eye to eye, but I always respected him. He had an immense impact on my archival education and career.

I had the great fortune to work with four women who took the rough edges off my personality and helped me appreciate the nuances of archives. They all worked for me at one time or another and they are all intelligent, hard-working, and motivated archivists or record managers. Laurie Gemmill Arp, Janet Carleton, Jennifer Seymour, and Jane Wildermuth have all had great influence on me and my career.

To say that I owe a lot to Kathleen Roe is an understatement. She has been a great friend and a great leader in the archival profession. The BACE course would never have come about without her efforts, connections, and skills. This book would never have come about without the efforts of Bob Beaty and John Marks of AALSH, Barbara Teague, executive director of CoSA, and Anne Ackerson of Creative Leadership & Management Solutions.

My children, Ben, Harry, and Emily, have taught me the meaning of life. My lovely wife, Laurie Gemmill Arp, has given me sage council on all matters. Her opinions have been of immense help in writing this book. My life would be empty without her encouragement and love.

Lastly, I commend you for taking the time to read this book. By doing so you have demonstrated your commitment to saving the history of your community, state, and our nation. Thank you for your efforts on behalf of history. Good luck with your life and archival endeavors.

Charlie Arp

Chapter 1

Introduction to Archives and Archivists

Organizations that hold historical records should have a historical records program in place that preserves those records in its care and assists people to use those records in a legally defensible and effective manner. The goal of this book is to provide you, as a caretaker of historical records, with the knowledge and tools to implement these basic requirements.

I hope that everyone reading this book uses it to conduct a thorough self-study and assessment to plan and take the appropriate actions to strengthen their historical records program. Developing a strong historical records program requires time, energy, resources, commitment, and, often, patience. But it's well worth the effort. A strong historic records program can make a difference in how our history will be defined and taught in the future.

The first chapter of this book provides an introduction to the archives, basic terminology, and key concepts. There are six sections in this chapter. In section I, "Records," I will define records, archival or historical records, and those who use them. In section II, "More about Historical Records," we will discuss the unique nature and format of historical records, their intrinsic value, and how to distinguish historical records from other records. Section III "Historic Records Collections" covers those who keep historical records and which types of institutions hold which types of materials. In section IV, I will go over the three meanings of archives. Section V defines what it means to be an archivist. The last section contains the chapter summary, additional resources, an exercise, and a quiz.

Section I: Records

People and organizations create and use records as they communicate with one another and conduct business. Records are produced as a result of what we do as individuals and as organizations. Records offer evidence of our activities and relationships, providing information about associated people, organizations, events, and places.

All records have value when they are created, but the value of most records decreases over time. Most records don't need to be kept beyond the period of time when they are of immediate use including the period of time during which they may be occasionally referred.

> *Records*—documents in any form containing information created by an individual or organization during the course of their activities. Records offer evidence of activities and relationships.

Others records have enduring historical value. These records are called *archival records (archives)* or *historical records*.

Examples of records include canceled checks, invoices, letters, diaries, files, financial ledgers, notes, photographs, drawings and illustrations, minutes, calendars, dockets, memoirs, rosters, resolutions, audio-visual materials, computer files, and email. All of these are *records* and some of them are *historical records*.

Historical Records

Records are the "by-product" of life's activities: what we do at work, at school, and at home; what we do as individuals and as groups. "Historical records" are distinguished from "records" by their *enduring historical value*. Typically, historical records are less than 5 percent of all records created. Yet the number of historical records in our communities, states, and nation are enormous, containing billions of pieces of evidence about the past. Despite the huge volume of these historical records, they give us just a tiny glimpse into the past. Many activities are not documented, and many sources of information have been lost or destroyed.

> *Historical Records* (aka archival records)—unique, unpublished resources that provide facts, opinions, viewpoints, and content that cannot be found in any other resource and are determined to have research value.

Historical records are created by both individuals and organizations as part of their normal work. People keep journals, write diaries and autobiographies, create family trees, and save business and personal letters and papers. Organizations create annual reports, legal contracts, meeting minutes, project files, and other business records.

When historic records are created, they are kept in a specific context and managed within logical groups, like a correspondence file, a series of personal diaries, or a family's photograph collection. Unlike a published book that can stand on its own as an information resource, historical records only make sense when managed and reviewed within their creative and historical context. This means that when historical records are managed as part of a historical records program, they are managed in groups, usually called "collections." Collections contain many records, all related to each other.

> *Collection*—groups of records related to each other or items brought together from a variety of sources based on a theme or the holdings of an archival institution.

Collection is a term used in archives in three different ways. As I said earlier, it is a group of records related to each other in some manner. It can also mean items brought together by a collector (an individual or organization) from a variety of sources with some unifying characteristic, usually a subject or topic. Finally, it can mean the entire holdings of an archives (i.e., the collections of the Smith County Historical Society).

Here are some examples of historical records:

- Thirteenth Annual Report, Pennsylvania Anti-Slavery Society notes, January 22, 1845, Wilbur H. Siebert Underground Railroad Collection held by the Ohio History Connection[1]
- American Community Survey, 2004: Population Data File, on magnetic tape cartridge, Series: American Community Survey (ACS) Public Use Microdata Sample Files, 1996–2015, Record Group 29: Records of the Bureau of the Census, 1790–2007, held by the National Archives and Records Administration[2]
- Correspondence: Germany, 1963–1964, Ruth Gage-Colby papers, held by the Minnesota Historical Society[3]

- Dwight D. Eisenhower's Inaugural Address and Ceremonies on audio tape/reel, Series: Personal Set of Sound Recordings, 1933–1952, Collection: Dwight D. and Mamie Doud Eisenhower Collection, 1911–1959, held by the National Archives and Records Administration[4]
- Email database of Thomas E. Samoluk, deputy director and associate director for communications of the Assassination Records Review Board, April 1, 1994 through September 30, 1998, held by the National Archives and Records Administration[5]
- Genealogical chart and a list of estates owned by the Gale family's ancestors in England and the United States (1614–1875) compiled by Nick Duff, Gale Family Collection, held by the Minnesota Historical Society[6]
- Letter from Jonathan Marsh, September 16, 1986, Buckeyes Singles Collection, held by the Columbus (Ohio) Historical Society[7]
- Letter from Lt. Henry O. Flipper to Representative John A. T. Hull, October 23, 1898, Lt. Henry O. Flipper Collection, held by the National Archives and Records Administration[8]
- Minutes of the Executive Committee 1910–1936, Burden Iron Works Collection, held by the Rensselaer County (NY) Historical Society[9]
- Peshtigo Fire, engraved image dated November 21, 1871, held by the Wisconsin Historical Society[10]
- Roswell Garst and Nikita Khrushchev photograph, Joe Munroe Collection, held by the Ohio History Connection[11]

Some Uses of Historical Records

Records are deemed to be historical records when they have enduring value. Who are the records valuable to? Who uses them? Historical records are valuable to community members, scholars, students, journalists, genealogists, lawyers, and others who want to know about people, places, and events in the past. They matter to individuals, organizations, communities, and government. How are they used? In lots of ways!

People use records to

- Understand their legal and civil rights
- Trace their family history
- Restore their homes or automobiles
- Find art or craftwork to use as examples for current work
- Authenticate items in their collections
- Research hereditary medical conditions
- Research historic reenactment characters
- Trace their titles to property

Organizations use records to

- Document their legal and fiscal obligations through time
- Defend themselves against lawsuits
- Understand decisions that were made in the past and why those decisions were made
- Celebrate anniversaries or special events in their past
- Plan for the future by learning about the past
- Create public relations and marketing campaigns

Communities use records to

- Celebrate their heritage and history
- Research the historic preservation of property in a particular area
- Promote tourism

One particularly important group that creates historical records is government—national, state, and local. Government records with enduring historical value are cared for by a variety of organizations at the local, state, and federal levels. Government records allow society to

- Document the responsibilities of government officials and agencies to hold them accountable for their actions
- Establish and document the legal rights and responsibilities of citizens
- Document decisions and why they were made
- Document benefits and entitlements
- Establish legal rights

Examples of historical records created by government include

- Congressional and state records documenting the creation of laws
- U.S. Geological Survey maps with handwritten annotations identifying possible Native American burial sites
- The birth, death, marriage, and divorce records kept by every county and state

Section II: More about Historical Records

Now that we've defined historical records, and you've had the opportunity to think about their continual creation in day-to-day life, we're going to discuss the following:

- The uniqueness of historical records
- The format of historical records
- The intrinsic value of historical records
- How to distinguish historical records from other records

Historical records programs—a program within an organization that follows basic requirements to ensure the preservation of the historical record collections in its care and assists people to use those records.

The Uniqueness of Historical Records

Historical records are unique. They are generally one-of-a-kind, and this makes them special. Historical records are unpublished. The information in them is the result of a person's or organization's activities, not a publication to be reproduced and disseminated to an audience.

This unique, unpublished information provides facts, opinions, viewpoints, and content that cannot be found in any other resource. It often offers important documentation and a unique perspective of the background, events, and ideas associated with the creator of the records.

A good example of the unique nature of historical records is a record book of the Female Tract Society of St. John's Episcopal Church of Worthington, Ohio. The book contains minutes of the meeting held at the home of Philander Chase on November 2, 1817, where the society was founded. Minutes from subsequent meetings over the next two decades highlight the religious and social lives of the women of Worthington.

The Format of Historical Records

Historical records can be found in many physical formats, such as paper, microfilm, maps, movies, photographs, drawings, cassette tapes, and videotapes. Historical records can be electronic files found on any medium, computer disks, hard drives, and even in the cloud! And they don't have to be old! Historical records can include

- An oral history of local veterans, recorded on audiocassette tapes
- A video recording of a local school band performance
- Digital photographs recording a community bicentennial celebration

Remember that just because something is old, it isn't necessarily a historical record. An old textbook, published in 1898, is *not* a unique, unpublished resource. It might be a "rare book," but it is not a historical record.

Once in a while, something published might be archival—for example, if you have a copy of the *Grapes of Wrath* where someone has written notes about how his or her family had a similar experience. That particular book becomes archival—because of the added comments that make it a unique and unpublished record of that family's specific experience.

The Intrinsic Value of Historic Records

Some historical records have *intrinsic value* that requires they be retained and preserved in their original format. The actual format of the records is important or has value because of the way it was made, the material it was made from, who made it, or its historical context. Records with intrinsic value may

- Have unique physical features
- Have artistic or aesthetic qualities
- Have educational potential based on their original physical format.
- Be associated with famous people, places, events, or issues

Examples of Intrinsic Value

- A map drawn on a piece of animal skin
- A letter signed by Martin Luther King Jr.
- The original constitution of Oregon

> *Intrinsic value*—some records have value as a physical item because of why they were made, who made them, or what they were made of, they have value as an artifact.

How to Distinguish Historical Records from Other Records

One of the biggest challenges that you face as a caretaker of historical records is deciding which records have enduring historic value and which do not. Remember that the vast majority of records created by individuals and organizations have only temporary value. Your role is to identify which records will be important to history.

Think of your own personal records. As soon as you don't need them anymore, you will throw away most of your records, such as receipts, ticket stubs, and canceled checks. But

> **Tip:** *Historical Records* are unique, unpublished resources, but they are not the only resources collected by an archives. Many published items are also collected by archives to provide historical context to the records they collect. Examples include period newspapers, pamphlets, posters, sheet music, county histories, lineage books, atlases, telephone directories, rare books, and historical books just to name a few. While these published items are not unique, they contain information of enduring historical value or information that helps people understand the historical records collected. In many cases these published items have survived in small numbers, or they were published in such small numbers that they are essentially unique. Such items are not archival records, but they clearly have value to an archival program and so deserve the care, preservation, and availability that being included in an archives brings.
>
> To ensure that those using your archives can find published items, they should also be given the same kind of descriptive treatment as your historical records (i.e., cataloging entries). Archival collections and published items held in an archives are never circulated, they are not "checked out" and taken out of the archives. The primary difference between an archives and a library is that historical records and published items collected by an archives are not circulated.
>
> The type of archival and published items your archives collects depends on the needs of the audience you serve. As an example, if genealogists (those working on family histories) are the primary audience your archives serves, you should also consider collecting published and unpublished family histories. Such items will benefit your users and it will encourage them to support your archives by donating their own research to you. Do not discount the importance of published materials to your archives.

other records will be more valuable to you, and you will care for them more thoroughly, things like the deed to your property, your birth certificate, and family photographs.

Selecting which records have enduring historical value and which do not is called *appraisal*. Appraisal is discussed more thoroughly in chapter 3.

Section III: Historical Record Collections

Who Keeps Historical Records?

Historical records are found in all types of organizations:

- Businesses
- Educational institutions
- Organizations whose membership is based on ethnicity, religion, nationality, and so forth
- Formal archives
- Local government offices
- Local historical societies and organizations
- Public libraries
- Regional museums
- Religious organizations
- Service organizations

These are just a few of the kinds of organizations that place a high value on historical records. The historical records programs within these organizations need to be able to provide a basic level of care and handling for the historical records they hold—they need to preserve and make their historical records in their care available for research. Throughout this book I will return to this over and over, *as archivists we need to preserve the records in our care while providing access to them*. Archives exist to collect, preserve, and provide access to historical records.

Historical records held by historical records programs are often referred to as "their collections." The term *collections* has other definitions, but for now think of a collection as a group of records with a unifying concept.

Three Examples of Historical Records Programs

The Local History and Genealogy Department of the Public Library of Steubenville and Jefferson County (Ohio) has more than 4,400 items, including a wide variety of how-to guides. It employs one library staff member to assist those who want to use these records.

The Saint Lawrence County Historical Association (New York) is a not-for-profit organization that researches, collects, preserves, and interprets the history of Saint Lawrence County. Among its resources for genealogical research are a card index, family file, business directories, county and township histories, and other reference books. The town files can be searched for information on non-genealogy related subjects. Its collections include the Walter B. Leonard Collection. Leonard was a vaudevillian, composer, and writer from Canton, New York. The archives contains his original manuscripts, music, playbills, ephemera, photos, correspondence, and posters from the early twentieth century.

The Alaska Native Language Center is a center for research and documentation of the twenty Native languages of Alaska. It is internationally recognized as the major center in the United States for the study of Eskimo and Northern Athabascan languages. The center houses an archival collection of more than 10,000 items, and includes virtually everything written in or about Alaska Native languages, including copies of most of the earliest linguistic documentation, along with significant collections about related languages outside Alaska.

What Types of Institutions Hold Which Types of Materials?

Organizations that hold historical records often also hold other types of materials that have historical significance—artifacts and published materials. These three types of materials—records, publications, and artifacts—are related. However, they are handled, managed, and preserved in different ways and with distinct professional standards and practices.

In this section, I will briefly define these types of materials for you. In the chapters and sections that follow, I will discuss the standards and practices relating to *historical records.*

Historical Records

Historical records, or *archives*, are made, received, or accumulated by a person or organization because they have enduring historic value. They include papers, documents, photographs, maps, digital files, and other unique materials. Historical records are commonly referred to as "archives." The organizations that collect and keep them and the building they are housed in are also often called archives. The word *archives* can refer to collections of historical records, the building where they are kept, and the program or organization that manages the collections.

Archives—three definitions:

1. Materials relating to the history of an institution that are kept for permanent preservation because of their evidential or informational value (e.g., documents, photographs, books, maps, blueprints etc.)
2. The place or building where archival materials are stored and cared for
3. The organization that cares for archival materials

There are secondary definitions of the word archives. The word can refer to the archives profession. It can be used as a verb—as in, "to archive a record," meaning to bring it into an archive, preserve it and make it available for use. Information technology (IT) professionals also use archive to signify taking a record offline. While all these uses of the word *archive* are valid. I will not use these secondary definitions of archives in this book.

Artifacts and Objects

Artifacts are tangible objects created for a certain purpose by individuals, organizations, and even nature. Artifacts may be collected and preserved by museums and other historical organizations, to document specific themes such as natural history, aviation, or music.

A *museum* is an organization that preserves and makes artifacts of historical value available as exhibits to the public for educational or aesthetic purposes. If you have artifacts in your collections, they need to be managed using museum practices.

Published Materials

Publications are printed materials that are created for distribution by individuals and organizations. They may include newspapers, books, magazines, and audio and video materials. Publications are collected and maintained by libraries.

A *library* is an organization that exists to collect and circulate published material. As stated earlier, there are many published items held in archives to provide context for the archival collections. The primary difference between an archives and a library is that the focus of a library is to collect published items and make them available for circulation. Items collected by an archive are not circulated. Things can get confusing as some libraries have small archives often focused on local history collections within their facilities.

Tip: Do not let the exceptions, the small collections that archives, museums, and libraries hold confuse you. An archives will hold documents with intrinsic value that are artifacts, like the constitution of a state. A museum will often hold archival collections that document the history of the artifacts it holds. A library may hold rare books or smaller archival collections. What distinguishes an archive, a museum, and a library from each other is their primary purpose, their overarching mission.

Table 1.1. Comparison Chart of Functions and Responsibilities of Archives, Libraries, and Museums

Category	Archival Collections	Library Collections	Museum Artifacts and Collections
Nature of collection	Unpublished, unique, groups of related items, significance related to other items	Published, available elsewhere, independent separate and individual items	Artifacts or objects that support broad collection themes
How materials are received	Considered and selected as a group	Selected as single items	Considered and selected as both single items and a group
How materials are arranged	Original order maintained if possible; archivist-determined arrangement otherwise	Predetermined subject classification system already established	Original order sometimes maintained; established by curator
How materials are organized and described	As record groups (collection of items)	As individual items	As individual items and as groups of items
How information about materials is provided	Guides, finding aids, inventories, indexes, online systems often using standardized descriptive information	Standardized descriptive information is available through a card or online public access catalog	Inventories and catalog entries through a card or online catalog
How materials are accessed and secured	Closed stacks, restricted access; items do not leave the archives' premises; special procedures allow researchers access while ensuring safety of records	Open stacks, most items may leave the library's premises	Restricted access, items usually available through exhibits, items do not leave the museum's premises except by special arrangement (loans to other institutions)
What items within collections are known as	Archival records, documents, manuscripts, ephemera	Books, magazines, maps, audio and video tapes	Artifacts, tangible objects
What those who care for the collections are known as professionally	Archivist	Librarian	Collections manager, registrar, or curator

Section IV: What Is an Archives?

Definitions

There are three primary definitions of archives, archives as records, archives as repositories, and archives as organizations.

Archives Are Records

"Archives" can refer to noncurrent records or groups of records collected and preserved by an individual or organization. In this case, archives are the papers, documents, files, photographs, and other materials created by individuals or organizations. They are the unique records people will want or need to use, now and in the future, to understand their history and society, to provide evidence for legal purposes, to prove ownership and rights, or to demonstrate how organizations operated and how people lived. In this case, "archives" are the historical records collected, preserved, and made available to researchers.

Archives Are Repositories

"Archives" can also refer to a building or part of a building where archival records are located. Here, "archives" refers to a physical location or facility. Archival repositories vary widely in size and structure, depending on the needs of the organizations and their budgets. They range from large, elaborate, well-funded physical facilities such as the National Archives to small, limited facilities such as a room at a local public library.

Archives Are Organizations

Finally, "archives" may also mean an organization, program, or agency that is responsible for managing and preserving historical records. I have referred to this earlier in this chapter as a "historical records program." For the purposes of this book, the two terms will be used interchangeably.

How many archival organizations can be found in the United States? The report, "Where History Begins,"[12] provides information from a 1997 survey that indicated there are more than 3,500 private, nonprofit repositories in the twenty-six states that responded to the survey. If you add to this the other states and all the local government archives plus archival organizations that have been created since 1997 that number could exceed 10,000 nationally!

Who Is in the "Archives Business"?

An *organization* may have its own archives responsible for the historical records of that organization.

A *state or local government* may have its own archives responsible for the historical records created by that government.

A *public library* may have a distinct historical records program that preserves local historical records.

A *historic house museum* may have historical records from the families that lived there.

A *county historical society* may have historical records as well as books and artifacts reflecting the history of the county.

What Is the Business of an Archives?

Archives are found in many different contexts: public and private; individual and organizational; profit and nonprofit; small and large; national and local. No matter what the circumstances, all archival programs have the same fundamental goals.

An archives:

- Ensures that historical records are collected, identified, organized, preserved, and made available for use
- Enables understanding the experience of others
- Provides information on history and cultural heritage
- Puts events and information into historical context

Section V: What Is an Archivist?

Archivists have formal training and experience in the management of historical materials. They may have received a formal education in archival administration in an academic setting or at a special archives institute or a series of workshops. Academic areas of formal study for archivists may include: library and information science, history, public history, or historical administration.

> *Archivist*—A person with formal training and experience in the management of historical records.

The Primary Tasks of an Archivist

While the focus of all archivists is to develop and maintain physical and intellectual control over historical records, an archivist may wear many hats. They may focus on one specific area of the archives field, or may even focus on one specific collection or kind of collection.

So, you may wonder, what are the tasks an archivist does?

Appraisal

Archivists *select* records. This process requires an understanding of:

- The historical context in which the records were created
- The uses for which they were intended
- Their relationship of the records to other sources
- The archival institution's collections policy

> *Appraisal*—the process of determining the value of records based on their current use; their informational value; their arrangement and condition; and their relationship to other records. An archival appraisal evaluates the enduring value of records for research use, not the monetary value of the records.

During this selection process, archivists distinguish between records and historical records and identify the historical records that should be collected by the archives based on its collections policy. Archivists refer to this process as *appraisal*.

Arrangement and Description

An archivist *organizes* and *describes* historical records. This is accomplished by *arranging* them in a logical order, *protecting* their condition, and *describing* them so users can find what they are looking for. Archivists call these functions *arrangement and description*.

Arrangement and description—the process of organizing historical records according to accepted archival principals and recording information about historical record collections in a standardized format.

Reference

An archivist helps users locate the records they need and helps them use the records. Archivists refer to these services as *reference services*.

Reference—activities that help users locate and properly use the historical records they need.

Outreach

An archivist promotes the historical records collections to increase awareness and the usefulness of the archives. Archivists refer to this as *outreach*.

Outreach—promoting archives and/or historical record collections to raise awareness of their existence and usefulness.

Preservation

An archivist ensures the safety and security of the records at all times, while encouraging their use for research and educational purposes. Archivists call this *preservation*.

Preservation—Practices and procedures designed to ensure the safety and security of historical records.

Other Activities

Most importantly, archivists are familiar with professional standards and practices and follow these in all aspects of their work.

Table 1.2.   How Is an Archivist Different from Other Related Professionals?

Archivist	Historian
Collects, preserves, and makes accessible historical records	Uses the historical records identified, arranged, and preserved by the archivist for historical research.
Archivist	**Librarian**
Collects, preserves, and makes accessible historical records	Collects, preserves, and makes accessible published materials
Employs professional standards and practices unique to archival collections	Employs professional standards and practices unique to published material
Archivist	**Museum curator**
Collects, preserves, and makes accessible historical records in paper, film, electronic, or others forms of documentation	Collects, preserves, and makes accessible mostly objects and artifacts

Section VI: Chapter Summary, Exercise, and Exam

"Of all the national assets, Archives are the most precious: They are the gift of one generation to another and the extent of our care of them marks the extent of our civilization."

—Arthur G. Doughty, Dominion Archivist, 1904–1935

Archival or historical records provide facts, opinions, viewpoints, and content that cannot be found in other resources. We keep archives because they serve as a memory—both to those who created them and to the wider community. They document transactions, actions, legal rights, and obligations and they provide organizations with a perspective upon which to base future actions. Archival records are also kept for historical or cultural reasons. Researchers use them to find evidence of the past. The photographs, films, letters, personal diaries, and official documents kept in archives tell us about different aspects of our collective history and culture.

Archivists follow standards and best practices to manage historical records collections. As you work your way through this book, you will learn about those professional best practices that can help you better care for your organization's historical treasures.

Additional Resources

The publications of the Society of American Archivists are very helpful: http://saa.archiv ists.org/store/items. Those titles marked with "AFSII" are the Archival Fundamental Series II. These publications are great foundational references that you will find helpful throughout your work in archives.

To learn more about the full range of archival training available, visit the websites of

- The American Association of State and Local History (AASLH)—Calendar: http://www.aaslh.org
- The Society of American Archivists—SAA Continuing Education Calendar: http://www2.archivists.org
- The Council of State Archivists—CoSA Webinar Series: http://www.statearchiv ists.org

Exercise

Think about all the activities you were involved in during the past twenty-four hours. List as many of these activities as you can remember.

For each activity on your list, write down what evidence, if any, your activities might have left behind.

Review your entire list, and what you wrote about evidence your activities left behind. Then answer these questions:

- Which of your daily activities were most likely to leave trace evidence behind?
- What, if any, of that evidence might be preserved for the future? Why?
- What might be left out of a historical record of your activities? Why?

What would a future historian be able to tell about your life and your society based on evidence of your daily activities that might be preserved for the future?

Chapter 1 Quiz

See the answers on page 323.

1. All of the below are records except:
   a. Canceled checks
   b. Published atlas from 1905
   c. Dockets
   d. Oral histories

2. Historical records are:
   a. Always on animal skins
   b. Always have intrinsic value
   c. Published
   d. Unpublished sources of unique information
3. Choose the historical record:
   a. Bank statements
   b. Old textbooks
   c. *Deepwater Weekly News*, 1923–present
   d. City council minutes
4. What kind of organization could be responsible for historical records?
   a. Local public library
   b. Mayor's office
   c. Religious organization
   d. All the above
5. The term archives means:
   a. Historical records preserved by an organization
   b. A building where historical records are located
   c. An entity responsible for managing and preserving historical records
   d. All of the above
6. An individual could use historical records to:
   a. Trace property ownership
   b. Complete their state income tax forms
   c. Look for a published obituary from 1987
   d. Find out what movie to see this weekend
7. A newspaper from 1957 is not a historical record because:
   a. It is at the local public library
   b. It is published
   c. It contains no useful information
   d. It is not very old
8. Town council minutes from 1876 through 1941 have been microfilmed. These minutes are historical records because:
   a. They have been microfilmed
   b. They are pretty old
   c. They provide unique official and unpublished documentation of the actions of the town council
   d. They were created by a government entity
9. An archivist's primary responsibility includes:
   a. Appraisal
   b. Arrangement and description
   c. Access
   d. Preservation
   e. All the above
10. When I complete this course, I will be a professional archivist?
    a. T
    b. F

Notes

1. Ohio History Connection, Wilbur H. Siebert Underground Railroad Collection, "13th Annual Report, Pennsylvania Anti-Slavery Society, Notes, Jan. 22 1845," accessed March 2018. http://ohiomemory.org/cdm/compoundobject/collection/siebert/id/28565/rec/4

2. National Archives and Records Administration, National Archives Catalog, American Community Survey, "2004 Population Data File," accessed March 2018. https://catalog.archives.gov/id/2945488

3. Minnesota Historical Society, Collection Finding Aids, Manuscript Collection, "Ruth Gage–Colby: An Inventory of Her Papers at MHS," accessed March 2018. http://www2.mnhs.org/library/findaids/00572.xml#a9

4. National Archives and Records Administration, National Archives Catalog, "Dwight D. Eisenhower's Inaugural Address and Ceremonies, Jan. 20, 1953," accessed March 1018. https://catalog.archives.gov/id/2173106

5. National Archives and Records Administration, National Archives Catalog, accessed March 2018. https://catalog.archives.gov/id/74887457

6. Minnesota Historical Society, Collection Finding Aids, Manuscript Collection, "Gale Family: An Inventory of their Family Papers at MHS," accessed March 2018. http://www2.mnhs.org/library/findaids/00319.xml#a9

7. Columbus Historical Society, Buckeye Singles Collection, "Letter from Jonathon Marks, Sept. 16, 1986," accessed March 2018. https://static1.squarespace.com/static/576ed3a8579fb313164109e6/t/59287799cd0f68ce1b64dd0c/1495824281787/Buckeye+Singles+Collection.pdf

8. National Archives and Records Administration, On-line Exhibits, "Letter from Lt. Henry O. Flipper to Representative John A. T. Hull, October 23, 1898," accessed March 2018. https://www.archives.gov/exhibits/featured-documents/henry-flipper

9. Rensselaer County Historical Society, "Burden Iron Works," accessed March 2018. https://www.rchsonline.org/finding-aids-1/burden-iron-works

10. Wisconsin Historical Society, "Peshtigo Fire, Nov. 25, 1871," accessed March 2018. https://www.wisconsinhistory.org/Records/Image/IM1784

11. Ohio History Connection, Ohio Memory, Joe Munroe Collection, "Roswell Garst and Nikita Khrushchev Photograph, 1959," accessed March 2018. http://www.ohiomemory.org/cdm/singleitem/collection/p16007coll15/id/203

12. Irons Walch, Victoria. 1998. *Where History Begins: A Report on the Historical Record Repositories in the United States,* Council of State Historical Records Coordinators. OCLC # 39853966

Chapter 2

Collections Policy

A collections policy is one of the foundational documents of an archival or historical records programs. It defines what kinds of archival or historic records your institution will and will not collect. In this chapter, you'll find out how and why to write an effective collections policy. There are four sections in this chapter. Section I defines what a collections policy is. In section II, I get you started writing your own collections policy by helping you assess your organization's capabilities and resources and show you some examples of collections policies. Section III goes over the elements of a collections policy. Section IV contains the chapter summary and exercise.

Section I: What Is a Collections Policy?

A collections policy is a practical statement that defines

- What your organization should collect
- How it should collect
- How to dispose of collections that are no longer valuable to your organization

Collections Policy—informs staff, users, and other interested parties about why and how your program collects historical records. Through this policy your organization defines the scope of its collections, specifies the subjects and format of historical records it will accept into its collections, and explains the process it will use to acquire and dispose of records.

There are common elements to all collection policies, but the key to an *effective* policy is that it takes into account the unique purpose and context of your institution. Your institution's collections policy may change over time to reflect changes in your organization. As you write or revise your collections policy, keep in mind that your goal is to create a practical document, based on a realistic assessment of your program's scope and capabilities.

When an organization accepts records that are not "quite" within its collecting scope, it is taking resources away from other records that are within its scope. Without a collections policy, your organization may find that

- It is competing with other repositories for similar records while no one collects other valuable records.
- It is using valuable resources on collections that aren't relevant to its mission.
- Its collections lack cohesion, and therefore are not as useful to researchers as they should be.

Section II: Assessing Your Capabilities and Resources

Before sitting down to write your collections policy, you should analyze your goals and resources. Remember that when your program accepts historical records collections, it is making a commitment to take care of and provide access to those collections *permanently*. Acceptance of a collection is a very real commitment of your resources, so your policy needs to be based on an honest assessment of those resources.

As you read through the assessment portion of this section, use the "Assess Your Resources Worksheet" provided as appendix A at the back of the book to record your answers to these questions for yourself and your program. The assessment you create will help you develop a new collections policy for your organization or review and revise your existing collections policy. There is also an electronic version of this form you can download from the American Association of State and Local History (AASLH) website at https://learn.aaslh.org/archivalbasics. You are free to modify and use this form as you wish. Save the "Assess Your Resources Worksheet" that you have filled out; you will use it later on in this chapter.

What Are Your Program's Financial Resources?

What money is available to cover ongoing operating costs, staff salaries, supplies, preservation, and other items? Given your financial resources, should your collecting program be small, medium, or large in size and scope? Archivists generally consider it unethical to collect materials that the organization cannot manage and make accessible.

How Much Space Is Available?

Is your storage area full or empty, or somewhere in between? How much more can you collect before your storage area is filled? Collections come in many sizes. If you have a limited capacity to store collections, your policy should set parameters for the size of collections that you can accommodate.

What Kind of Material Can You Take Care Of?

Most programs collect historical records on paper. Other formats that can be collected include photographs, video, audio, microfilm, or digital records.

All of these formats require special storage and handling that may be beyond the resources of some programs. For example, if you do not have microfilm readers and reader/printers, it is wise to specifically state in your collecting policy that you will not accept microfilm. If you cannot preserve or provide access to digital records should your archives collect them? Your collections policy should be specific about what formats you will and will not accept based on what formats you can preserve and provide access to.

Can Your Program Support Materials in Poor Physical Condition?

Materials that are deteriorating and in poor condition may require reformatting and/or work by a conservation specialist in order to ensure their survival and accessibility. Can you afford to reformat records? Can you afford to hire or contract with a conservation specialist?

Does Your Program Have Enough Staff with Training to Manage the Records and Make Them Available?

For example, if your program decides to collect historical records written in a native tribal language or records on a particularly complex subject (molecular biology), will your staff (volunteer or paid) be able to understand and help users with the collections?

Who Uses Your Collections?

The interests of those using your collections should impact your collecting practices. If your users are mostly genealogists, then collecting annual reports and scientific lab reports from a local business will not serve them well. This is a very practical concern for historical records programs; the need to collect material that users want.

Is there a collecting theme or focus that your historical records program wants to, or is mandated to, pursue? Should you focus on a specific geographic area, a particular time period, a particular group of people, or a specific event? Do you have a formal mandate to collect particular materials?

Before getting started reviewing or writing your institutions collections policy, it will be helpful for you to look at some examples of collection policies. There are two collection policies given as examples. The Mills Archives collections policy is appendix B and the Local History Collections of the Hamilton Public Library is provided appendix C. If you want more examples of collections policies, I have also included citations for collections policies that you can search for and find via the internet as appendix D. As you review these examples, you might jot down any notes that you think will be helpful when you review or write your own collections policy.

Section III: Elements of a Collections Policy

A collections policy has seven elements:

Element 1: The name of the program and its parent organization (if applicable)
Element 2: The purpose of the program
Element 3: A description of the types of historical materials the program collects and the topics and areas of emphasis that the program specializes in. This should include the subjects, people, timeframes, and geographic regions your program focuses on.
Element 4: A description of the formats the program can responsibly manage (e.g., manuscripts, audio materials, visual materials, photographs, digital records)
Element 5: A description of how those historical materials are acquired
Element 6: A description of procedures used to remove materials from collections
Element 7: A description of procedures used when materials are loaned

As you read through these elements again in more detail, you can use the Collections Policy Worksheet provided as appendix E forms to create or revise your own collections policy. There is also an electronic version of this form you can download from the AASLH website at https://learn.aaslh.org/archivalbasics. You are free to modify and use this Collections Policy Worksheet form as you wish. As you review each of these seven elements, I suggest you have a copy of your "Assess Your Resources" from the first section to help with your work.

Element 1: The Name of the Program and Its Parent Organization

State the complete name of your program. Include hierarchical details up to your parent organization, if you have one. Also include the governing authority for your program, such as a board of directors, trustees, and so forth. This information will be incorporated into the next element, the statement of purpose.

Element 2: The Purpose of the Program

All organizations that maintain a historical records program have a purpose for collecting those records. This purpose, often called a mission statement, may be specifically stated, or it may be an informal understanding.

Your purpose can be influenced by many factors including

- The nature of your organization itself
- Your geographic location
- Your organization's intended audience

Your collections policy should contain your organization's statement of purpose. The statement should be short and concise, summarizing why you have a historical records program.

Your statement of purpose should answer these four questions. Take a moment to answer them for your organization:

1. What subjects, groups, or region should your collections document?
2. What types of material should your organization collect?
3. How should the material you collect be used?
4. Who are the primary users (audience) of the collections?

Now that you have answered these questions, you can use your responses to craft your statement of purpose. You can use the following format to help you:

The purpose of the *[name of program and parent organization]* is to document the *[subjects, groups, region emphasis about which the program collects]*.

The *[program name here]* identifies, collects, preserves, and makes available historical records documenting *[scope here]* for use by *[audience]*.

Element 3: Describe in More Detail the Types of Historical Materials Collected and the Program's Topics and Areas of Emphasis

This description should include the subjects, people, timeframes, and geographic regions on which your program focuses. You should also describe the types of materials your organization collects, such as records, manuscripts, photographs, and maps. Together the subjects of your collection (people, timeframes, regions) and the types of material your organizations collects (formats) are called the "scope" of your collections.

Some collection policies include this information in the statement of purpose section. Others include more specific collecting information as a separate section of the policy. Whichever method you choose, be sure that your description is specific enough to guide selection decisions.

Most often, a program focuses on one or more subjects or themes—people, events, geographic areas, and so forth. The area of collecting focus for your program should relate to your audience. What subjects are they interested in? What types of collections are they interested in?

You should also consider what nearby or related programs collect. Try to avoid overlapping or duplicating collections. This will avoid competition for materials and will ensure that a broader historical record is maintained in an organized and complementary way.

Element 4: Acceptable Formats

In this section, you will describe the formats the program can responsibly manage. You have already considered this question in the "Assess Your Resources" worksheet.

Be specific in this element; indicate both what formats you will accept and those you will not accept.

Element 5: Methods of Acquiring Historical Materials

In your collections policy, you should include general information about how your program will acquire records. The specific forms to use, approvals needed, and other pertinent information are not necessary at the policy level. I will discuss in detail some of the common ways to transfer records to your program in chapter 3.

Keep in mind that acquisition of archival records involves the legal transfer of property and other rights from the owner to you—all records pertaining to archival acquisitions are retained permanently.

As you create this element of your policy, you should investigate how your program currently receives records and consider whether the current practices are sufficient. Consider if you will accept records based on their ownership being transferred to you, or will you take in records as a temporary loan? In normal circumstances, archivists recommend accepting records only with ownership so that you have the final authority about arrangement, use, and disposition of the records. You should avoid temporary loans unless the loan is for exhibit purposes.

Will you accept restricted or confidential material? A balance between the privacy of the creator and the rights of the public needs to be struck. Archivists recommend accepting as few restrictions on access as possible, in part because it is difficult to justify spending a historic records program's limited resources preserving a collection that cannot be immediately made available to researchers.

A quick note on restrictions. If you must accept a restriction(s) to get a collection, try to limit the restriction to a specific portion of the collection and try to limit the time period of the restriction to a defined period of time. It is much easier to manage a restriction defined as "ten years after date of receipt" than it is "after the author's death," as this restriction forces you to keep track of when the author passes. Restrictions with event-based time periods are difficult to manage. These kinds of restrictions increase the likelihood of a mistake in providing access to portions of a collection that are closed.

State, in general terms, how collections can be acquired by your program. You might try using this format to get started: *Materials may be acquired by gift, bequest, purchase, or any other transaction that passes title of the materials to [program name here].*

If you need some help understanding methods of acquisition, take a look at chapter 3, where I discuss methods of acquiring materials; then come back to complete this element of your collections policy.

Historical records are generally transferred to an archive in one of the following ways:

Donation—can be a straightforward gift with no strings attached or come to you via a bequest or gift with specific requirements.

Purchase—many organizations support acquisitions through purchase from private or commercial vendors.

Transfer—government records are often transferred using standard forms such as records transfer forms, certificates of records disposal, and records retention schedules.

Element 6: Removal of Unwanted Materials from Your Collections

You may find that your organization holds collections that fall outside its collections policy. When this occurs, you will need to decide whether or not you want to continue to use your program's limited resources to maintain these out-of-scope collections. If you choose not to keep these records in your collection, you will need to remove them from your holdings.

Your collections policy should provide guidelines for when it is appropriate to remove materials. Generally, removal should occur when either the materials fall outside the collecting scope or the organization cannot support the materials. In archival terms, this removal process is called *deaccessioning*.

Should you need to remove items from your holdings, first check to see if there were disposal instructions included in the acquisition documents. For example, a gift agreement might specifically state that if the organization no longer wants to retain the records, they should be returned to the donating family.

If no such disposal instructions are available, then your organization should follow its process for disposal and documentation of that disposal. Your collections policy should explain these practices.

For element 6, you should describe in general terms the process for removing materials from your collections. This section should include

- What kinds of materials can be removed from collections
- Who has the authority to decide what materials to remove

Element 7: Loaning Records from Your Collections

Your collections policy should state clearly the terms under which you will loan records to other organizations. It should include

- What kinds of materials will be loaned
- How long records can be on loan
- Care and handling terms for the loaned records
- Terms under which the loan can be ended
- Who has the authority to loan material
- How will loans be documented
- How loaned items will be insured

Loans are described in more detail in chapter 11.

As you use the collections policy worksheet to create or revise your collections policy, remember that this is your policy. A worksheet cannot meet all of your particular needs, so you should revise it appropriately, adding the elements you need, expanding on sections if needed, until you have made it your own.

If you are creating your collections policy for the first time, show the worksheet to other staff members and work on your policy together. Once your collections policy is completed, your governing body should officially approve it.

Remember to review your collections policy on a regular basis. Use it as the guiding principles for the management of your collections. It is truly a fundamental document to a historical records program.

Section IV: Summary and Exercise

A collections policy is one of the foundational documents of a historic records program. It defines what your archives will collect based on your organization's mission statement, capabilities, and resources. It describes the types and topics of the historical records you will collect, and it defines how you will acquire and remove historic records from your collections. Your collections policy is authorized by your organization's governing body and it should be reviewed on a regular basis.

The ABC Department of Archives Exercise

This exercise demonstrates how a collections policy can guide decision making about what to collect.

The ABC Department of Archives Collections Policy

The ABC Department of Archives is a department within the ABC Public Library. The ABC Department of Archives identifies, preserves, and makes available for research materials relating to the environment and its connection to the people of the ABC community. This area of interest includes the waters and wetlands surrounding the ABC community, as well as land use in the region. The department is particularly interested in documenting the impact of environmental change on the community, including its industries such as fishing and agriculture.

The department will acquire unpublished records and papers, books, pamphlets, periodicals, maps, and photographs related to the areas of interest noted above.

The department will work cooperatively with historical societies and other community groups to gather and preserve the history of the community without duplication.

Materials may be acquired by gift, bequest, purchase, or any other transaction that passes title of the materials to the ABC Public Library. In order to maintain and improve the quality of the collection, materials may be deaccessioned due to irrelevance, lack of space, duplication, or irreparable condition. This will be done only with the approval of the ABC Library's board of directors.

Based on this collections policy, decide whether or not the ABC Department of Archives should accept or reject the following groups of historical records.

Group 1

Sailing Association Records, 1915–1972, twenty-two cubic feet. A voluntary association of people interested in boating. The collection contains minutes, membership lists, photographs of members and events, and publicity materials. Accept or reject?

Group 2

ABC Environmental Coalition Records, 1975–1983, ten cubic feet. This group is concerned with the preservation of local wetlands. The collection contains lobbying records, press releases and clippings, correspondence, and financial records. Accept or reject?

Group 3

ABC Bakery Records, 1912–1970, three cubic feet.
A local, family-owned bakery shop, well known in the community until it closed in 1970. The collection contains financial data, letters from customers, and recipes. Accept or reject?

Group 4

Literary Association Records, 1958–1969, twenty-five cubic feet. A local association of authors, teachers, and readers. The collection includes correspondence with authors, reviews of books, meeting minutes, photographs, and audiotapes of lectures. Accept or reject?

Answers

Sailing Association Records—Accept, these records would most likely be accepted into the collection because they provide documentation of the people of the area. They would be a particularly good fit if they also included information relating to the environment—this kind of information would most likely be found within the Minutes.

ABC Environmental Coalition Records—Accept, these records meet the criteria of the collections policy very well, documenting local wetland preservation efforts.

ABC Bakery Records—reject. This is a good example of an interesting and important local history collection. It certainly documents the local people; yet does not have content relating to the wetlands or environment. The best decision here is most likely to try to find another program where this collection is a better fit. However, if there are no other programs, you might decide to accept the collection, even without a perfect fit, because it is important. You might also decide that your program doesn't have the resources to care for this collection which is marginally related to your collections policy and mission.

Literary Club Records—reject. This collection is an interesting local history collection that documents the local people, but without a focus on the environment. It also contains audiotapes, which are not supported by the program. The best decision in this case would be to find another program that would accept these records, particularly one that can properly care for the audiotapes.

Chapter 3

Appraisal

When records are offered to your historical records program, often your first inclination will be to say, "Yes!" Instinctively, you see a value in the records and want to preserve them and make them accessible to researchers. However, remember that before you can accept the records, you need to review them to make sure the records really belong in your program. This review process is called *appraisal*.

This chapter discusses appraisal. Section I defines it, section II covers making appraisal decisions; in it you get an Appraisal Scorecard to help you structure and document your appraisal decisions. In section III, I will discuss other factors to consider when making appraisal decisions. The chapter ends with a summary and the "Riveroaks Historical Society and Museum Appraisal Exercise" in which you review the appraisal decisions of Cliff Rahmad, a fictional archivist.

Section I: Defining Appraisal

Appraisal involves analyzing records to see if they are appropriate for your program. Appraisal looks at the historic, legal, administrative, fiscal, and intrinsic value of records and their relationship with other records to see if they fit the criteria of the organization's collection policy. The term does not, in this context, refer to placing a monetary value on records. The value being considered is historical worth, not monetary worth.

Making appraisal decisions about the historical importance of records is a complex process. You can usually find a reason to accept records; the appraisal process evaluates the necessity of accepting them.

You may find it helpful during the appraisal process to consult with others who know about or have a particular interest in the records. These people could be colleagues, other archivists, historians, specialists, or researchers. Whether you have this kind of assistance or not, you need to apply a systematic evaluation process to appraisal decisions.

> The *appraisal process* is analyzing the historic, legal, administrative, fiscal, and intrinsic value of a group of records and their relationship with other records, based on an organization's collections policy.

Section II: Making Appraisal Decisions

By asking a series of five questions about the records you are evaluating, you can collect important information on which to base your appraisal decision. During the appraisal process, you are reviewing the records as a group, not as individual items. Your final decision will be based on the answers to these questions for the entire group of records, not on one particular document that is part of a group of records.

These are the five questions:

1. When were the records created?
2. Why were the records created?
3. What kind of information is in the records?
4. Who created the records?
5. How do these records fit with your program?

The Questions

Let's take a moment to expand upon each of these questions.

When Were the Records Created?

Are the records old? Are they scarce or rare? Do they cover an important period of time in the subject matter? Do they cover a short or a long period of time? If you're collecting policy limits your collections to a particular time period, do the records fall within that period?

Why Were the Records Created?

What office, group, or person created the records? What are the principal activities of that office, group, or person? Do the records document the main activities or functions of that office, group, or person? Do the records document activities, events, or people that are included in your collection policy?

What Kind of Information Is in the Records?

Do the records document important activities or events? Are they routine or nonroutine? Do they document things identified in your collection policy? Are the records an important source of information on the topic? Are they the only source? The best source? A credible source? Do they offer a viewpoint that is different than that of other records? Do they provide unique information?

Who Created the Records?

Do the records reflect a common or an individual point of view? Was the creator a decision maker? Did the creator have unique or unusual experiences? Was the creator personally involved in the events recorded? Was the creator biased? Do their records focus on one point of view? Does the creator exhibit a perspective different from the mainstream?

How Do the Records Fit in Your Historical Records Program?

Do the records fit with your program's collection policy? Do they duplicate, complement, or enrich your current holdings? Will they be useful to your researchers? What is the condition and size of the materials? Can you accommodate them and commit to both access and preservation? Can you support storage costs and the staff who will make them accessible to the public?

Answering the Questions

The answers to these questions form the primary argument for accepting or rejecting the records offered to your program. Generally speaking, the older and rarer the records, the better. Having said that, be careful; do not overlook a historic record just because it is new or dated relatively recently. The more important the person or office, the better. Records from prominent people or high-level offices are important in documenting how policies and decisions are made and their impact on people and communities. However, equally important are the records of everyday citizens and organizations that document common people's lives and experiences. While the significance of the person or office give you some idea of the importance of the records, it is the information the records contain that is of real importance. The more credible, rare, and detailed the information in the records, the better. Most important, the more the records fit the criteria of your collections policy, the better.

Section III: Other Factors to Consider

There are three other factors you need to consider. The responses to these questions may *contradict* the decision that would have been made based on the five primary considerations listed above.

If these questions lead you to make an exception to your collection policy, be sure to document the mitigating factors carefully so that you justify the exception and don't set a precedent for not following the policy.

These are the three questions:

1. Are there *political* considerations in accepting or rejecting the records? If you accept these records will other records not be offered to you? Will the point of view documented in the records offend other donors, researchers, or the public at large? It is important to remember that while some collections might offend some people, if the collection accurately portrays what happened, if it contains historical facts and points of view, it has merit. As archivists we want to document all of history, both the good and the bad. I am not saying you should not take a controversial collection. I am saying you need to be aware of the ramifications of taking a controversial collection. While all of us would like to believe political considerations do not have a place in appraisal decisions, in some cases they do.
2. Consider who the *donor* is. Could there be positive or negative repercussions for accepting or rejecting the records? Will you lose a potential funding source if you do not accept the records?
3. What *precedent* will be set if these records are accepted or rejected? Will you have other sets of records offered to you if you accept these records? Will you not have records offered to you if you accept these records? Will you be compelled to take other records because you have accepted these records?

After you have considered all these questions you will come down to two fundamental questions:

1. Are the records *historically valuable*?
2. Are the records *appropriate* for your repository?

The decision to accept records into your program is guided by your collection policy. If the records are historically valuable, and they meet the criteria that you established for your policy, then you should probably accept them. Why do I say probably? Because there are always exceptions to the rule!

Using an Appraisal Tool

Many historical records programs guide and document their appraisal decisions by using a scorecard. I have provided you with an Appraisal Scorecard as appendix F. There is also an electronic version of the Appraisal Scorecard form you can download from the AASLH website at https://learn.aaslh.org/archivalbasics. You are free to modify and use this scorecard as you wish.

The scorecard has a column for "score" and another for notes. I score appraisal decisions 1 to 5, with 1 being a no and 5 being a yes. While numeric scoring is still subjective, it does give you the ability to document your appraisal decisions with some precision. Some historic records programs will create a cut-off appraisal score, meaning they will not accept collections that score less than seventy (or whatever score they choose). I kept appraisal scorecards as part of a collection's administrative records. I also kept the appraisal scorecards of those collections that were rejected. It is helpful to show that you have been consistent in applying your collections policy over time. Appraisal scores can also be used to prioritize preserving and describing collections.

We have been discussing the appraisal of the private papers of individuals, organizations, or institutions. There is a different appraisal process used by governmental and corporate entities that have records management programs to make appraisal decisions. Records management deals with the maintenance of records from their creation through their destruction or selection for permanent preservation. Records management programs define or help define which records are of enduing historical value by the creation and maintenance of a records retention schedule.

A records retention schedule lists all the records created by the organization along with how long those records should be kept—their retention value. The records retention schedule is created by looking at how long each series of records needs to be maintained for operational, fiscal, legal/regulatory, and historical reasons based on the function of the office. This analysis is often supported by examples of how long other institutions are keeping similar records. The resulting retention periods documented on the records retention schedule are approved by the management of the organization.

A records retention schedule can make an appraisal decision on a series of records or it can ask for further input on that decision. As an example, the records retention schedule for the State Bureau of Vital Statistics gives birth, death, and marriage records a permanent retention value, meaning that these records are to be kept forever. No appraisal decision by an archivist is needed. In other cases, the records management program may request appraisal input from the archival component by putting something like "Review by archives for historical value" in the records schedule. In this case the records retention schedule alerts the archives that the records in question may be of enduring historical value.

Section IV: Summary and Exercise

There are some key points to remember. To appraise the appropriateness of a potential acquisition to your organization ask and answer five questions:

1. When were the records created?
2. Why were the records created?
3. What kind of information is in the records?
4. Who created the records?
5. How do these records fit with your program?

You might want to make an exception to your collection policy because of political considerations, because of who the donor is, or because a precedent might be set by accepting or rejecting them. If you make such an exception be sure to document why you made the decision you did. The final, fundamental questions to answer are these:

- Are the records *historically valuable*?
- Are the records *appropriate* for your repository?

An appraisal scorecard can help you make your decision and document that decision for future members of your organization

If your appraisal decision is to accept the records, then you will proceed with a formal transfer of the records and move them into your collections. I will talk about that in the next chapter. If your appraisal decision is to reject the records, you should do the following:

- Thank the potential donor.
- Explain your decision in brief, general terms.
- If appropriate, refer the donor to another historical records program where the records might be a better fit.

Riveroaks Historical Society and Museum Appraisal Exercise

About the Organization

Founded in 1868, the Historical Society and Museum has a small historical records collection that is kept in the society's headquarters, the Horatio House (a Victorian house, c. 1888), which is open to the public on weekends. The collections include personal papers of local artists whose works are represented in the museum; genealogical records; and documentation, photographs, and ephemera from the society's sponsorship of the annual Old Riveroaks Day event for the past fifty-two years.

Collection Policy

The purpose of the historical records program is to document the history of the community of Riveroaks and the region and to support the collections of the museum. The archives identifies, collects, preserves, and makes available records and personal papers of enduring value from Riveroaks residents, organizations, businesses, and related groups from 1700 to the present. The archives makes its collections available upon request and by appointment.

The Historical Society accepts records and personal papers in paper formats (bound volumes, papers, and photographs) only. The organization cannot support materials in other formats.

The historical records program acquires materials by gift, bequest, purchase, or other transactions that pass title of the materials to the Riveroaks Historical Society and Museum.

Materials will be removed from the historical records program if the records do not fall within the collecting scope of the program. The curator will make a recommendation for removal of material. The board of directors will approve or reject this recommendation for removal. When materials are removed, the historical records program will offer the materials to other community organizations before destroying them.

The historical records program does not loan its materials, except by action by the board of directors

About the Town of Riveroaks

Riveroaks was founded in the early eighteenth century by the Podgamessqua Tribe, who used the area as its summer fishing grounds. In the late eighteenth century, a small town developed around a natural pooling of the Hiltonia River; this area eventually was named Deepwater. In 1906, the town of Deepwater was officially incorporated as the City of Riveroaks.

By the early twentieth century, the town had grown in prominence, both economically and politically. Five major factories were built between 1901 and 1916, including the J&M Tayson Luggage Co., and the town's population swelled to 27,000. However, the Great Depression hit Riveroaks and the Hiltonia Valley hard, and the growth in population slowed for the next five decades.

Recently Riveroaks has undergone a small revitalization. Passenger rail service was restored two years ago. An old mill and two abandoned factories have been renovated for new uses, including residential spaces that have attracted commuters from the nearby city of Hiltonia. The town's population currently is 41,000.

The Riveroaks Historical Society and Museum Appraisal Scorecard

Now that you've learned about the town of Riveroaks and the organization's history and collections policy, we're going to look over Cliff Rahmad's shoulder as he examines three sets of papers that have been offered to the Riveroaks Historical Society and Museum (see table 3.1). As you can see, his scorecard follows the "five question" format we described earlier in this chapter. Given his answers, do you agree with his decisions?

Table 3.1. Three Sets of Papers to Consider Adding to the Collection

	James Tayson Papers	Charlotte Tomlinson Papers	Artist Lisa Smith Papers
When were the records created?			
1a. Are the records old?	1910–2000	1940–2000	1920–1970
1b. Are the records scarce?	No–routine business records	Some	Yes
1c. Are the records from a significant time period?	Yes	Yes	No
1d. Do the records cover a long or short period of time?	Long	Long	Relatively Long
Why Were the Records Created?			
2. Do they document the principal activities or functions of the creator?	Yes	No	Yes
What Is in the Records?			
3a. Do they document important activities?	No	Yes	Yes
3b. Are they the only source of information?	No	Yes	No
3c. Are they the best source of information?	No	No	Yes
3d. Do they dispute other records?	No	Yes	No
3e. Do they provide unusual information?	Yes	Yes	Yes
Who Created the Records?			
4a. Do the records reflect a routine or unusual point of view?	Routine	Unusual	Unusual
4b. What was the position of the creator?	Founder of local manufacturing company	Local collector and historian	Local artist
4c. Was the creator personally involved in the activities recorded?	Some	No	Yes
4d. Did the creator possess the necessary expertise to understand the events recorded?	Yes	Yes	Yes
4e. Does the creator display a bias?	No	Yes	No
How Do the Records Fit with Our Program?			
5a. Do the records meet the requirements of our collection policy?	No–not historically valuable, just routine records	Yes	Yes
5b. Where is the geographical focus?	Riveroaks	Riveroaks	Hiltonia Valley
5c. Do they duplicate or support current holdings?	Some duplication	Some duplication	Support
5d. What is their research potential?	Low	Extraordinarily high	High
5e. Do they meet researchers' needs?	No	Yes	Yes
5f. What is the condition and size of the group of records?	Twenty-five cubic feet; fair condition; stored in file cabinets	Forty cubic feet; fair condition; stored throughout house in various boxes	Twenty cubic feet; good condition; stored in steamer trunks
5g. Can we support the storage and staff costs, necessary preservation and conservation of the records?	Yes	Yes	Yes
5h. Are there political considerations in accepting or rejecting these records? Any positive or negative repercussions from donor? Any precedent set if accepted?	Possibly negative repercussions if we reject, but we should be able to avoid	Yes	No
Accept or Reject Records?			
6. Are there records valuable and appropriate for our program?	No	Yes	Yes

Chapter 4

Accessioning

You now know how important it is to have a collections policy, and you've taken the first steps toward writing and implementing your own policy. You have also learned about the process of appraisal—selecting records that you want to include in your historical records program based on your collections policy.

Now you're ready to accession. In the archival world, formally bringing historical records into your archives is called *accessioning*. Accessioning is a two-part process. First, you transfer legal ownership of the records; second, you document the content of the materials and manage their physical transfer and storage. During this process you gain physical and intellectual control over the records.

Accessioning—formally accepting records into an archives.

Section I of this chapter discusses the importance of having clear legal custody over your records and how to do it. Section II focuses on how to bring records under the physical and intellectual control of your organization. In section III, we will look at the importance of documenting your accessions. The chapter ends with section IV, a summary.

Section I: Transferring Legal Ownership of the Records

It is vitally important that your historic records program can prove that it has the legal rights to the collections under its care. Many programs have had legal issues because they could not prove they had the legal rights to all of their collections. Such issues range from simple disagreements over the rights to collections expressed verbally to court cases costing significant amounts of money. Once you are in a court battle, the reputation of your program will suffer regardless who wins the legal case. Many historic records programs have lost the time and money invested into the description and conservation of a collection because they could not prove they had legal right to it. It is worth your time to do this step right.

To prove you have the legal rights to a collection you need to document the legal transfer of the papers, books, audiotapes, videotapes, or other physical media and their content to your organization. This legal transfer portion of the acquisition process can be documented by using the following:

- Purchase agreements
- Deposit agreements
- Deed of gift agreements
- Record of transfer

Purchase Agreements

A purchase agreement is used when your organization buys the records for a specific sum of money. Before you purchase historical records, you'll need to make sure the person selling the records has clear ownership of them. This can be difficult when purchasing family records (papers).

The documentation of a purchase may be as simple as a bill of sale or as complex as a formal contract. Your legal counsel should review bills of sale, especially if it is a contract, before the purchase is made in order to protect your interests. Whatever documentation is used at minimum it needs to include the following:

- Who purchased the records
- Who sold the records
- A description of the records (sufficient to identify them in court if needed)
- The amount paid for the records
- The date of the sale

If at all possible, include a statement of the seller's right to sell the records.

Deposit Agreements

A deposit agreement documents when records are placed in your physical custody without an actual transfer of title. With a deposit agreement, you have the records in your collection, but you do not actually own them. It's similar to a bank account: you deposit money with the bank, so the bank has physical custody of it; but you maintain ownership and control of the funds.

Most programs try to avoid deposit agreements unless the collection is very valuable and there is no other way to ensure its safekeeping. Why do archivists avoid them? Your organization may end up spending its resources to manage, store, and provide access to a collection, only to have the owners change their mind and want the collection returned at a later date.

Some deposit agreements state that ownership will pass to the historical records program at a certain time. If you are dealing with an individual, it is best to have the deposit agreement state that title will pass to your program upon the individual's death or earlier if possible.

> **Tip:** If you decide to use a deposit agreement to acquire materials, it should answer these questions:
>
> 1. Who provides insurance for the records against loss?
> 2. What type of archival work needs to be done for the collection, and who is responsible for paying for it?
> 3. Is access permitted to the collection? Are there access restrictions?
> 4. If there are access restrictions, who is able to grant access?
> 5. If the depositors remove the records before transferring title, do they have to reimburse your program for its costs in managing the collection?
> 6. Is your program responsible for accidental damage to the collection?

There is an example deposit agreement between the Riveroaks Historical Society and Museum and Charlotte Tomlinson as appendix G for you to review. There is also a "Blank Deposit Agreement" provided as appendix H. There is an electronic version of this form you can download from the AASLH website at https://learn.aaslh.org/archivalbasics. You are free to modify and use this form as you wish.

Deed of Gift Agreements

A deed of gift is a signed document that outlines a voluntary transfer of ownership of records without money changing hands. The records being transferred to you are a gift, and the deed of gift documents that fact. A deed of gift doesn't have to be fancy or long; it can be simple and straightforward, but it does have to be specific.

Many programs use a standard deed of gift form that can be modified to meet special circumstances. Using a standardized form simplifies the process for the staff and tells the donor that you are running a well-established historical records program. The elements of a deed of gift usually include

- Name of the donor and the relationship of the donor to the records creator
- Name of the recipient of the records
- Date of transfer of ownership
- Summary details on the records being transferred (titles, dates, amount, and general description)
- A specific statement that transfers rights to the physical and intellectual property (It is vital to detail the name of the person or organization that holds copyright to the records and the time period covered under copyright)
- A statement of access restrictions. (Sometimes collections are closed for a period of time or request other stipulations on the use of the collection. Be sure your program can meet any requested restrictions before accepting the collection. It is in the best interest of your program to limit restrictions and/or limit the time period restrictions are in effect.)
- A statement defining how the collection will be used by the historical records program. (The program should state that it will have free use of the collection for research, exhibit, and any related educational purposes.)
- Disposal criteria and authority. (What are the options and procedures your program must take if you decide to dispose of any of the material?)
- Dated signatures of the donor and the recipient

This may seem pretty formal—it is! The deed of gift is a binding legal contract. Your legal counsel should review your deed of gift forms, as well as any deed of gift that deviates from your normal template document.

After a deed of gift is completed, you should send a letter of acknowledgement to the donors to confirm the donation and thank them for it.

There is a sample "Deed of Gift Agreement" between Elbert Marvel and the Quill College Archives provided as appendix I.

There is a "Blank Deed of Gift (Simple)" provided as appendix J. An electronic version of this form you can download from the AASLH website at https://learn.aaslh.org/archivalbasics. You are free to modify and use this form as you wish.

It is important that your program establish who can sign purchase agreements, deposit agreements, and deeds of gifts on behalf of your organization. Remember to have your legal counsel review the forms I am providing to you and any modifications you make to them before use as they are legally binding agreements.

Record of Transfer

In the previous chapter I touched on records management. If your archives works in conjunction with a records management program to collect the historic records of your parent organization, you will use a record of transfer form to document the transfer of records from the agency of origination (the creating entity) to the archives. The intent of record of transfer forms is the same as a deed of gift, a purchase, or deposit agreement—to document the change of legal ownership and responsibility for the records from the creating entity to an archives. The informational elements for a record of transfer include the following:

- Office creating the records—include as much of the institutional hierarchy as needed to identify the office without question. As an example, "Legal Division, Office of the General Counsel, Department of Regulatory Affairs."
- Include name and contact information of the individual transferring the records including title, office address, email address, and telephone number.
- Description of the records—use as much detail as necessary to accurately identify the records. The description usually includes the title of the records, date spans, volume, retention period from the records retention schedule, and media on which the records are transcribed (e.g., paper, microform, electronic). It may include the purpose of the records, the specific format of the records if they are digital records, how the records were created (work process), how the records were transferred (picked up by, transferred via thumb drive, transferred via email, etc.) and the physical condition of the records.
- Transfer of ownership statement—include a statement something like "The ownership of the records described above are hereby transferred to [name of the archives] for their use and/or destruction."
- Add signature of individual transferring the records including the date of record transfer.
- Add signature of individual from the records management office or archives accepting the records including title, contact information, and date of acceptance.

Once these agreements or transfers are completed, regardless if they are deeds of gifts, purchase agreements, deposit agreements or records of transfer forms, they become vital business records that you should maintain as a permanent part of your archives. They are legally binding documents that prove your program's rights to the records and protect you from litigation. If ownership of records ever needs to be traced, these forms also offer evidence of the previous ownership of the records.

Section II: Gaining Physical and Intellectual Control of Your Records

Once you have legally transferred a collection to your program, the next step in the accessioning process is to establish what archivists call "physical and intellectual control" over the records. What does that mean? It means making sure you know what you have and where it is.

This second step of the accessioning process takes place after the legal agreements have been made and the records are in your physical custody. At this point, a staff member should be made responsible for reviewing the records and creating the documentation that your program will rely on to know what you have acquired and where it is stored.

This accession documentation should be created as soon as possible after you receive physical custody of the records—preferably the same day you take custody of the records. After all, you don't want to lose the records or get busy with something else and forget about them. Many programs have a designated area for accessioning records so that if you do get pulled away from accessioning, the records you are working on will not get mixed up with other records. Creating accessioning documentation is usually a fairly quick task; it will go faster the more you do it.

Records that you acquire will vary widely in their size and intellectual content. Sometimes you will acquire a single volume; another time you may bring in many boxes of materials. Some records may be additions to existing collections, while others may be new collections. At this stage, you need to have a general understanding of what records you have acquired, how much material there is, and how to manage it until it can be processed and fully incorporated into your collections.

Should You Divide the Records into Groups?

Your first task is to make a high level evaluation of the best way to manage the records during the accessioning process. With small acquisitions—a single volume, a couple of boxes of records—there is no need to consider doing any preliminary organization of the records. You can answer the "what," "where," and "how much" questions without much trouble. But if you have brought in a large group of records—twenty, thirty boxes or more—you may want to break down the contents of the boxes into smaller units in order to help you answer the "what," "where," and "how much" questions. Breaking down the records is done by *identifying record series*. A record series is a group of records that logically belong together, are created, filed, and maintained together, and that serve the same function.

> A *record series* is a group of records that logically belong together: they are created, filed and maintained together because they serve the same purpose or document the same activity.

These are some common examples of record series:

- Meeting minutes
- Press releases
- Budget records
- Birth records
- Death records
- Correspondence
- Subject or reference files
- Monthly reports
- Grant applications

Since it may be some time before the records that are being accessioned will be ready for researchers, it's important to create accessioning documentation that provides a general understanding of the records. Identifying the record series that the creating entity employed to file and use the records will help you and your researchers to understand the intellectual content of the records. It will be much easier to understand and manage records described as and consisting of "Minute Books, 1900–1975," than to understand "Green Valley Environmental Association, Miscellaneous Records, 1900–1975."

Begin by looking at the records. Are there obvious types of records that make a logical group, such as set of minute books, a group of photographs depicting related events or people, or financial records? These items form record series—groups of related records that make logical sense, are filed and maintained together, and that serve the same purpose.

For example, let's say you have acquired the personal papers of John Smith, a prominent local scholar. There are fifty boxes of material. When you look at the materials, you find that the papers mostly consist of (1) financial records, (2) personal diaries, (3) family scrapbooks and photographs, and (4) academic papers and writings. Each of these four groups of records can be easily identified as a record series.

You should divide records into series if

- The records are well organized, labeled, and filed
- The series are easy to identify
- You can do the job quickly

Do *not* divide up records into series if

- The record series are not easy to identify
- If you have to do refiling and reorganizing to accomplish the task

If you cannot easily identify different series, if there is any doubt in your mind about the series in the accession, it is better to leave the records as they are and come back to the identification of record series later—when you are arranging and describing the collection. It is very difficult, if not impossible, to undo rearranging records, so if you have any uncertainty about moving records into series at this point, leave the records in the order in which they were sent to you.

If you have divided the acquisition into record series, you should physically segregate the series so they can be described and stored as separate accessions. The term *accession* refers to a group of records that have been identified as a single unit to be managed and stored together. An accession is a thing, the result of the process of accessioning.

> *Accession*—records transferred to an archives as a unit at a single point in time.

Doing the Paperwork

Now you can begin recording information about each accession using an accession form or database. This documentation helps you control your archival holdings. The accession documentation should include these elements for each accession:

- Noting where each accession is located
- Describing the content of the records and thus providing a temporary way for staff to find what they are looking for

The accession form should include the following elements for each accession.

Accession Number

Assign a unique number to each accession. Using this accession number, records are recognized, physically located, and tracked in storage. Accession numbers are often based on the year followed by a simple sequential numbering system. For the year 2003, the first accession would be numbered 2003-001; the second accession 2003-002, and so on.

Title of the Collection

Provide a descriptive title for the records you are accessioning. Titling collections calls for more precise use of records and collections along with the use of new terms.

We have defined records as documents in any form containing information created by an individual or organization and collections as groups of records with a unifying concept or characteristic. A more exact definition of records are official documents created by governments, institutions, or corporations. Records created by an administrative unit can be referred to as a record group. As an example, the records of the State of Ohio Department of Health would be called the Ohio Department of Health Record Group, with individual record series within the group. You can also have subgroups. As an example, the Ohio Department of Health (record group), Division of Vital Statistics (subgroup) with different series of records within the subgroup.

Records created by individuals or families are more precisely called "papers." An example might be "The Papers of Charlie Arp, 1972–2017," (documents created by Charlie Arp dated from 1972 through 2017) or "The Arp Family Papers 1929–1973," (records created by various members of the Arp family dated from 1929 through 1973).

Collections have been defined earlier in three ways. The definition of collection used in titling is "items brought together by a collector (individual or organization) from a variety of sources with a unifying theme, usually a subject or topic." The Charlie Arp Collection could be documents brought together by Charlie Arp. An example might be the "Charlie Arp Collection of British Sports Car records, 1939–1972," various documents concerning British sports cars dated from 1939 through 1972.

You do not have to use records, papers, and collections this precisely when titling collections, but it does give those looking at titles a better idea of what an accession or collection contains.

Definitions used in titling

Records—official documents created by governments, institutions or corporations
Papers—personal documents created by individuals or families
Collection—items brought together from a variety of sources with a unifying theme
Record group—a collection of records that share the same provenance (creator)

Name and Address of the Source of the Collection/Donor

You can get this information from the transfer documentation, if you aren't already aware of it.

Date the Collection Was Accessioned

This is not the date from the transfer document, but the date that you are filling out the form.

Amount of Materials/Records

How many boxes, books, and so forth, are there?

Description of the Materials/Records

Write a sentence or two describing the content of the material and its characteristics.

Comments about Restrictions to the Materials/Records

If the materials are restricted, this should be noted along with a description of the restriction including how long the restriction lasts. Are there particular people who can look at the restricted records? Are the records health or student educational records restricted by law? If so, give the legal citation that restricts the records.

The Location Where the Material/Records Will Be Stored

Use a standard way of noting where the records are stored such as a shelf location, box numbers, and so forth. Give enough information so that the records can be found easily.

Some programs use individual forms to record this information; others use notebooks; and others use database programs. Notebooks (also called logs) and databases assure that all the accession records are kept together. Accession forms enable you to create files for each of your collections. The method you use isn't as important as making sure that you keep good records. We'll talk more about recordkeeping and documentation in section III.

There is a sample accession form provided for you as appendix K. There is also a sample accession form for you to download and modify as needed for use in your program at the AASLH site at https://aaslh.org.

Working with Your Accession

As soon as you assign an accession number to a group of records, you need to include that number on the accession itself. In other words, write the accession number on each box, or, for bound volumes, put a strip of paper in each volume with the accession number written on it. Label each physical container with that accession number so that you don't lose anything. Here are the three critical steps in order:

1. Assign the accession number
2. Create the accession record (documentation)
3. Label each physical container for that record group

Do these three things for each accession you have identified. When the process is complete, the boxes should be physically moved to appropriate storage space. In storage, the accession numbers should be clearly visible, so that staff can locate the material as easily as possible.

Section III: Documenting Your Accessions

You've probably noticed by now that a historical records program generates lots of forms and paperwork. At minimum, you will have collection policies, correspondence, legal documentation of records transfers, and accession forms.

All this paperwork provides the documentation you need to establish ownership and manage your collections effectively. Documenting your collections, where they came from, what they are, where they are, and how they can be used, is vital to managing them.

Archival programs vary in how they keep records of their collections. In this course, I suggest a simple, streamlined approach to recordkeeping, with a minimal need for cross-referencing. It should work for most small- and medium-sized historical records programs. At minimum you should keep donor files and accession files.

Donor Files

Donor files are typically arranged alphabetically by last name. They should include donor contact information and correspondence. Keep files for donors and potential donors together. These files should also contain the transfer documentation for collections that have been donated.

Governmental and organizational archives working with a records management program may not need to maintain a donor file. If record of transfer forms are used, they can be filed alphabetically by the name of the unit. If record of transfer forms aren't used, you can document where the records were transferred from in their accession records by adding a copy of the deed of gift or transfer form.

Accession Files

You should have one accession file for each accession that you hold. This file should contain the following:

- A completed accession form
- Supporting documentation, such as inventories, if available

Accession files may eventually also contain finding aids and disposal information. You will need to determine an appropriate order for these files based on your workflows and numbering systems. I suggest ordering the files by accession number. These records may also be maintained in a notebook or database.

The Better Documentation Option

You may want to consider a more complex filing system that cross-references your files. Many historical records programs use a system that includes donor files, potential donor files, accession books or files, and collection files. This seems like a lot more work, but it gives you better access to the information you need to manage your program. In this case, your file system might look something like this.

Donor Files

Contain correspondence and related documentation relating to donors and the collections they have donated; including transfer documentation.

Potential Donor Files

Contain correspondence and information relating to potential and pending donor relationships.

Accession Files

Contain the accession record elements and related material such as inventories of materials, including donor name so you cross reference to your donor files. There is one accession record for each accession.

Collection Files

Finding aids, inventories, and other related information pertaining to your processed collections. These should include a reference to an accession number so you can cross

> **Tip:** Many institutions keep accession and donor files in a database so they can be searched or sorted in multiple ways.

reference back to accession records and donor information. There is more about finding aids in later chapters.

No matter how simple or complex your documentation filing system, it is vital that you maintain the appropriate information about your collections. As years go by, and staff changes, and more collections are added, you will rely on these records to manage and understand your collections.

Section IV: Summary

There are two parts to accessioning new collection into your program—documenting your legal right to the records and establishing physical and intellectual control over them.

It is vital that you have legal control over the records in your program. There are four kinds of documents that give you legal control over your records:

- Purchase agreements
- Deposit agreements
- Deed of gift agreements
- Record of transfer

Important points to remember:

- Gaining physical and intellectual control of your acquisitions means knowing what you have and where it is.
- Accessioning should be completed as quickly as possible after you receive physical custody of the records (i.e., the same day if at all possible).
- Sometimes dividing your acquisitions into record series will make them easier to understand and manage.
- Your organization should use a consistent accession documentation—that includes accession number, title of collection, source, date accessioned, amount of material, description, comments on restrictions, and location of material.
- Assign the accession number, create the accession record, and label the containers.
- At minimum, you need donor files and accession files.
- Accession files contain accession information/forms; donor files contain donor contact information.

Chapter 5

Arrangement

You have gained some control over the records you have acquired by accessioning them. You know who donated the records to you, you have a very basic understanding of what is in the records, and you know where they are located. Now you need to gain a more detailed understanding of the records so that you can help researchers use them. Researchers need to know how the records are organized, where they came from, and how to locate the exact information they seek. Organizing and describing the records so they can be easily understood is called *processing*. Processing records gets them ready for researchers to use them. It also helps to protect and preserve them.

There are three tasks involved in processing an archival collection of records:

- Arrangement: organizing the records
- Preservation: taking actions to prevent and slow down deterioration of the records
- Description: creating tools to help researchers locate the information they need from the collection

Accomplishing these three tasks will help you better understand and preserve the records. Arranging and describing the records makes it easier for researchers to find the information they seek, preserving the records makes it possible for generations of researchers to use them. The next three chapters goes over these processing tasks separately. This chapter covers arrangement, chapter 6 discusses preservation, and chapter 7 goes over description.

This chapter has three sections, including a quiz. The first section defines some of the terms you need to know to arrange archival collections. Section II goes over four steps you need to take when you arrange an collection. Section III is the summary and quiz.

Section I: Terms

Arranging records organizes them to reveal their content and significance. It involves figuring out how a person or organization filed the records when they used them and then restoring that order if it has been disturbed.

You should be aware of and use two fundamental principles when arranging records—provenance and original order. You will also need to understand how archivists implement arrangement using the "collections" and "series" concepts first introduced in chapter 4, "Accessioning." In this chapter, we'll discuss these concepts, provide a check-list, and lay out the steps to follow in arranging your records.

Provenance

Provenance refers to the practice of keeping groups of records together based on who created them. This means that collections should be maintained based on the creator of the records. Records from different creators should not be reorganized into collections based on subject or classification schemes created by someone else.

Have you been to your local public library lately? You probably noticed that in a library, the books are organized by subject—with all the books about a particular topic placed in the same location. Archivists don't organize their collections this way. They organize them based on provenance, the creator of the records. Why do archivists do this? Because archivists try to organize archival collections in a way that answers the widest variety of potential questions. Organizing records based on provenance provides context to the records. If you know who and why the records were created, you understand their value, meaning, and biases more clearly.

> *Provenance*—the practice of keeping groups of records together based on who or what office created them. Collections should be maintained based on the creator of the records.

For example, suppose you decided to organize the records of an environmental group in your area by subject. Records that were created by the director, the finance department, the field specialists, and the public relations/lobbying departments would be broken apart and intermingled with each other and with the records of other departments. This would make it easy to respond to a request such as, "I need all the records relating to wetlands." Other questions, however, would be difficult if not impossible to answer:

- How did the director manage the organization and make decisions?
- How did the public relations (PR) department function?
- What did the PR director know about potential problems with legislation and regulations?
- What were the various advertising approaches used over time?
- Did the various advertising approaches emphasize the positive aspects of programs over the negative aspects?
- What were the successes and failures of the public relations department?

Keeping the records separated by creator down to the subunit, the individual, office, or department that created them, helps answer the most questions and the most important questions that might be asked of the collection. Provenance is independent of series or collections, meaning a subunit, individual, office or department can have multiple series or collections—all of which have the same provenance.

Provenance seems like a simple concept, but it can get confusing when an individual collects the records of a company or a public office. The provenance of a collection or a series of records is the entity that created or received those records and maintained them together in order to accomplish some task, not the person who collected or donated them.

Original Order

In keeping with the idea of provenance, you also should try to keep the original filing structure of the records. This is called the "original order" of the collection. Whenever possible, records should be maintained in the order in which the creator maintained them. It's all right to correct obviously misfiled folders, but leave the basic organizational structure of the collection as it was originally set up.

If you are working with collections of relatively modern "office" types of records, original order refers to the order of the whole filing system—not the order in which individual documents were placed in file folders.

Other collections, such as diaries, personal papers, and photographs often aren't filed in this "office" like way. In these cases, original order is most often chronological—the order in which the materials were created. Having said this, such records can be organized by topic—so be sure to look!

Original order—whenever possible, records should be maintained in the order in which the creator maintained them.

Even if the reason behind the organizational scheme isn't immediately obvious to you, the creator had some rationale for it. Maintaining original order helps archivists present a collection to the researcher that shows how the creator used the records. Sometimes figuring out and maintaining original order just won't be possible. I will discuss what to do when that happens later in this section.

Provenance and original order are the principles upon which arrangement and description are based. But when it's time to think about the actual work of arrangement, when you are preparing to process the records of an accession, collections and series are vital concepts to understand.

How Records Are Organized

In the titling section of chapter 4, "Accessions," I talked about records as the documentation created by governments, institutions, or corporations. If the government, institution or corporation collects, preserves, and makes its own records available to researchers, those records are often organized into record groups and subgroups. I then defined papers as the documentation created by individuals or families. Sets or series of papers can be organized into collections. Collections are defined in three different ways: as a group of records with a unifying concept, as items brought together from a variety of sources with a unifying theme, and as the holdings of an archival institution. In this context, we are talking about a group of records with a unifying concept.

Using the terms *records* or *papers* and *record groups* or *collections* to describe and organize records and/or papers can get confusing. If the Smith County Historical Society holds the records of the Smithville Methodist Church, should that set of records be referred to as a record group or a collection? I would say "collection" because the Methodist Church is not collecting, preserving, and making the records available to researchers—the Smith County Historical Society is. But it really doesn't make a difference.

How your archival organization choses to refer to sets of records is up to them, there is no right or wrong way, just different ways. Going forward in this discussion of arrangement, description, and preservation, I am going to use the terms *collections* and *series* to keep things simple. It is enough for you to know that other organizational concepts like record groups, subgroups, and papers exist and that you can use them as circumstances dictate.

Collections

When you examine records of an accession, it is important to remember that you may have more than one collection within an accession. There is not a one to one relationship between an accession and collections and/or series. You can have multiple collections and/or series within one accession, and you can also have one collection and/or series over multiple accessions. Here are some examples of collections:

- Board of Trustees Records, 1956–1973
- Sailing Association Records, 1934–1978
- John Smith's Personal Papers, 1824–1875
- Canal Photographs, 1880–1900
- Montville Methodist Church Records, 1868–1956

> *Collection*—A collection is a group of records that have the same provenance and are related to each other.

Series

Some larger collections may consist of several "series." A record series is a group of records that logically belongs together, are filed and maintained together, and are created to serve the same function. Let's look again at one of the previous examples to see how collections and series work together.

Sailing Association Records, 1934–1978

This collection consists of several series. They include (1) minutes, (2) membership rosters, (3) correspondence, and (4) photographs of events. If this collection is very small (a box or two), you would describe it just at the collection level, noting the series into which it is divided. For example, Sailing Association Records, 1934–1978. These records consist of minutes, membership rosters, correspondence, and photographs.

But if it is a larger collection you would need to describe the collection as a whole, then explain each of the four series. That would look like this:

> *Series*—A record series is a group of records that logically belong together: they are created, filed and maintained together because they serve the same function or document the same activity.

Sailing Association Records (collection A)

Minutes (series 1)
Membership Rosters (series 2)
Correspondence (series 3)
Photographs of Events (series 4)

Generally, the larger and more complex the records are, the more appropriate it is to break the collection into several series, if that is how the creator used the records.

Now we will move on to look at the steps you should go through when arranging your records.

Section II: Arranging Records

Step 1: Research

Arranging archival collections begins with research and review. It's vital to know as much as you can and understand the arrangement you want *before* moving any files. Why? Because it's very hard to "undo" any refiling and rearranging once you have started. It's better to research and review the records thoroughly before physically moving anything.

The first thing you need to do is look up the accession record and learn what you can about the records: Where did they come from? How were they acquired? How much is there? Then you need to begin learning about the creator of the records. What did the person/group do? Why did they create the records? How did they use the records? Answers to these questions will help you understand what is and isn't important in the records.

To help you, I have a preprocessing checklist for you to use (appendix L). It asks you to answer three questions to help you understand more about who created the records and why they were created.

1. Who was the creator or accumulator of the records?
   Learn who created the records: their lifespan, birthplace, vocations, education, special events, and family life. Look for biographical information. Do the records have an attitude or bias that may affect the content and interpretation of the information in them?
2. Why and how were the records created and used?
   Learn about the organization that created the records: mission, functions, dates of operation, special events, board members, and locations. What was the purpose of the records? Why were they created and how were they used?
3. What do you know about the time, place, and subjects of the records?
   Research the subject that is the focus of the records. Learn about the time period in which the records were created, events that transpired, and the setting or locale in which they were created.

Locating the Information

Where are you going to find this kind of information? Sources include newspapers, biographical dictionaries, local histories, census records, and organizational histories. Websites like Ancestry.com, GenWeb, or even Wikipedia can be a great source of information. Most current organizations and many historical organizations have web sites that include varying amounts of historical information. People who knew the individual or worked for the organization may also be able to suggest sources.

Make sure you check your holdings as well. Do you have other records from this source? Do these records fill a gap in your holdings from that source? Are they continuations of series you already have?

Once you know who created the records and you have learned as much about them as possible, it's time to use your notes and knowledge and begin the actual organizing and arranging of the records. But don't start unloading boxes yet!

Step 2: Looking for Collections and Series

In this step, you are looking for an overall sense of how much work and what kind of work processing this particular collection is going to involve. This initial review is crucial. You may be opening the boxes of an accession and looking at the records in detail for the first time. When you are done with this initial review you should have

1. Identified collections and record series and physically divided the records into collections and series as necessary
2. Decided whether or not maintaining original order is possible

When you open the boxes, you will most likely find one of three situations.

Case 1) The records are well organized, record series are easy to determine, and the arrangement necessary seems almost obvious.
Case 2) The records are relatively organized, but more work needs to be done to analyze collections and record series.
Case 3) The records are a mess.

Let's look at these situations one at a time and go over what steps you need to take for each of them.

Case 1

The records are well organized, record series are easy to determine, and the arrangement necessary seems almost obvious. When you look through the records ask yourself these questions: Are the records in good order? Can you identify the original order? Do they make up a single collection? Are the record series obvious? If all your answers are yes, then you can move right on to step 3!

Case 2

The records are relatively organized, but more work needs to be done to analyze collections and record series. If the records need to be divided into collections and series, you should do so now.

1. Decide whether the records should be organized as multiple collections or as one collection with several series.
2. If you decide to organize the records into multiple collections, physically separate out the various collections, then look for series within the individual collections.
3. If you decide to organize the records as one collection, identify the record series that exist.
4. Evaluate the size of each series.
5. If more than one series, physically separate out the series if possible (keeping the records in their original order within each series) and label them with temporary labels so you can keep track of them (series 1, box 1; series 1, box 2; so forth and so on).
6. If you cannot physically separate out series from one another take notes describing the series you see.
7. Answer these questions:

   - Are the records in good order?
   - Can you identify separate series?
   - Can you identify the original order?
   - What should the order be if original order is unclear?

Make sure you jot down your observations and notes about the arrangement; then move on to step 3. If the original order isn't apparent and the records still seem like a mess to you, take a look at case 3 to learn how to handle these more complex situations

Case 3

The records are a mess. Unfortunately, sometimes records are accessioned in great disarray, as if someone dumped the contents of a desk or file cabinet into a box and shipped them off to you. This can be a daunting and time-consuming situation. Just making sense of the records may seem almost impossible. Take your time. Go through the materials, take notes on what you find, and look specifically for series if you can find them. Sometimes you can identify series by looking for similarly labeled files or files documenting specific functions or activities such as financial management or grant administration. Try to get an overall sense of the kinds of records you have. If you can identify the record series, go through the same steps listed in case 2:

1. Decide whether the records should be organized as multiple collections or as one collection with several series.
2. If you decide to organize the records into multiple collections, physically separate out the various collections, then look for series within the individual collections.
3. If you decide to organize the records as one collection, identify the record series that exist.
4. Evaluate the size of each series.
5. If more than one series, physically separate out the series if possible (keeping the records in their original order within each series) and label them with temporary labels so you can keep track of them (series 1, box 1; series 1, box 2; so forth and so on).
6. If you cannot physically separate out a series from one another, take notes describing the series you see.
7. Answer these questions:

    - Are the records in good order?
    - Can you identify separate series?
    - Can you identify the original order?
    - What should the order be if original order is unclear?

If it is not possible to identify series or original order and the records cannot be used by researchers without some arrangement, what should the series and order be? Archivists generally create series based on the following:

- Types of materials. Records are divided into series based on what they are. Correspondence, diaries, photographs, or minutes, for example.
- Functions or roles of the creator. Records are divided into series based on activities. A college professor's papers might be divided into personal life, teaching and research, professional service, and community service.
- Topic. Topics are clearly identified, and the records grouped by topic. The topics should reflect the person's life or activities—not the subjects the archivist thinks people will want to research because research trends change over time.

Archivists generally arrange series based on

- Chronology—all the records within a series are placed in chronological order.
- Alphabetical order—all the records within a series are placed in alphabetical order.

Be careful! If you must impose an order on the records, pick one of these arrangement schemes per series and stick with it. If you must impose an order on the records, seek advice and input from a professional archivist (if possible) and/or your colleagues before you start rearranging records. Imposing order on a set of records is a huge processing decision, it is very difficult and time consuming to try to reverse this decision once it is made. Be very sure about this decision before you proceed.

As you are working with the collection, keep your eye out for any information that might be sensitive, including medical or student educational records or portions of the collection where access has been restricted by the donor. Make sure to note where such information is in the collection so that decisions can be made about providing access to these materials.

Step 3: Decide an Arrangement Scheme and Plan for Preservation

Finally, take another look at the records in order to make final decisions about arrangement. Begin thinking about what kind of preservation work needs to be done. You will start to create an informal plan (more about this in step 4). When you're done, you should be able to answer these questions:

- What is the original order of the records?
- What kind of information is in the records?
- Why might the records be organized this way?
- What kinds of formats are within the collection?
- What kind of supplies will you need to process the collection? (More about this in a minute.)
- How will you address "document level" arrangement?

Up until now we have discussed arrangement and order in terms of the filing system. Now you will need to consider the documents themselves.

Most often it's best to leave the individual documents in their original order. If, however, that order has obviously been lost (the contents of the folders were spilled in the boxes, for example), you may need to create an order—chronological order often works best at the document level.

Step 4: Make a Plan

Based on your reviews of the records, create a brief plan for how you want to arrange the records. It shouldn't be formal or lengthy; just notes on a pad of paper will be fine. But writing it down will make clear how you want the final arrangement to work and it will help keep you from too much back-tracking if you get called onto another project and don't get back to this particular collection right away.

For each collection you have identified, your plan should include

- The corresponding accession number
- The records series you have identified within the collection (if applicable)
- A description of the original order; or the order you will impose if there is no useable original order—and why you chose the arrangement that you did
- Types of formats in the collection and an estimate of the kinds and amounts of processing supplies you will need
- Your thoughts as to what should be processed first and any problems that might be encountered

Section III: Summary

Whenever possible, box and label the records yourself when they are being picked up from the donor, before they are physically moved to your location. This is the best way to understand and preserve the original order of the collection. When doing this, you can often identify collections and series on the spot and label boxes so that they can be identified later.

There is not always a one-to-one relationship between an accession and a collection or series. It is possible that one accession contains multiple collections and multiple series. It is also possible to have multiple accessions that contain portions of one collection or one series. When records are picked up from a donor or accessioned has no impact on how the records are organized into series or collections.

When in doubt, don't rearrange records. If you're not sure what the original order is or if it seems not to make sense, be cautious before changing it. It is very hard to reorganize records back into the original order.

Keep it simple. If there is no original order, or if there is an original order that is unusable, contact a professional archivist whenever possible or your colleagues to help make this decision. When making arrangement decisions follow these general guidelines, (1) never impose order on records unless the original order cannot be restored, (2) do as little rearranging as possible to make the collection usable, and (3) use the simplest order possible.

Quiz

See the answers on page 323.

1. Provenance is:
   a. The practice of keeping groups of records together based on who created them
   b. A province of France
   c. The practice of keeping groups of records together based on subjects
2. Provenance is important because it:
   a. Makes it easier to organize records
   b. Provides context to the records
   c. Makes searching for subjects easier
3. Is provenance important beyond the main entity that created the records? Does provenance extend to the subunits that created the records?
   a. Yes
   b. No
4. Is provenance defined by who donated the records to you?
   a. Yes
   b. No
5. Original order means organizing records:
   a. By subject
   b. As the creating entity did
   c. Chronologically
6. If you cannot figure out the order of a set of records, and if the records are in complete disarray and unusable by researchers, you should:
   a. Leave the records in disarray and describe them the best you can.
   b. Impose some order on the records.
7. If you cannot figure out the order of a set of records, if the records are is complete disarray, and you decide to impose some order on the records, you should:
   a. Arrange the records in any order that suits you.
   b. Arrange the records in the order that makes it easier for the researchers to finds what they need.
   c. Arrange the records based on type, function, topic, or chronology and make a note in the finding aid saying that you have imposed an artificial order on the records.

8. A collection of records are:
   a. Records donated to your institution by an individual or entity
   b. Records donated to your institution by an individual that were created and/or received by an individual or entity
   c. Records donated to your institution by various individuals with a common theme or that are related to each other
9. A record series is a group of records:
   a. Created by the same entity
   b. Maintained in original order
   c. That logically belong together, are filed and maintained together, and are created to serve the same function
10. Are record collections and/or series defined by when they were accessioned:
    a. Yes
    b. No

Chapter 6

Preservation

Now that we understand the concepts that guide arranging archival collections we can begin the physical work of implementing an arrangement scheme: refiling materials, moving folders from one location to another, and generally putting the collection in the order decided upon. As you do this arrangement, you will also perform some tasks that will help preserve the collection. Preservation during the arrangement process involves examining the condition of materials in a collection, removing unsafe containers and replacing them with containers that will help keep the collection safe and in good condition.

This chapter has four sections. In section I, we examine several common types of material found in archival collections. Section II covers rules for handling archival items during processing and some of the supplies you will need for processing. Section III discusses how to handle specific materials during processing and the steps you need to take to preserve and process them. Section IV is the chapter summary and quiz.

Section I: Preservation of What?

Assuring that archival collections are preserved is one of the primary activities of archivists. The underlying philosophical theme of archival work is that *archivists need to preserve collections while providing access to them*. Archival materials require preservation in order to keep them in the best condition possible for as long as possible. Even formats like paper and photographs need special care and handling to assure that they survive as long as possible. Let's take a closer look at these formats.

Paper

Paper created before the 1840s was made primarily from cotton and flax rags turned into pulp. This paper is strong and quite stable. When stored correctly, this paper can last for hundreds of years.

After 1840, modern paper production used trees as the source of pulp. This paper produces acid when exposed to air and moisture, and it turns brown and brittle over time. Depending on the production methods and materials used, this kind of paper may start to show signs of deterioration after only ten years.

Photographic Materials

Photographic images are formed by the action of light on chemical compounds. Photographic materials are made up of many layers (supporter, binder, and image-forming layer), each of which responds differently to the environment.

The supporting and binding layers of photographs can readily absorb and lose moisture, which can lead to deterioration. If any one of these layers fails, the image can be lost.

Section II: Handling Archival Materials during Processing

Archivists take preservation actions during processing to slow the deterioration of collections. Nothing can completely stop deterioration, but good preservation practices can slow down the ravages of time dramatically. Good preservation practices start with how archival materials are handled during processing. The basic handling practices are these:

- Handle records as little as possible and always with great care.
- Records being processed should be returned to storage when they are not being processed for an extended period of time, even overnight.
- Label folders using number 2 pencil (not pens!) or with computer-generated labels as long as the labels do *not* come into contact with the records.
- Clean hands with soap and water before working with records. Do not use hand lotions or sanitizers.
- Keep supplies, equipment, and work areas clean.
- Keep food and drink out of work areas. They increase the likelihood of vermin infesting your archives and sooner or later you will spill something on a record.
- Use archival quality supplies from reputable vendors whenever possible.
- Different formats will require different handling; make sure you understand proper preservation techniques for the material.

For more detail on how to handle archival material, see the Northeast Document Conservation Center (NEDCC) Preservation Leaflet "4.1 Storage and Handling Practices."[1]

Processing Supplies

Before you start, set up your processing work area with the appropriate tools and supplies. Basic processing supplies include the following:

- Acid-free, lignin-free, buffered file folders
- Acid-free, lignin-free, buffered paper for interleaving
- Acid-free, lignin-free, buffered archival storage boxes
- Polyester (mylar) or acid-free, lignin-free, buffered enclosures for photographs
- Number two pencils and a good gum eraser
- A dust brush

Acid-free, Lignin-free, and Buffered

Before going any further, I want to define "acid-free, lignin-free, buffered," which is used to describe archival quality paper products. Acid free refers to chemically purified paper products that are more stable. These product have a pH rating of 7 (half way between acid and alkaline). Paper products made from wood fibers contain lignin. As lignin deteriorates, it creates acid; lignin-free paper products have the lignin removed. Buffered paper products have an alkaline buffering agent added during production. This buffering protects against migrating acids. So acid-free, lignin-free, buffered paper products have any existing acids washed from them, they will not create any new acids, and they have chemical agents added to them to slow or stop acids moving from item to item. (See the National Park Service Conserve-O-Gram No. 4/9 "Buffered and Unbuffered Storage Materials" dated July 1995[2] for a more complete discussion of these terms.)

There are some cautions about using buffered materials. Buffered materials should not be used with blueprints or colored prints. Some say that that since the buffered materials absorb the acids from the items that reside within them and become acidic themselves they need to be replaced on a regular basis. I have not heard of any institution replacing buffered materials and the NEDCC in their preservation pamphlet, "4.1 Storage Methods and Handling Practices"[3] advocates the use of buffered materials, so I don't put much credence in that argument. Still, you should be aware of those concerns.

As I said earlier, preservation work performed during processing depends on the type of materials being processed and paper and photographic materials are very different. They require particular handling precautions and preservation actions during processing.

Ideally, every collection would be processed and preserved using specialized archival quality supplies. In reality, many programs can't afford these kinds of supplies. So what can you do to balance reality with the ideal?

If you can only purchase a limited amount of processing supplies, first purchase the supplies *that come in direct contact with the historical records*. These include acid-free, lignin-free, buffered folders for paper-based materials. Enclosures for photographic materials can be made of acid-free, lignin-free, buffered paper or of polyester, polypropylene, or polyethylene. Photographic materials have specific needs that are detailed later in this chapter.

Partial List of Archival Suppliers

Archival Methods
655 Driving Park Avenue
Suite #5 / Dock #8
Rochester, NY 14613
Phone: 1.866.877.7050
Fax: 1.585.334.7067
https://www.archivalmethods.com

Archival Products
PO Box 1413
Des Moines Iowa 50316
Phone: 1.800.526.5640
Fax: 1.888.220.2397
https://archival.com

Gaylord Archival
PO Box 4901
Syracuse, NY 13221-4901
Phone: 1.800.448.6160
Fax: 1.800.272.3412
http://www.gaylord.com/c/Preservation

Hollinger Metal Edge
9401 Northeast Dr.
Fredericksburg, VA 22408
Phone: 1.800.634.0491
Fax: 1.800.947.8814
https://www.hollingermetaledge.com

Light Impressions
2340 Brighton Hennrietta Townline Rd
Rochester NY 14623
Phone: 1.844.656.4876
Fax: 1.866.592.8642
http://www.lightimpressionsdirect.com

University Products Inc.
517 Main Street
Holyoke, MA 01040
Phone: 1.800.628.1912
Fax: 1.800.532.9281
https://www.universityproducts.com

Section III: Preservation as Part of Processing

Now, let's look at some of the most common types of materials and the preservation work that should be done when processing them. In each case I will list how the material should be handled and the tasks you should undertake while arranging these materials.

Before going through this list, we need to discuss what to do with items that need the services of a conservator to preserve them. If your organization is lucky enough to have a conservator on staff use them in accordance with your organization's internal procedures. If you don't have a conservator on staff, you can hire the services of a conservator. The Library of Congress[4] has information on preservation online, including the ability to ask a question of their conservators and how to find a conservator in your area. Conservation On-Line[5] (a.k.a. CoOL) has a free directory you can use to find a conservator in your area as well along with lots of information on conservation including techniques. NEDCC[6] has a wealth of information on conservation, including how to use their services if needed.

Loose Paper

Handling

When handling loose papers, remember to support them on a stable surface. Do not lean on or write on (over) loose papers. Do not use pressure-sensitive tape to mend loose papers as it will grow brittle and yellow over time damaging the papers. It is easy to misplace loose papers so remove the entire folder from a box before looking for an individual document.

Processing Tasks

If the papers are dirty, use a dust brush to gently remove excessive dirt and dust. Note any badly damaged pages and place them in separate folders to protect them. These pages can be given to a conservator for individual treatment. If the damaged pages can be photocopied without further harm, photocopy them on acid-free, lignin-free, buffered archival paper and insert the copies into the collection. Make a note on the collection finding aid regarding the copies.

Refolder the papers using acid-free, lignin-free, buffered archival quality file folders. Select appropriate sized folders that are larger than the documents and be careful to not overfill folders. Folders should be labeled with number 2 pencils. Place folders in archival quality, acid-free, lignin-free, buffered boxes. The boxes should be filled but not packed tightly.

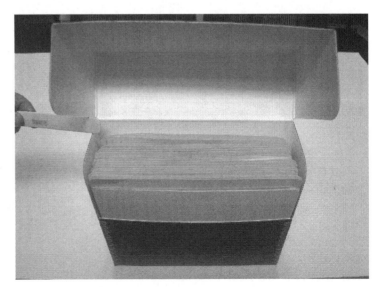

Figure 6.1. Small archival box (12.5" × 10.25" × 5") containing the correct amount of file folders. Notice how all the folders stand without any bending.
Photo by Laurie Gemmill Arp, courtesy of Columbus Metropolitan Library

You should unfold loose papers that are folded and remove papers from envelopes. Use a "bone folder" to smooth out folds on papers that have been folded for long periods of time. Bone folders are available through archival supply companies. If a fold won't "unfold," don't push it! Call a conservator or professional archivist in your organization before proceeding! Never take an action on an item that will harm it.

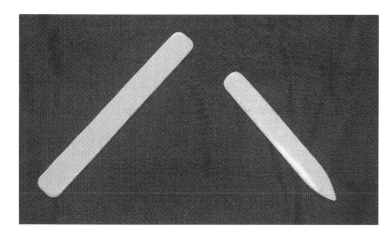

Figure 6.2. Bone folders
Photo by Laurie Gemmill Arp, courtesy of Columbus Metropolitan Library

If possible, you should remove staples from papers. Staples rust over time and they frequently cause physical damage to papers. Use a "spatula" to lift the staple folds from the back and then carefully pry the staple out from the front. Spatulas, sometimes called microspatulas, are available through archival supply companies. Remove any metal paper clips and replace them with inert plastic clips. Staples or other metal fasteners should be left in place if removing them will harm the papers. For more detailed information on removing staples see the NEDCC Preservation Leaflet 7.8 "Removal of Damaging Fasteners from Historic Documents."[7]

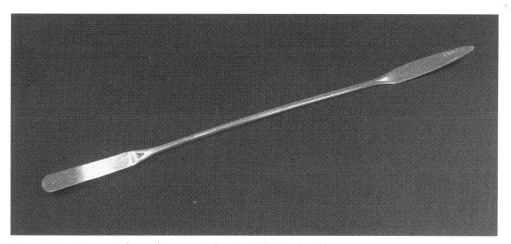

Figure 6.3. Microspatula used to pry staples, typically 8 inches long
Photo by Laurie Gemmill Arp, courtesy of Columbus Metropolitan Library

It may be impractical to remove the staples from a large collection. The decision to remove or not to remove the staples from a collection should be made by taking into account the physical condition of the collection (i.e., Are the staples rusty? Is it likely that you will tear pages removing staples?), the volume of the collection, the amount of collections awaiting processing, the number of individuals processing collections, and the historical importance of the collection being processed. The volume of governmental and institutional records and the probability of harming the records by removing the staples from them makes it difficult to justify removing the staples from these kinds of collections.

Many archival institutions enclose high use archival documents inside polyester film using a process called encapsulation. At one time, it was fashionable to laminate documents to protect them. Lamination uses heat to bind documents between plastic sheets and is no longer an accepted preservation technique because heat can damage the documents and there is no easy way to remove a document from lamination. Encapsulation does not create a bond between the document and the polyester film holding the document. It seals the edges of the polyester around the document. Encapsulation done well works but it can be relatively expensive. Even encapsulation has its problems. NEDCC states that "the deterioration of acidic materials is accelerated by encapsulation, and leaving corners of the encapsulation open has little if any effect on this problem. In some situations the need to protect materials during handling may outweigh this concern."[8] Do not use lamination on archival documents and consider encapsulation only if done by a conservator or those trained by a conservator. Encapsulation is not hard to do but it does require some training to do it correctly.

Bound Volumes

Handling

When removing bound volumes from shelves, support them from the bottom of the spine. Always use caution when turning pages and use book cradles and supports if possible. Many old bound volumes suffer from red rot, the result of the degrading of vegetable-tanned leather.[9] Red rot can make it very difficult to handle bound volumes without harming them. It weakens the spines and covers of old bound volumes by turning the leather into a felt-like red powder.

Figure 6.4.   The lighter red areas of this leather bound volume are the result of red rot.
Photo by Laurie Gemmill Arp, courtesy of Columbus Metropolitan Library

Processing Tasks

If the pages of the volume are dirty, use a dust brush to gently remove excessive dirt and dust. It is almost impossible to clean red rot from the spines or covers of bound volumes. Do not use pressure sensitive tape to mend bound volumes as it will grow brittle and yellow over time damaging the items.

You should unfold any folded pages using a "bone folder." If a fold won't "unfold," don't push it! Call a conservator or professional archivist in your organization before proceeding! Never take an action on an item that will harm it.

If possible you should remove staples from bound volumes using a "spatula" to lift the staple folds from the back and then carefully pry the staple out from the front. Remove any metal paper clips and replace them with inert plastic clips. Remember that staples or other metal fasteners should be left in place if removing them will harm the original item.

Depending on size, bound volumes can be stored in boxes. They can be placed in acid-free, lignin-free, buffered folders or they can be stored on shelves. If stored in boxes, place the volumes with the spine facing down. If stored in upright boxes, the volumes should be placed with the spine down to avoid having the text block pulling away from the spine. Larger volumes should be stored flat to remove stress from the spine of the volume.

Maps, Architectural Drawings, and Other Oversized Documents

Handling

Think of oversized documents as just another type of loose paper. When handling oversized documents remember to support them on a stable surface. Do not lean on or write on (over) them. Do not use pressure sensitive tape to mend oversized documents as it will grow brittle and yellow over time damaging the documents. It is easy to misplace oversized documents so remove the entire folder or box of oversized documents before looking for an individual document.

Remove any staples and metal paper clips and replace them with inert plastic clips. Staples or other metal fasteners should be left in place if removing them will harm the documents.

Processing Tasks

Oversized items need to be stored by size. This means that if the oversized item is part of a collection with normal sized items, it must be removed from the collection and stored separately. If this is the case, you should insert an acid-free, lignin-free, buffered separation sheet within the collection where the oversized item was removed, describing it and noting where it is stored.

If possible, oversized items should be enclosed in appropriately sized, acid-free, lignin-free, buffered archival quality folders labeled with collection information. You can also get wide-format jackets to hold oversized items from archival suppliers. It may not be possible for you to purchase such folders or jackets because of cost. If this is the case, try to separate oversized items with appropriate sized sheets of acid-free, lignin-free, buffered paper. If you do not use folders, it is very important that each oversized item is labeled with collection information on the back using a number 2 pencil or on a buffered label that is affixed to the item with an inert clip. For more information on labeling oversized items see the NEDCC Preservation Leaflet, "4.9 Storage Solutions for Oversized Paper Artifacts."[10]

Not labeling or losing the label from an item breaks the connection between the item and the collection from which it came. This removes the collection information or context from the item. An item without context has less historical significance. Given that searching for and finding items is based on collection information it can also be very difficult or impossible for users to find items without context. Not labeling, incorrectly labeling, losing a label or failing to permanently attach labels to folders holding oversized items is a common mistake that has rendered many historically meaningful items almost useless.

If possible, group oversized items by size and store the folders holding them horizontally (flat) in large-sized, acid-free, lignin-free, buffered archival quality boxes or in metal storage cabinets designed for maps and oversized materials. Storing oversized items in flat drawer cabinets in acid-free, lignin-free, buffered boxes and/or folders is ideal for maps and other oversized documents.

Figure 6.5.   Cabinet holding oversized maps
Photo by Laurie Gemmill Arp, courtesy of Columbus Metropolitan Library

If flat storage is not possible, and the documents are flexible, you can store them by rolling them, wrapped in large sheets of acid-free, lignin-free, buffered paper around alkaline tubes at least four inches in diameter; do not use narrow tubes as these will cause the documents to curl tightly, resulting in difficulty in flattening for use. Do not use wooden dowels as acid in the wood will harms the items. You can then store the rolled items in acid-free, lignin-free, buffered archival quality containers. These kind of containers are expensive. If you cannot afford them, you can also store the rolled oversized items horizontally on shelves. Be careful that rolls do not stick out beyond the end of the shelf. If you have to store oversized items vertically (standing on end), do not overcrowd or crush them.

Photographic Media

Handling

Handling photographs correctly is very important. If possible, wear white, lint free, or nitrile (synthetic rubber) gloves when handling photos. Touching a photograph with your fingers will leave oil from your skin on it and over time this oil will mark the photograph. Avoid bending or creasing photographs and pick them up by the edge using both hands. Light is harmful to photographs so keep them covered when they are not being viewed.

Processing Tasks

Getting the correct enclosures for photographic materials can be complicated. Paper enclosures must be acid-free, lignin-free, and buffered for black and white photographs and older color photographs. Contemporary color photographs should be housed in acid-free, lignin-free, and unbuffered enclosures. Paper enclosures for photographs must pass the Photographic Activity Test (PAT).

You can create your own folders for the photographs by folding a piece of acid-free, lignin-free, buffered archival quality paper in half. When storing photographs using this type of folder, make sure it is well supported, so the photograph doesn't bend or curl.

The positives of using paper enclosures for photographs is that they are relatively cheap, and you can label the paper enclosure rather than the actual photograph. The negative side of paper enclosures is that you have to handle the actual photograph to view it. There are some types of photographs that should not be enclosed in buffered paper or folders. The NEDCC states in preservation pamphlet "5.5 Storage Enclosures for Photographic Materials" that "unbuffered paper enclosures are recommended for storage of color images, cyanotypes, and albumen prints due to their sensitivity to alkalinity."[11]

You can also use plastic enclosures made of polyester, polypropylene, or polyethylene for photographic materials. These enclosures should not be coated or contain plasticizers or other additives. Plastic enclosures are expensive, but you can view the photographs without handling the actual photo.

Getting the right enclosures for photographic materials can get complicated. For additional information on this topic see the NEDCC Preservation Pamphlet "5.5 Storage Enclosures for Photographic Materials" and the Library of Congress Preservation site under Collections Care, Photographs.[12]

Photographs generally come to an archives as separate photographic collections or as part of larger paper-based collections. If you are keeping photographs within a paper-based collection, place the photograph in the appropriate enclosure and label it with the collections information in case the photograph gets separated from the collection. Label enclosures with pencil only. If it is necessary to mark a photograph, write lightly with a soft lead pencil on the reverse of the image.

If you pull photographs out of a paper-based collection insert a separation sheet within the collection where the photograph was removed describing it and noting where it is stored. If the collection photographs have been digitized, you can print a copy of the photographs on acid-free, lignin-free, buffered paper and place it within the collection as a convenience to the researchers.

Keep cased objects, such as daguerreotypes and ambrotypes, in their original cases or frames. If possible, encase them in custom-made, four-flap paper enclosures to reduce wear and tear on fragile cases. Daguerreotype used from the late 1830s until 1860 was the first commercially successful photographic process. Daguerreotype images are on a metal plate housed in a case rather than on paper.[13] Ambrotypes, which are also kept in cases, are negative images on glass plates with dark material behind the image. Ambrotype images were used from the early 1850s until about 1865.[14]

After being placed in Mylar envelopes or other enclosures, prints, negatives, and cased objects should be put in acid-free, lignin-free, buffered durable boxes to give them additional protection from light, dust, and potential environmental fluctuations.

Nitrate Film Base

Everyone and every institution collecting photographs and negatives needs to know about the dangers of cellulous nitrate negative film stock. Cellulous nitrate negative film stock is highly flammable and releases hazardous gases as it deteriorates. Cellulous nitrate negative film stock has caused numerous fires and should be dealt with immediately. At minimum, cellulous nitrate negative film stock should be separated from other film stock and stored in low humidity cold storage. Ideally, cellulous nitrate negative film stock should be copied onto modern film stock and then destroyed.

Eastman Kodak sold cellulous nitrate negative film stock from 1889 until the early 1950s. The NEDCC Preservation Pamphlet "5.1 A Short Guide to Film Base Photographic Materials"[15] describes the deterioration of cellulous nitrate negative as

> Nitric oxide, nitrous oxide, and nitrous dioxide are all released as gases from the decomposition of cellulose nitrate. In the presence of atmospheric moisture, these gases combine with water to form nitric acid. The formation of nitric acid acts to further degrade cellulose nitrate film, and it can destroy enclosures in which the negatives are stored. It can even damage materials stored in close proximity to the collection.

For information on identifying and dealing with cellulous nitrate negative film stock, see the NEDCC Preservation Pamphlet "5.1 A Short Guide to Film Base Photographic Materials"[16] or "Preserving Your Collection of Film-based Photographic Negatives" by Paul Messier of the Rocky Mountain Conservation Center.[17]

Scrapbooks

Handling

Scrapbooks should be stored individually on shelves because of their unique conditions, weights, and sizes. Support and pull scrapbooks (or other bound volumes) from the bottom when removing them from shelves. Pulling them from the top can harm the spine of the volume. Use caution when turning the pages of scrapbooks as they may be brittle and use book cradles or supports to hold the volumes whenever possible.

Processing Tasks

If the scrapbook is in good physical condition, store it in an acid-free, lignin-free, buffered archival box. If it is in poor condition photocopy, microfilm, or digitize the scrapbook to document its original order and then dismantle it. Preserve the dismantled pages of scrapbooks by placing them in acid-free, lignin-free, buffered folders.

News Clippings within a Collection

Handling Tips

Handle news clippings carefully so they don't rip or tear—newsprint is very fragile.

Processing Tasks

Note where the clipping is filed within the collection to ensure it gets refiled in the correct place. Remove the clipping, photocopy it onto acid-free, lignin-free, buffered paper, and place the photocopy in the collection in lieu of the original clipping. I would be very reluctant to encapsulate clippings because of the cost. As stated earlier, do not use lamination and consider encapsulation only if done by a conservator or someone trained by a conservator.

What do you do with the original clipping? It is very difficult if not impossible to preserve original clippings. Newsprint is too fragile and it contains too much acid (which is what turns it brown and brittle) to make preservation economically feasible. You can preserve original newspapers and clippings, but you need to consider the cost vs. the benefit of doing so as well as the potential impact on other projects (i.e., less time and resources to spend on other collections). In most cases the information on the clippings is of importance, not the clippings themselves. Copying the clippings preserves the information. While it goes against our nature as archivists, in most cases the correct decision, once you have made preservation quality copies, is to discard (destroy) the original clippings. It is just too expensive to preserve them and in most cases they have little or no intrinsic or artefactual value (value as physical things). Having said that, there are always exceptions. Several institutions use original clippings to demonstrate the aging process of historical materials to users.

Informational value versus artefactual value is an ongoing argument in archives with no right answer. If an archives copies, digitizes, or microfilms a collection, should they spend resources preserving the original items in the collection? If the only value the collection has is the information it contains, the answer is no. However, this is seldom the case and some people will get angry very quickly should they discover that an archival organization is destroying original items just because they have been copied.

If your organization is considering destroying original items because they have been copied, I urge you to evaluate the items very carefully before proceeding. The look and feel of original items is very difficult to duplicate and photocopies, microfilm, and digital surrogates fail to convey that look and feel to users. If you are convinced that the original items have no artefactual value and you plan to destroy them, I would follow and document that I followed, the internal procedures your organization has to deaccession the items. If possible, I would return the items to the donor rather than destroy them.

Microfilm and Microfiche

Handling

Master negatives get special treatment because they are the preservation copies of the film, they are used to create the copies of the film used by researchers. Store the master negative in a secure location in appropriate environmental conditions. (Master films should be stored at maximums of 65°F, 35% RH, ±5 percent.) Wear gloves when handling master negatives. Handle all microfilm and microfiche, including use copies, by the edges or leaders. Resleeve fiche immediately after use. Do not pull film rolls tight on the reel as this can scratch the film.

Processing Tasks

Microfilm reels should be individually boxed. The film should be held in the wound position by a preservation-quality paper tag secured with a string and button tie (rubber bands contain residual sulfur, a source of film and emulsion damage, and must never be used). Storage containers should be made of acid-free, lignin-free, buffered paper.

Storage containers should be adequately labeled and should accurately reflect the contents of the roll. Microfiche should be sleeved with the emulsion side away from the interior edges of the enclosure to prevent abrasion (this also adds protection from adhesives on sealed edges). If you are storing the master negative and using copies, maintain an index that allows you to understand where each is stored and that shows the relationship between the master negative and the use copy.

Figure 6.6.   Cabinet holding microfilm reels
Photo by Laurie Gemmill Arp, courtesy of Columbus Metropolitan Library

Audio and Video Magnetic Tapes

Handling

Minimize handling tapes. Handle tapes only by the housing supports, never touch tape surfaces. Avoid contamination of the tape by dirt, dust, food, cigarette smoke, and airborne pollutants. Assure proper threading and mounting on playback equipment. Rewind tapes with even tension. Take care not to drop tapes and/or cassettes.

Processing Tasks

Rewind tapes completely. Store tapes in labeled, protective, inert plastic containers. The preservation of magnetic tapes is covered in chapter 13, Digitization.

Section IV: Summary

The preservation decisions you will make are based on a careful examination of the materials. Different materials require different preservation procedures and materials. It's critical that you remove containers that are unsafe for the storage of historic materials and replace them with containers that promote the preservation of the items. In most cases this means purchasing and re-housing historic materials in acid-free, lignin-free, buffered containers.

Now that we've covered the handling of materials, we'll move on to the documentation of your collection in the next chapter—writing descriptions and finding aids.

Preservation Quiz

See the answers on page 323.

1. The underlying philosophical theme of archival work is that, as archivists, we need to preserve the collections in our care while providing access to them. Which is more important:
   a. Preserving archival collections
   b. Providing access to archival collections
2. Early paper was made from cotton or rag stock and is very stable. When paper started being made of wood pulp, it started deteriorating relatively quickly because of its acid content. When did paper start being made of wood pulp?
   a. The 1880s
   b. During World War II
   c. The 1840s
3. Why do archivists keep food and drinks out of archival work areas?
   a. Food in work areas increases the likelihood of vermin infesting those areas.
   b. It is easy to spill drinks and/or food on archival collections while working on them, thus harming or destroying items.
   c. Both A and B
4. If you can only purchase a limited amount of processing supplies:
   a. Purchase archival boxes first.
   b. Purchase those materials that come in contact with the archival items first—things like acid-free, lignin-free, buffered folders or polyester photographic sleeves.
   c. Purchase bone folders first.

5. Why should you wear cotton gloves when handling photos?
   a. You want to keep the photos clean.
   b. Oil from your skin (fingers) will mark the photos.
   c. Both A and B
6. Mylar sleeves for photos are expensive. What can you do to house photos if you cannot afford Mylar sleeves?
   a. Use acid-free, lignin-free, buffered paper to create your own sleeves for photos.
   b. Put the photos in folders without sleeves.
   c. Use everyday copy paper to create your own sleeves for photos.
7. What is the best way to store maps, architectural drawings, or other oversized documents?
   a. Rolled up and vertical (standing on end) in a bin
   b. Rolled up and horizontal (laying down on its side) on a shelf
   c. Lying flat in an oversize cabinet
8. What is the most efficient way to preserve news clippings?
   a. Encapsulate them in a clear polyester envelope.
   b. Photocopy the news clipping onto acid-free, lignin-free, buffered paper.
   c. Deacidify the news print and then encapsulate the clipping in a clear polyester envelope.
9. Should a microfiche/microfilm master negative get special storage treatment?
   a. Yes
   b. No
10. If you cannot afford oversized cabinets to store maps, architectural drawings, or other oversized documents, how should you store them?
   a. Rolled up and vertical (standing on end) in a bin
   b. Rolled up and horizontal (laying down on its side) on a shelf

Notes

1. Northeast Document Conservation Center, Preservation Leaflet, "4.1 Storage Methods and Handling Practices," accessed March 2018. https://www.nedcc.org/free-resources/preservation-leaflets/4.-storage-and-handling/4.1-storage-methods-and-handling-practices

2. National Park Service, "Conservo-Gram 4/9, July 1995," accessed March 2018. https://www.nps.gov/museum/publications/conserveogram/04-09.pdf

3. Northeast Document Conservation Center, Preservation Leaflet, "4.1 Storage Methods and Handling Practices," accessed March 2018. https://www.nedcc.org/free-resources/preservation-leaflets/4.-storage-and-handling/4.1-storage-methods-and-handling-practices

4. Library of Congress, Preservation, accessed September 2018. https://www.loc.gov/preservation/

5. CoCOL, accessed September 2018. http://cool.conservation-us.org/

6. Northeast Document Conservation Center, accessed March 2018. https://www.nedcc.org/

7. Northeast Document Conservation Center, Preservation Leaflets, "7.8 Removal of Damaging Fasteners from Historic Documents," accessed March 2018. https://www.nedcc.org/free-resources/preservation-leaflets/7.-conservation-procedures/7.8-removal-of-damaging-fasteners-from-historic-documents

8. Northeast Document Conservation Center, Preservation Pamphlet, "7.5 Conservation Treatment for Works of Art and Unbound Artifacts on Paper," accessed March 2018. https://www.nedcc.org/free-resources/preservation-leaflets/7.-conservation-procedures/7.5-conservation-treatment-for-works-of-art-and-unbound-artifacts-on-paper?fontsize=4

9. Wikipedia, "Red Rot," accessed March 2018. https://en.wikipedia.org/wiki/Red_rot

10. Northeast Document Conservation Center, Preservation Leaflets, "4.9 Storage Solutions for Oversized Paper Artifacts," accessed March 2018. https://www.nedcc.org/free-resources/preservation-leaflets/4.-storage-and-handling/4.9-storage-solutions-for-oversized-paper-artifacts

11. Northeast Document Conservation Center, Preservation Leaflet "5.5 Storage Enclosures for Photographic Materials," accessed September 2018. https://www.nedcc.org/free-resources/preservation-leaflets/5.-photographs/5.5-storage-enclosures-for-photographic-materials

12. Library of Congress, Preservation, Collections Care, "Photographs," accessed March 2018. https://www.loc.gov/preservation/care/photo.html

13. For more information on daguerreotypes see Daguerreobase, Collective Cataloging Tool for Daguerreotypes, "What is a Daguerreotype," accessed March 2018. http://www.daguerreobase.org/en/knowledge-base/what-is-a-daguerreotype

14. Wikipedia, "Ambrotype," accessed March 2018. https://en.wikipedia.org/wiki/Ambrotype

15. Northeast Document Conservation Center, Preservation Pamphlet, "5.1 A Short Guide to Film Base Photographic Materials," accessed September 2018. https://www.nedcc.org/free-resources/preservation-leaflets/5.-photographs/5.1-a-short-guide-to-film-base-photographic-materials-identification,-care,-and-duplication

16. Northeast Document Conservation Center, Preservation Pamphlet, "5.1 A Short Guide to Film Base Photographic Materials," accessed September 2018. https://www.nedcc.org/free-resources/preservation-leaflets/5.-photographs/5.1-a-short-guide-to-film-base-photographic-materials-identification,-care,-and-duplication

17. Conservation On-line (Cool), "Preserving Your Collection of Film-based Photographic Negatives" Paul Messier, accessed September 2018. http://cool.conservation-us.org/byauth/messier/negrmcc.html

Chapter 7

Description

Description takes what you have learned about a collection during arrangement and preservation to create a roadmap to the collection for researchers. Without a good description the most historically valuable records will go unused because researchers won't know they exist or how to find them. Good descriptions are also vital to the ongoing management of your collections.

This chapter has four sections. Section I goes over description in detail. Section II is a discussion of finding aids. Section III is a finding aid exercise in which you will be asked to make arrangement, preservation, and description decisions based on information provided. You can then compare your decisions with mine. The chapter ends with section IV, the chapter summary.

Section I: Description in Detail

You began descriptive work when you accession records. At that stage you started to understand and document the contents and physical nature of the records. You continued to gather descriptive information when you arranged the collection by researching the creator, reviewing the records, and deciding on an arrangement scheme. The preservation work you do on a collection also affects the description. The work you do refoldering and relabeling items will help you create a list of folders, which serves as an inventory to the records.

A description of the collection should provide enough information to allow you both to manage and to provide appropriate access to it. The description includes information about the location of the collection within the archive so that staff can find it, along with the source and content of the collection.

What Descriptive Tools Do You Need?

Descriptive tools range from catalogs to sophisticated computer systems that organize information about the collections held by an archival program. In this book, I will offer a simple, streamlined approach to description that you can adapt to your own program's needs and existing processes.

Catalogs

Most historical records programs use some kind of catalog to point researchers to the collections they are looking for. Your catalog may take the form of a card catalog made up of index cards arranged in specific ways, a database, a complex, computerized public access system, or even a simple list of collections. No matter what form it takes, your catalog is the main point of access to your collections.

Figure 7.1. Traditional card catalogs are still very useful.
Photo by Laurie Gemmill Arp, courtesy of Columbus Metropolitan Library

Catalog Entries

You will create a catalog entry for each collection that has been processed and is available for research. At minimum the entry should contain the following informational elements:

- Title of collection
- Provenance (creator or source) of the collection
- Dates the collection covers
- A unique collection number
- A brief (one or two sentence) description of the contents of the collection, if the title is not an adequate description

The library and archival communities have created rules and tools for creating catalog entries. If you want to learn more about these formalized cataloging rules, take a look at *Describing Archives: A Content Standard. Second Edition (DACS),* published by the Society of American Archivists (www.archivists.org).[1]

Is a Catalog Entry Enough?

Some collections may only need a catalog entry to make them accessible for researchers. Small collections, consisting of a single or few items, are often described using only a catalog entry.

How do you know if a catalog entry is the only description needed? Put yourself in the researcher's shoes. Ask yourself how people looking for the information contained in a collection would find it. What would they need to know in order to identify the collection as the source of information they need? Generally, if a collection consists of a single record series and is relatively small in size a catalog entry will be adequate. Some examples include

Ada Elder Autograph Book 1920
One volume
Call number: MSS 98

William Banister School Records 1910
1 cubic foot
Call number: MSS 45

Christ Church Baptismal Records 1930–60
Arranged alphabetically by last name.
Box 1: A–H
Box 2: I–R
Box 3: S–Z
Call number: MSS 151

In these cases, researchers gain enough information from the catalog to understand what the records are, where they came from, and whether they are likely to contain useful information. A catalog entry alone won't provide adequate information to a researcher when collections are larger and more complex. For example,

Jenny Fox Collection 1906–1910
10 cubic feet
Call number: MSS 130

Burleigh Company Records 1880–1940
7 cubic feet
Call number: MSS 40

Barbara Jones Papers 1875–1900
15 cubic feet
Call number: MSS 202

In these cases, a catalog entry does not provide enough information for researchers to know what is in the collection. When researchers need a more detailed description of the contents of a collection, you will need to create a *finding aid* for them.

Section II: Finding Aids

Finding aids are also referred to as *inventories* or *registers* by some historic records programs. Finding aids provide detailed information about collections, describing not just the content of the collection, but the context in which it was created. They answer questions such as these:

- Where did the records come from?
- Why were they created?
- How do they relate to other records?
- Why are they significant?

Elements of a Finding Aid

The informational elements of a finding aid will vary. The core elements of a finding aid are:

- Name of the historic records program that holds the collection
- Unique collection number
- Collection title
- Collection dates
- Name of creating entity
- Biographical sketch or organizational history
- Records description
- Access restrictions
- Inventory—list of boxes and folders

The finding aid is what you and your researchers will use to get an idea of whether or not the collection has the information they seek.

Archivists don't just sit down and write a finding aid. Instead, as they research, take notes, and learn about the collection, they do so with the understanding that they will be creating a finding aid for the collection at some point. When the collection has been processed, they take their knowledge and their notes in hand to create that finding aid.

This means that as you process a collection, you will need to keep the elements of a finding aid in mind to make sure you gather and keep track of the information you need for the finding aid. Let's take a look at each core element in more detail.

Unique Collection Number

Each collection being processed should be assigned a unique collection number. Programs create and assign collection numbers in different ways depending on how their collections are organized. In many cases the collection number is as simple as the next sequential number. The first collection processed is collection 1, the second collection processed is collection 2, so on and so forth.

Record Creator

The record creator is the person or group responsible for creating or using the group of records, not the individual items within the collection. Use the name by which the person or group is most commonly known. For example, use Stevie Wonder, not Steve Morris.

Collection Title

The collection title is a descriptive title you assign to the collection. In cases where you just create a catalog entry for the collection, this will be the only information a researcher uses to decide if they want to use the collection, so the title needs to convey some idea of what is in the collection. Usually the title is made up of a combination of the name of the record creator and the predominant type of material that is in the collection. Be as specific as you can, while still accurately reflecting the content of the collection. Use the terms records, papers, and collection as defined in chapter 5. Records are created by institutions or governments, papers are created by individuals or families, collections are items brought together by a unifying concept.

For example, the *James Tayson Personal Papers* would be an accurate title for a collection that included letters, diaries, and personal financial records. However, if the collection consisted only of letters from World War II, a better title would be the *James Tayson World War II Letters*. The *ABC Bakery Records* might be more appropriately called the *ABC Bakery Financial Records*. The *Linda Smith Photograph Collection* might be more appropriately called the *Linda Smith Family Photograph Collection*.

Collection Dates

The dates of the records should be included in the finding aid. Often the dates are included as part of the collection title—James Tayson Financial Records, 1923–1958.

Many archivists use the abbreviation circa, given as ca. or c. before or after collection dates to note uncertainty about a date. Circa is Latin for around or about and it is used when specific dates are not known.[2] If you see circa used before a date—ca. 1775—it means the actual date is not known but it is believed to about 1775. So a collection date of c. 1775 to 1813 means the archivists who processed the collection believes the collection materials date from around 1775 to 1813.

Biographical Sketch or Organizational History

This section contains a brief overview of the main events in the history of the creator, providing the researcher with enough information to understand the context in which the records were created. You gathered this information when you researched the collection's provenance.

Description

This element should describe the collection, including the types of materials, dates, and information about how it has been arranged. It should also discuss the strengths, weaknesses, and gaps in the collection; and it should note any significant subjects, people, or organizations. The best descriptions bring out what is hidden in the collection—bringing to light what might not be obvious to the researcher.

You gather this information from your processing notes, from the preprocessing research you did, and from your own knowledge of the collection.

Access Restrictions

If there are any access restrictions and/or copyright statements that pertain to this collection, they should be noted in the finding aid. This information should be part of your accession, acquisition, or processing records. If portions of the collection are restricted for legal reasons, if for example the collection contains medical or student education records, note the appropriate legal citation.

Inventory—List of Boxes and Folders

The inventory element acts as a detailed table of contents to the collection. It usually consists of a listing of the folder title, folder number, and box number. The goal of the inventory is to allow the researcher to identify precisely what box or folder is needed.

It might look something like table 7.1.

Table 7.1.   Box 1

Minutes	January 1955– June 1955	Folder 1
Minutes	July 1955–November 1955	Folder 2
Minutes	December 1955– May 1956	Folder 3

See appendix M "Example Finding Aid–Pearl Nye." The core elements are identified in this finding aid for your reference. There are finding aids you can use as examples at every archive. Many archives have finding aids online for you to review including the National Archives and Records Administration,[3] the Minnesota Historical Society,[4] the OhioLink Finding Aid Repository,[5] and the Massachusetts Historical Society.[6] Some finding aids that I think are good examples include the "Laura Riding Jackson Papers, 1924–1984 (bulk, 1970–1984)" at the New York Public Library,[7] the Guide to the Atomic Scientists of Chicago Records 1943–1955" at the University of Chicago Library,[8] and the "Anita Pollitzer Family Papers 1845–1979" at the South Carolina Historical Society.[9]

Section III: Practice with Finding Aids

Now that you have learned about the core elements of a finding aid, you are going to create one on your own. I have provided background notes about the collection below (think of them as the processor's research notes) to get you started.

About the Collection

Your organization is the ABC Department of Archives and Local History. The collection is the Local Sailing Association Records.

The Records

- Two cubic feet minutes from Local Sailing Association, 1899–1960
- Accessioned four years ago
- Related Sailing Association records: membership rosters, correspondence, and photographs of events

The Sailing Association

- Voluntary social club prominent in the local community
- Incorporated in 1899—membership comprised of mostly wealthy individuals

- Depression—fewer people had sailboats; broadened membership to many socio-economic groups who shared an interest in sailing
- Focus changed to families and recreation plus sharing tips on sailing information and techniques
- Disbanded in 1960

Sailing Association Minutes

- Organized chronologically by date
- Entire history of the association
- Early twentieth century—significant amount of social commentary; detail on policy debates
- Local call number: Series 169

Minutes are arranged as follows:

Box 1

- Folder 1 Minutes, 1899–1905
- Folder 2 Minutes, 1906–1910
- Folder 3 Minutes, 1911–1915
- Folder 4 Minutes, 1916–1920
- Folder 5 Minutes, 1921–1925
- Folder 6 Minutes, 1926–1930

Box 2

- Folder 7 Minutes, 1931–1935
- Folder 8 Minutes, 1936–1940
- Folder 9 Minutes, 1941–1945
- Folder 10 Minutes, 1946–1950
- Folder 11 Minutes, 1951–1955
- Folder 12 Minutes, 1956–1960

There is a "Finding Aid Worksheet" provided as appendix N. Using it and the background information provided above, draft the elements of your finding aid now. There is an electronic version of the "Finding Aid Worksheet" you can download from the AASLH website at https://learn.aaslh.org/archivalbasics. You are free to modify and use this form as you wish.

Results

Now that you have created your own draft of a finding aid for this collection, take a look at the "Local Sailing Association Records" provided as appendix O. Compare yours with appendix O and make any revisions you think are appropriate. Keep the researchers' point of view in mind when you make your revisions. What would they be looking for and how would they look for it?

Remember a good finding aid is

- *Intended for the researchers.* A finding aid must help researchers find the materials they are looking for.
- *Objective about the collection.* The bias of the processor or the collecting program should not be reflected in a finding aid. It should describe the collection without commentary.
- *Aware of the needs of many researchers.* A good finding aid anticipates how different researchers will approach the collection.

- *Includes notices of any restrictions.* A good finding aid includes information on what items are restricted and why those items are restricted.
- *Clear, concise, and consistent.* Avoid using jargon in your finding aids. Consider creating a finding aid template that will enable you to write finding aids that are organized consistently. This consistency will make it easier for researchers to use your collections.
- *Efficient.* A good finding aid is easy for researchers to scan and grasp the information necessary as quickly as possible.

Section IV: Processing Case Study

Now that you understand arranging, preserving, and describing a collection, I will integrate all three tasks and examine a case study of an archivist processing a collection. I will work my way through processing with a sample collection, pointing out the appropriate steps along the way.

I will give you information about the collection being processed in *italic font*. I will ask you questions about various aspects of processing this collection. My answers to these questions will follow in roman font.

Scenario

You are a processor at the Riveroaks Historical Society and Museum. You recently appraised and accessioned a collection of papers from a local artist, Lisa Smith. The accession record for this collection contains the following information:

Accession number: 2002-013
Title: Lisa Smith Papers
Description: This collection consists of five cubic feet of records relating to the art of Lisa Smith. Lisa Smith was a local artist, recognized nationally, for her work depicting rural life. The records consist of exhibit files that include extensive notes and background material for each work exhibited, photographs of each exhibit, news clippings about each exhibit, and exhibit catalogs.
Dates of records: 1972–1999
Source of collection: Emily Smith
Accession date: April 12, 2002
Amount: 5 cubic feet
Restrictions: None
Location: Back storage room, shelf 3

Background Research

Before you process the collection, you need to learn about it and research its provenance. To do that use the preprocessing checklist referenced in chapter 5. That checklist asks three questions:

1. Who was the creator or accumulator of the records? What do you know about the people (individual or organization) who created and used the records?
2. What was the purpose of the records? Why were they created? How were they used?
3. What do you know about the time, place, and subjects of the records?

You research the collection using resources such as newspapers, biographical dictionaries, local histories, census records, and by interviewing the donor if possible. In this case, you locate several articles in the local newspapers that discuss the life of Lisa Smith and her work. For the first question, who was the creator or accumulator of the records, you learn that *Lisa Smith created this collection herself as a record of her work on various exhibits held both locally and nationally. Exhibits were held at galleries and museums. Lisa was very involved in the exhibition of her artwork and created and maintained detailed exhibit files, documenting how the exhibit was put together, reactions to it, what it looked like.*

For the second question, what was the purpose of the records, why were they created, you learn this: *The records were created between 1965 and 1999. They document exhibits of artwork held at several locations including but not limited to the Riveroaks Museum; the West Side Gallery in New York, NY; the Cleveland Museum of Art; the Museum of Modern Art; and the Gallerie de Francaise in Paris, France.*

The files contain information about each venue and each piece displayed at that venue, including the artist's handwritten descriptions and background of each painting. These were later edited and incorporated into exhibit catalogs, brochures, and other descriptive information. Most files contain photographs of each piece of artwork included in the exhibits and some contain photographs of the exhibit venue. Also included are newspaper clippings, exhibit catalogs and brochures, and correspondence between the artist and exhibit organizers.

Answering the third question, what do you know about the time, place, and subject of the records, you learn this: *Although the collection was created as a record of exhibits by the artist, its greatest strength is the artist's own descriptions of each piece, in which she details how the piece was created, the settings, the intent of each piece, and the meanings each piece had for her. These descriptions provide insight into the mind of the artist, how she was affected by the political and social events that occurred, including the Vietnam War, the social upheaval of the 1960s, the environmental movement, and local issues such as plant closings in Riveroaks in the 1970s, and economic development in the region.*

To identify the original order of the collection, you must look through each box and evaluate what you see. *In this case, when you look through the records you find that each file folder is labeled by the exhibit venue and date; however, the files are not in any particular order within the boxes and look somewhat disheveled, possibly indicating that they were hastily boxed without regard for the original order.*

Identify Your Arrangement Options

You should identify three arrangement options based on this review. Think about what those options might be, you have three choices:

1. You can leave the records in the order they are, assuming that this was the creator's actual filing system.
2. Because the file folders are labeled by name of venue, then date, you can decide that the artist used an alphabetical (by venue name) filing system.
3. You think that the files were created as each exhibit occurred, so you can decide to arrange the records by exhibit date.

The factors you must consider when deciding the arrangement choice to use are what the most likely original order is and how will researchers want to look for information?

It seems most likely that these records were filed either alphabetically or chronologically. Unfortunately, you cannot identify the logical order of the records because the records were boxed hastily. You try contacting Emily Smith, Lisa's daughter, who donated the collection. Unfortunately she doesn't know how the files were organized.

Without any clue to how the records were arranged, you must consider the needs of the researchers. How will they use the collection? What will they be looking for? What arrangement will most effectively meet their needs?

You speculate that most researchers of the collection will be researching the development of the style of the artist or will be researching a particular painting. What arrangement will facilitate access to those kinds of research questions? What about chronological order?

Arranging the collection chronologically would highlight the development of the artist's style and the development of her career (as demonstrated by the increasing prestige of the exhibit venues). Further, if a researcher knew the approximate date for a painting (which is likely), a chronological order would make searching easier. A chronological arrangement also seems a likely original order, since each file was created as each exhibit occurred through time.

What about alphabetical order? Arranging the collection alphabetically by venue name keeps the arrangement simple and straightforward. But, it would not highlight the artist's developing style or the increasing prestige of her career. Researchers looking for information on a particular painting would have to know where the painting was exhibited, which seems unlikely. What arrangement scheme would you chose?

My decision is this: I would arrange the collection chronologically by date of exhibit. Since each folder is labeled with both venue name and exhibition dates, the folder list that I create will include both venue name and exhibition dates. I could create an alternative index to the folders by venue name. Since it's not clear whether or not the researchers would need such an index at this point, and I have other collections to process, I simply make a note of this possibility.

Review the Records for Preservation Needs

Now that you have decided on your arrangement scheme, take a second look at the collection to decide what supplies you will need and how much preservation work will be necessary. *You note that the records are in good condition although they are quite dusty; there are news clippings; there aren't any materials larger than 8½ × 14 (legal size); there are many photographs within the collection; papers are held together using both staples and paper clips and there is no rust on them; there are some soft cover bound volumes (exhibit catalogs) within the collection.*

Based on the review above, you need to make the following preservation decisions. First, should the photographs be removed and stored separately or housed in archival quality folders and stored within the collection? Second, should the staples and paper clips be removed? Finally, what preservation supplies will you need?

What to Do with the Photographs?

You estimate that there are approximately 300–400 photographs within the collection. Removing them will require extensive cross referencing and labeling that will substantially increase processing time. Further, the photographs are integral to understanding the records and researchers will rely on them. So removing them may be highly frustrating for the user. Maintaining the photographs within the collection will provide a better user experience and will maintain the cohesion of the records. What would you do with the photographs?

My decision: If I had limited resources, I would store the photographs within the collection, using folders created from folded acid free paper to protect them. Since the photographs are such an important part of this collection, if I had the time, expertise, and resources, I would digitize the photographs, remove the original photos from the collection, and replace them with digital images printed on acid free, lignin-free, buffered paper. The digital images would have information about where to find the original photograph on the back of the image. I would also consider putting the digital images on the institution's website to raise awareness of the collection and our archives. I would then place the original photographs in Mylar envelopes in acid free, lignin-free, buffered boxes and create a second index to them based on subject.

Should You Take the Time to Remove All Staples and Paper Clips?

Although time consuming, the best practice is to remove all staples and paper clips. What do you think you should do?

My decision: Since the staples and paperclips are not rusty and you have a limited staff available for processing, I would decide to save processing time by leaving the paperclips and staples in the collection. There is one exception: if a clip or staple is holding photographs together, that clip or staple will need to be removed so that the photographs can be physically separated using acid free, lignin-free, buffered paper, or folders.

What Preservation Supplies Will You Need?

Based on your review, your supply list should look like this:

- Five archival quality cubic foot boxes
- Acid-free paper for photocopying news clippings and foldering photos
- Approximately 200 legal sized acid free file folders
- Number 2 pencils for labeling folders
- Spatula (archival staple remover)
- Dust brush

What's Your Plan?

By this point you should have a good idea of how processing will move forward. You should have a file containing background information and notes (which will be incorporated into your descriptive aids later) and a list of supplies. It's a good idea to include an informal plan for the processing of the collection. This plan should include the arrangement scheme you have decided on, the reason for your decision, and preservation decisions. It's important to get this down in writing in case you are interrupted and don't get back to the collection for some time, or in case another person takes over the processing for some reason. Your informal plan for processing this collection might look something like this.

Arrangement

It was not possible to determine the original order of the collection so arrangement will be chronological by exhibition dates. Arranging the collection chronologically would highlight the development of the artist's style and the development of her career (as demonstrated by the increasing prestige of the exhibit venues). Further, if a researcher knew the approximate date for a painting, a chronological order would make searching easier.

Description

I am considering creating an index to the collection based on venue location. It's not clear at this point if this will be helpful to the researcher or not, so I will wait and see how researchers use the records. If it seems further indexing would be helpful, I can create it later.

Preservation

Photographs are integral to the collection and will be maintained with the collection—not removed. They should be stored in archival paper folders.

The Research is Done—Let's Get to Work!

You're now ready to roll up your sleeves and get your hands on the collection.

> **Tip:** Before you get started, make sure you have adequate workspace that is clean and secure. Gather your supplies and have them in the processing area ready to use.

Physically Arrange the Collection

You have already decided the appropriate arrangement for the collection. Now you should do the physical arrangement. In this case, the file folders are labeled with venue title and exhibition dates, making the physical arrangement relatively easy.

Just look through each box, identify the files in chronological order (from 1965–2001), then move the files, in order, to new boxes. When you have one box filled with arranged records, put a temporary label on the box noting the date span, so it's easy to keep the boxes in order.

When you're done, you should have five cubic feet of records arranged chronologically by exhibition dates. You should take a look at the arrangement and double check it to see if there are any mistakes.

Arrangement Decision

You happen to notice that there are two instances where exhibition start dates are the same:

> *Riveroaks Museum, September 1971–December 1971*
> *Art World, September 1971–January 1972*
> *Smith's Gallery, March 15, 1981–June 31, 1981*
> *Cleveland Museum of Art, March 15, 1981–August 1, 1981*

What ordering principle will you use to file them?

My decision: I think it would be easiest for researchers of the collection if I filed these materials chronologically, then alphabetically by venue. So this is what the filing system looks like:

Art World, September 1971–January 1972
Riveroaks Museum, September 1971–December 1971
Cleveland Museum of Art, March 15, 1981–August 1, 1981
Smith's Gallery, March 15, 1981–June 31, 1981

Start the Preservation Work

The files are arranged now, so it's time to begin the preservation work on the materials. You begin by removing the first folder from the first box—Riverpark Art Gallery, February 9, 1965 to March 31, 1965—reviewing the contents to determine preservation actions and taking the appropriate actions. Make sure to maintain the order of the documents and items within the folder.

You begin by removing the first folder from the box and working your way through the contents of the folder, taking appropriate preservation actions as you go, and making sure to maintain the order of the documents and items within the folder. Begin work by starting with the first box. Remove the first file and review the contents to determine preservation actions. The first file is labeled Riverpark Art Gallery, February 9, 1965 to March 31, 1965.

You begin your preservation work by handling each item and taking appropriate action on it. Note that the items are all quite dusty and dirty, so at a minimum, cleaning is required. You may wish to review the preservation instructions in chapter 6 before beginning the exercise below.

For each of the nine items in the folder, decide upon the correct preservation actions to take. I have listed the appropriate preservation actions for each item in italics.

1. A folded letter inviting Lisa Smith to exhibit five paintings at a local artists' exhibit at the Riverpark Art Gallery. *You should carefully unfold the letter, wipe gently with dust brush, and place upside down in pile.*
2. A unfolded letter accepting the invitation. *You should wipe the letter gently with dust brush and place in pile upside down on top of first item.*
3. An unfolded letter and attached materials (including a photograph of the exhibit space) describing the exhibit (stapled together). *You should carefully remove staple, remove photograph, and house in folded sheet of acid-free paper. Clip materials with archival quality clip.*
4. Notes made on legal pad paper by Lisa Smith, listing paintings to be exhibited and brief descriptions of them. *There is really no action necessary. Clean if needed and place the notes in pile.*
5. An unfolded letter from Lisa Smith to the Gallery with attached list of paintings and descriptions of them (stapled). *There is really no action necessary. Clean if needed and place the letter in pile.*
6. A trifolded brochure from the exhibit. *You should unfold the brochure, clean it if needed, and place in pile.*
7. Photographs of each painting as displayed at the exhibit. *You should place each photograph in folded acid free paper folder and place in pile.*
8. Newspaper clippings from local papers about the exhibit and artists. *You should photocopy clippings onto acid-free paper and place in pile—or note the titles of each clipping on a sheet of paper, separate clippings for later photocopying, when photocopied return copied clippings to the appropriate place in the collection.*
9. An unfolded thank you letter from the gallery to Lisa Smith. *There is really no action necessary. Clean if needed and place the letter in pile.*

Filing

Copy the original folder label exactly onto an archival quality folder using a number 2 pencil in clear handwriting. Place the items in the labeled folder. Folders can be creased along edge lines to ensure the documents don't bend. Most file folders have score lines that run parallel to the center fold. If you crease the folder along one of those lines, the folder expands to accommodate more documents.

> **Tip:** If the contents of one of the original folders is too large for a single archival folder, use a second folder. Label both folders identically (per the original), and note "folder 1 of 2" and "folder 2 of 2."

Boxing

Place the processed folder in an archival box of the appropriate dimensions. (In our scenario, we are using cubic foot boxes.) You will find that it may be helpful to place the box on its side so that the folders lay flat as you continue filling up the box—this keeps the documents from bending. Continue to work your way through each file folder within the collection. Fill the box so it is snug and the documents don't bend when the box is sitting in the correct position. Don't overfill! Folders should slip easily in and out of the box without forcing or bending. Put a temporary label on the box to help you keep track of it.

Figure 7.2.   Archival box (12 × 15 × 10) containing almost too many file folders. The folders stand without bending but they do not slip easily out of the box.
Photo by Laurie Gemmill Arp, courtesy of Columbus Metropolitan Library

> **Tip:** If you finish a collection and have some room left over in the last box, use a smaller box or use a box spacer to support the documents within the box and prevent them from bending. Box spacers are available from archival suppliers or you can make your own.

The Finishing Touches

Once you have completed the preservation work on the entire collection, you will need to create permanent box labels and, if you haven't already, assign the collection a permanent collection number according to your existing internal practices.

Permanent box labels should be adhered directly to the box with appropriate archival adhesives. The label should, at a minimum, include the unique collection number and the sequential box number within the collection. If you are certain there will be no additions to the collection you can also include the number of boxes in the collections (i.e., box 1 of 4). A sample box label could look like figure 7.3.

Figure 7.3. Box label with minimal information
Photo by Laurie Gemmill Arp, courtesy of Columbus Metropolitan Library

The Finding Aid

With the accession record and your research and processing notes handy, you are ready to write a finding aid for this collection. Feel free to use the "Finding Aid Worksheet" provided as appendix N. There is also an electronic version of this form you can download from the AASLH website at https://aaslh.org to draft your own version of the finding aid for this collection. When you are finished, take a look at our version of the finding aid, appendix P, "Lisa Smith Finding Aid," and see how yours compares.

If your program uses catalogs, you should create the finding aid first, and then create the catalog card or record based on the finding aid.

Different Levels of Processing

What I have described in this case study is full processing. While it is important for you to understand full processing, very few collections deserve or need this level of processing and description. Most institutions have a backlog of processing such that they cannot afford the time and resources needed to process their collections to the item level. It is important for you to discuss with your colleagues the correct level of processing at your institution along with what level of processing each collection warrants. Many institutions have a processing manual that describes their processing standards, including how their finding aids are written. If such a manual exists at your institution, it will be important that you follow it. If your institution does not have a processing manual, consider creating one to ensure consistent processing practices.

I was always told that the goal of archival processing and description was to put the box containing what a researcher is looking for in front of them. A view of processing called "more product less process" (aka MPLP), calls for minimal processing of collections to the level needed to make them usable for researchers.[10] The trick is finding that minimal level and defining usable. The point of MPLP is that backlogs of unprocessed collections that cannot be used by researchers are no good to archival institutions or to researchers. In the MPLP world, it is better to have simple high level descriptions of collections so they can be used by researchers than it is to have a few carefully crafted finding aids with 60 percent of an institutions collections unavailable to researchers because they have not been processed. I agree with the philosophy behind MPLP, but its implementation can be difficult.

The level of processing and description your institution employs depends on the resources available to it and the nature of the collections being processed. A few collections merit an item by item description of their contents because of their historical significance or the importance of their authors. For the vast majority of collections, a folder-by-folder description is more than sufficient. Some government collections can get by with a box-level description because of the nature and volume of their records. The collection being processed and how researchers will use it define the correct level of processing needed by that collection. How much processing is needed by a collections must be determined on a case by case basis.

The level of preservation a collection receives is also dependent on the merit of the collection and the resources the institutions has. It would be nice if every staple was removed from every document in every archival collection, but that is just not possible.

Processing collections takes time, effort, and resources. Because many archival institutions lack sufficient resources they have a backlog of collections awaiting processing. Whenever possible, avoid allowing public access to unprocessed collections lacking sufficient finding aids. Unprocessed collections might contain private/confidential information such as social security numbers, and health or student educational records that you might be unaware of and that should not be made available to the public. As well, the more you know about the contents of your collections, the easier it is to prove that something belongs to you. This is important if someone steals items from your collections.

Section IV: Summary

Arranging, preserving, and describing your historic records collections are core archival activities. These activities, together called *processing*, result in collections that are well organized, preserved from deterioration, and accessible to your researchers.

Arrangement and description must be done with the user in mind. Providing a collection that reflects its creation (*provenance* and *original order*) allows researchers to more fully understand why and how the records they are using were created; giving them a context for their research. The cataloging tools and finding aids that you create for your collections are the only means for helping researchers locate what they want.

The preservation work that is done during processing assures that your collections will stay in the best possible condition. Preservation work requires time and resources. Most historic records programs have to make decisions about just how much preservation work they can afford to do during processing. If you can only afford one thing, try to make sure that the materials that come into direct contact with the records are of appropriate archival quality. The folders, enclosures, and boxes that house your historic records collections provide the first line of defense against deterioration.

The level of processing your institution uses depends on the resources available to it, the backlog of collections waiting to be processed, the nature of the collection being processed, and the needs of the researchers using the collection. You want to do enough processing so you can put the box containing what a researcher is looking for in front of them.

In the next chapter, we will continue looking at preservation, but from a broader perspective. Your materials are affected by the building and storage conditions in which they are located and by the potential disasters that could occur. We will look at these factors in depth, and help you to decide what changes you should make in the physical environment of your facility and how you can plan for potential disasters in order to help preserve your historical records.

Notes

1. Society of American Archivists, Bookstore, *Describing Archives: A Content Standard (DACS) Second Edition,* accessed March 2018. https://saa.archivists.org/store/describing-archives-a-content-standard-dacs/223/

2. Wikipedia, "Circa," accessed March 2018. https://en.wikipedia.org/wiki/Circa

3. National Archives and Records Administration, Research Our Records, "Regional Guides and Research Aids," accessed March 2018. https://www.archives.gov/research/guides/regional-resource-aids.html

4. Minnesota Historical Society, "Collection Finding Aids," accessed March 2018. http://search.mnhs.org/?brand=findaids

5. OhioLink, "Finding Aid Repository, Browse, Title," accessed March 2018. http://ead.ohiolink.edu/xtf-ead/search?browse-title=first;sort=title

6. Massachusetts Historical Society, Collections Guides, "Search Collection Guides," accessed March 2018. https://www.masshist.org/collection-guides/

7. New York Public Library, Archives and Manuscripts, "Laura Riding Jackson Papers, 1924–1984 (Bulk 1970–1984)," accessed March 2018. http://archives.nypl.org/brg/23210

8. University of Chicago Library, Special Collections Research Center, Finding Aids, "Guide to the Atomic Scientists of Chicago Records 1943–1955," accessed March 2018. https://www.lib.uchicago.edu/e/scrc/findingaids/view.php?eadid=ICU.SPCL.ASCHICAGO

9. The South Carolina Historical Society, "Anita Pollitzer Family Papers 1845–1979," accessed March 2018. http://www.southcarolinahistoricalsociety.org/wp-content/uploads/2013/01/Anita-Pollitzer-family-papers-12101.pdf

10. Greene and Meissner, 2005. "More Product, Less Process: Revamping Traditional Archival Processing." *The American Archivist*, Vol. 68, No. 2, Fall/Winter 2005.

Chapter 8

Housing Collections

Historical record collections are composed of unique items that may be fragile. These items require special care to enhance their preservation. In this chapter, we will look at ways to protect archival records by evaluating and improving the facility and the environment in which those records are housed.

The ideal facility for historical records is a repository that has been specifically planned and constructed to hold archival collections in a location far from any hazards—hazards like rivers or lakes that might flood, mines that could collapse, volcanoes that may erupt, or coastal areas prone to hurricanes. The reality is that most historical record collections are housed in buildings that were constructed for other purposes, buildings that serve many functions, or older buildings with less than state-of-the-art systems. Often these buildings are located in historic districts with little regard for the physical dangers of their location.

In this chapter, I will look at ways to protect archival records by evaluating and improving the building and environment in which they are stored. The goal of this chapter is to help you find a reasonable medium between the ideal and the real world so that you can create the safest and most secure conditions possible for your collections. In section I, I cover what to look for when inspecting buildings and storage areas. Section II goes over the measures you need to take within the building—climate, air, light, and pest controls; storage equipment and protections from fire and water damage. I will also define the bottom-line protective measures you need to take, measures that should be your first priority. The chapter ends with section III, a short summary and quiz.

Section I: The Building

Your Building's Bio

Let's get started by doing a quick evaluation of your facility. See "Your Building's Bio" worksheet (appendix Q) and fill out the checklist (items 1, 2, and 3). As you read through the rest of this chapter, think about your building and note any actions to take and improvements you need to make. You can record these on the "Your Building's Bio" worksheet," under item 4. If, at the end of the chapter, you're interested in doing a more in depth evaluation of your building, see appendix R, "Facility Assessment Questionnaire," and fill out one questionnaire for each location where records are stored.

Your Building

The building is the outermost protective layer for the preservation of your collections. You should budget for routine maintenance tasks and perform them. Performing these tasks will prevent or delay the need for more expensive repairs. You or your maintenance staff, if you are lucky enough to have them, should periodically inspect your building and keep a log of building problems noted during these inspections to see which are reoccurring. Reoccurring problems need to be addressed. During inspections you should look for specific problems in different areas.

On the roof, check for:

- Cracking
- Buckling
- Deteriorated flashings
- Standing water
- Damaged or clogged gutters and drains
- Damaged seals and caulking around skylights (if you have them)

On the exterior, check for:

- Missing shingles
- Blistered or peeling paint
- Deteriorating mortar
- Cracks in the foundation
- Damaged seals and drains in the foundation

In the interior, check for:

- Water leaks around windows
- Water leaks on interior walls
- Water leaks on ceilings
- Indications of rodents or insects
- Indications of mold

Storage Areas for Archival Collections

The area and environment in which archival collections are stored is vital for the protection and preservation of those records. The right conditions will help ensure the preservation of the records and that the information within them remains accessible. Let's take a look at the storage area itself first, then look at the storage equipment in section II.

As you may recall from chapter 6, "Preservation," the first key action to take with archival records is to put them in the proper acid-free, lignin-free, buffered storage containers regardless of where they are going to be stored. Proper archival storage containers provide the records with a "microenvironment" that protects them from light, dirt, and moisture and hinders deterioration. The importance of storing archival records in archival quality acid-free, lignin-free, buffered folders and boxes cannot be overstated. They are the first line of defense for your archival collections.

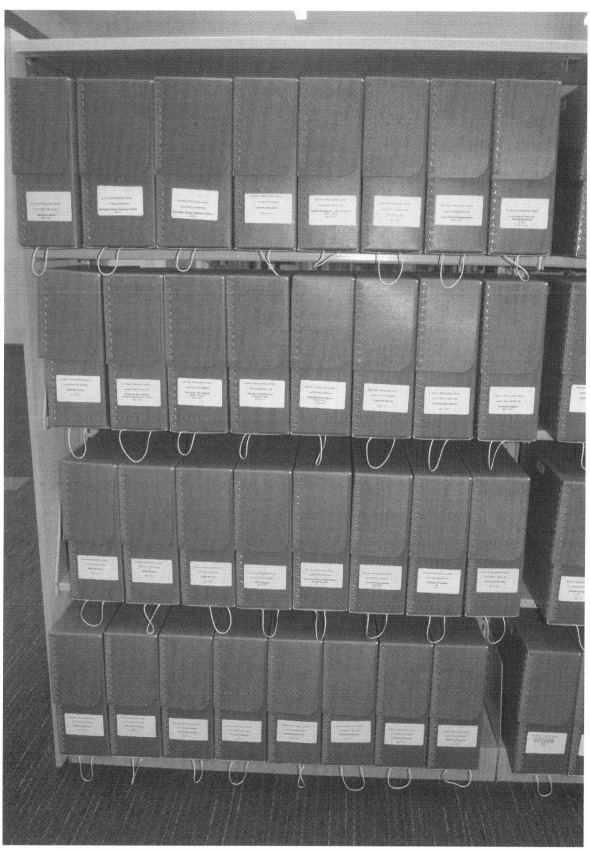

Figure 8.1.   Stack area with small archival boxes (12.5" × 10.25" × 5"). Notice how the bottom shelf is 4 inches off the floor.
Photo by Laurie Gemmill Arp, courtesy of Columbus Metropolitan Library

Storage Spaces to Avoid: Attics and Basements

Attics are a common and seemingly convenient place to store archival collections, but they are not a suitable area for storing archival records. There are four reasons to avoid attics as a place to store your archival collections. First, attics are hot in the summer and cold in the winter. These drastic cyclical changes in climate are very damaging to archival collections. Second, roofs often leak and the water gets to the items in the attic first, resulting in collections being ruined by water or infested with mold. Third, attics often have low relative humidity, resulting in your collections becoming dry and brittle. Dry and brittle collections can literally crumble. Finally, archival collections stored in attics are fire hazards.

Basements are another common records storage area that should be avoided. There are three reasons to avoid basements as places to store your archival collections. First, basements usually have high relative humidity levels, resulting in collections that deteriorate and warp. Second, basements are "pest friendly," they are often home to bugs, rodents, molds, and mildews, which can destroy archival records. Finally, basements are prone to the "trickle down" effect. Any leaks or water problems above will end up going down to the basement, causing water damage and mold and mildew damage to your records.

Avoid attic or basement storage for your archival collections if at all possible. If you have no choice but to store your archival collections in the attic or basement, you should take as many precautions as possible to protect your collections from the damaging effects of those environments. Attic or basement storage precautions include the following:

- Store your records in archival quality acid-free, lignin-free, buffered boxes so there is an extra layer of protection between the records and the environment.
- Store the records four to six inches off the floor to protect them from flooding and twelve inches away from walls to promote circulation.
- If leaks from above are a problem, place plastic sheeting material over the boxes to protect them from falling water. Plastic sheeting is not a long-term solution for leaks. It is a short-term solution for an immediate problem.
- Monitor for pests and rodents.
- Install a dehumidifier in the basement or a humidifier in the attic to help stabilize the relative humidity.
- Avoid electrical fires by monitoring all electrical equipment appropriately. Don't use equipment if having electric appliances in these areas is dangerous.
- Install water monitors if you can afford them. Otherwise check for water problems on a routine basis.
- Install fire extinguishers and smoke detectors or other fire detection and suppression equipment.
- Contact your local fire department to have them inspect the areas and offer their own suggestions.

Section II: Within the Building

Climate Control

Climate control is important because high temperature and relative humidity (RH) can severely limit the lifespan of archival records. High temperatures increase the speed of the chemical reactions that cause the deterioration of archival items. High relative humidity provides moisture to fuel these reactions. The higher the humidity, the more quickly deterioration proceeds. Relative humidity that is too low can cause documents to dry out and become brittle.

Temperature and RH are interrelated, a change in one will bring about a change in the other. Managing temperature and relatively humidity levels is referred to as *climate control*. Archival institutions should try to maintain stable conditions year round as the first step toward limiting the deterioration of historical record collections. A good climate for historical record collections has a temperature no higher than 70°F and RH between 30 percent and 50 percent. The lower temperature, the better it is for your collections. RH should not be allowed to get too low or the collections may experience damage from drying out. Generally, you should try to keep RH no lower than 30 percent.

Fluctuations in temperature and relative humidity harm your collections. To take this a step further, the more rapidly the fluctuations occur, the worse it is for your collections. Roads are good examples of the effects of temperature and humidity fluctuations, the more the roads get wet and dry and the more they heat and cool, the faster the pavement buckles and breaks. The goal is to maintain the most stable storage climate possible for your collections.

If you had a choice of two storage climates for your records, which of these would you choose?

Environment 1

This storage area is located near an office work area with heating and cooling systems. Although the temperature and relative humidity aren't monitored, the climate is generally people friendly—with temperature between 65 and 70 degrees with a stable humidity level.

Environment 2

This storage area is one of those rooms that is "hot in the summer" and "cold in the winter." During the cooler months of the year, the temperature stays between 50 and 60 degrees Fahrenheit and RH is generally around 60 percent. During the warmer months, the temperature stays between 70 and 80 degrees and RH is generally about 40 percent.

Answer: Although neither of these storage areas is ideal, if you had to choose, Environment 1 would be your best option. Although the climate isn't monitored and probably fluctuates, it's generally more stable.

How Can You Tell if the Climate Is Okay?

Many monitoring devices can help you monitor your climate. The key to monitoring your climate is to record the measurements systematically. Once you have recorded measurements over a period of time, several weeks at a minimum, you can evaluate your climate and determine whether or not you need to take action.

At a minimum you need reliable thermometers and humidity monitors in all your storage areas. These don't have to be expensive, but they do have to be reliable. Humidity can be measured using humidity indicator cards, available from many archival suppliers. These cards usually cost less than $10 for a package of five cards. Or for about $70, you can purchase a hygrometer. For about $100, you can purchase a simple thermohygrometer (also called a hygrothermometer) that measures both temperature and RH.[1] If you want to monitor continuously instead of just at specific moments in time, you can purchase a hygrothermograph. You can also purchase digital monitoring devices or data loggers, which can record continuously and create a variety of graphic reports of your environmental conditions.

Your equipment doesn't have to be complex and digital. You can monitor climate using a reliable thermometer and hygrometer for about $100. If you combine this relatively inexpensive equipment with a chart where you write down the temperature and humidity readings every day for several weeks, you have a sound climate control system. Remember to monitor climate in all your storage areas. You can purchase climate monitoring equipment from a variety of vendors, including traditional archival supply companies and scientific instrument companies. For more information, see the NEDCC preservation pamphlet "2.2 Monitoring Temperature and Relative Humidity."[2]

If your climate is less than perfect, you should consider taking actions to improve the situation. First think about the removal of collections from attics, which tend to be hot, or basements, which can be damp. If this is not possible, you could install central environmental controls, or use portable air conditioners, humidifiers, and/or dehumidifiers. You can also look at improvements in insulation and building seals. Be sure to continue to monitor the conditions once you've made changes so you can make any additional necessary adjustments.

Lights

Light levels in storage areas should be low. Light accelerates deterioration of historical materials. It weakens paper fibers and makes them brittle. It can cause the paper or ink to bleach, yellow, fade, or darken. Any exposure to light, even for a brief time, is damaging, and the damage is cumulative and irreversible. Ultraviolet (UV) light is particularly damaging and should be avoided whenever possible.

Visible light levels are measured in lux (lumens per square meter) or footcandles. One footcandle equals about 11 lux. Ideally, visible light levels should be maintained at 55 lux (5 footcandles).

Monitoring Light Levels

There are specific devices that can be used to monitor light levels. Light meters measure visible light levels; and UV meters measure ultraviolet light levels. UV is particularly damaging to collections. Basic light meters can be purchased for just over $100. UV meters are significantly more expensive, costing over $1,000. Some meters measure both visible light and UV; these are, of course, more expensive.

Because light meters, particularly for UV levels, are expensive, your best choice is to take some precautions to keep light levels at a minimum. Since damage caused by light is a result of both the intensity and duration of exposure, your goal is to reduce both whenever possible. There are cheap and easy things you can do. For example, lights should be turned off when no one is in the room. If the room has windows, the incoming light should be blocked using heavy curtains, blinds, or shades. Collections should be exposed to light only when they are being used (or processed). When they are not in use, collections should be stored in a "light-tight" container or in a room where light exposure is minimal.

In areas where archival collections are exposed to light, incandescent bulbs or LED lights should be used. LED lights do not emit UV or infrared radiation and they are cheap to operate so they would seem a good fit for archival institutions. Most fluorescent lights emit a significant amount of UV rays that are harmful to archival materials. If you must use fluorescent lights or expose your records to natural light, you can purchase UV filters for light fixtures and windows from archival suppliers. You can also purchase versions of fluorescent lights that emit low amounts of UV rays. Check the manufacture's specifications for these bulbs.

The law of reciprocity says that limited exposure to a high-intensity light will produce the same amount of damage as long exposure to a low-intensity light. For example, exposure to 100 lux for 5 hours would cause the same amount of damage as exposure to 50 lux for 10 hours. For more information on light and the damage it causes see the NEDCC preservation pamphlet "2.4 Protection from Light Damage."[3]

Protection from Fire

Libraries, archives, museums, and historic structures contain books, manuscripts, records, artifacts, film stock, magnetic media, combustible interior finishes, cabinets, furnishings, and laboratory chemicals. All of these materials are fuel for fires. The buildings that house collections also provide potential sources of ignition, such as electric lighting and power systems, heating and air conditioning equipment, heat producing conservation and maintenance activities, and electric office appliances. To protect your archival collections from fire, you should eliminate all existing fire hazards possible and hold regular fire drills. Equip all storage areas with portable fire extinguishers, ensure staff know how to use the fire extinguishers and have them inspected annually. Equip all storage areas with smoke detectors and if possible, install manual alarm stations.

Most local fire departments will provide fire inspections and can assist you in developing a fire safety program. If the fire department is familiar with the building and collections in advance, there is a greater chance that fire-fighting strategies may be able to take collection priorities into account.

Tip: Arson, unfortunately, is one of the most common cultural property ignition sources. It must always be considered in fire safety planning.

See the NEDCC Preservation pamphlet "Emergency Management 3.2, An Introduction to Fire Detection, Alarm, and Automatic Fire Sprinklers"[4] for more information on fire prevention.

Protection from Water

Historical records collections are highly susceptible to water damage. Mold growth in moist conditions is an additional problem for archival collections and those who work or use them. The best steps to take against water damage are regular inspections of roof coverings and flashings, with repair and/or replacement as needed. Make sure that the gutters and drains are cleaned frequently and avoid storing collections underneath water or steam pipes, bathrooms, mechanical air-conditioning equipment, or other sources of water. It is important that you keep collections at least 4 inches off the floor on shelves or pallets to avoid damage caused by common flooding events like burst pipes and leaky equipment or roofs.

Figure 8.2.   Stack area with various sizes of archival boxes. Notice how the bottom shelf of each rack is 6 inches off the floor.
Photo by Laurie Gemmill Arp, courtesy of Columbus Metropolitan Library

If possible, avoid storing collections in basements or other areas vulnerable to flooding. If storage in such areas is necessary, you can install water-sensing alarms so that quick detection of flooding is assured. At a minimum, you must inspect the areas routinely and often. Staff should also familiarize themselves with the location and operation of water mains and shut-off valves so they can shut off the water supply during an emergency. These locations can be diagrammed and posted for quick reference. Consider providing digital versions of these files to staff so they can store them on their smart phones and tablets.

Tips:

- Label the pipes in your storage areas (hot, cold, sewage) so if there is a leak you know what is leaking out of the pipe.
- Staff should know where and how to turn off the water supply.
- You should avoid storing collections in areas that have water or waste pipes running through them. Pipes can be difficult to avoid.
- If collections are stored near pipes, protect them by keeping the records in boxes, on shelves, or in drawers and keep them off the floor. If water falls on the records that are in boxes or on shelves, the boxes and the shelves will help shed the water and protect the records.

Air Quality

Good air quality is important to archival collections and to the people who care for and use them. If you have air and ventilation systems, they should always be on to assure proper air quality, and you should use filters or vents to eliminate gases, dirt, and solid particles in the air.

Whether you have air and ventilation systems or not, make sure that you keep chemicals out of archival work and storage areas. These chemicals include cleaners with ammonia/chlorine and polyurethane/oil based paints. See the NEDCC Preservation Pamphlet "The Environment 2.1 Temperature, Relative Humidity, Light, and Air Quality: Basic Guidelines for Preservation"[5] for more information.

Pest Control

Insects and rodents aren't popular in most quarters, and they certainly aren't welcome in collection storage areas. Pests are attracted to the components of archival materials, cellulose, paste, glue, sizing, emulsions, and adhesives. Pests are also attracted to food and drink and plants, so keep these out of storage areas and keep the storage areas clean. It is also best practice to keep food, drinks, and plants out of archival work spaces for the same reasons.

If you have insects and rodents in your work or storage areas, try to get rid of them naturally, using traps and thorough housecleaning before resorting to chemicals. The chemicals contained in sprays and repellents can be damaging to historical records. If you have to use chemical sprays, make sure that your archival records are protected by storing them in boxes with plastic sheeting over them while spraying is taking place. Don't spray anything directly on the boxes and remove the plastic sheeting once the spraying is done. For more information on pests and how to deal with them see, *Integrated Pest Management: A Selected Bibliography for Collections Care.*[6]

> **Tip:** Common pests in archives include silverfish, firebrats, booklice (psocids), cockroaches, and mice.
>
> - Silverfish and firebrats can reach a half inch in length. They feed on paper sizing and adhesives, chewing holes in paper, book bindings, and wallpaper to get to the adhesives underneath.

Figure 8.3. Silverfish
Credit: arlindo71

- Booklice are small, less than a tenth of an inch in size. They feed on mold growing on paper, pastes, and glue.
- There are thirty kinds of cockroaches that infest human habitats, and most grow to about a half an inch. Cockroaches will eat anything but they are especially fond of starchy materials and protein.

Figure 8.4. Cockroach
Credit: Backiris

- Mice grow from five to six inches long with tails from two to four inches long. Mice are generally nocturnal, confine their activity to about a ten-foot range, and live in family groups. Mice are omnivores. They will eat anything.

Good, Better, Best Storage Areas

Your storage area needs to be the best it can be; but it will probably never be perfect! So based on the notes you took on "Your Building's Bio" worksheet, take a minute to determine what actions you think should be your first priorities in improving your facility. Keep in mind that the actions you list should be practical things that are feasible for your specific situation. Your goal should be to meet the following "Good" criteria for all your storage areas. These are minimum standards for storage of archival collections.

Good—The Bottom Line in Storage

- Keep a locked storage area.
- Maintain a steady temperature with as little daily fluctuation as possible.
- Maintain a steady relative humidity level with as little daily fluctuation as possible.
- Shelves should be constructed so they are at least four inches off the floor to ensure they are protected from minor flooding and twelve inches from walls to promote circulation.
- Maintain a low light level, keeping lights turned off as much as possible and sunlight out of the storage area.
- Smoke alarms should be installed in every storage area and on every level of the building; they should be routinely checked.
- Fire extinguishers should be placed in every storage area and routinely checked; staff should be trained in how to use them.
- Conduct regular fire drills.
- Seek inspection and input from the local fire department.

- The area should be as clean as possible. No food, drink, trash, cleaning supplies, etc., should be maintained in the storage area. All attract pests such as insects and rodents to the storage area.
- Monitor for pests.

Table 8.1.

Good	Better	Best
Keep a locked storage area.	See Good section	See Good section
Maintain a steady temperature with as little daily fluctuation as possible.	Maintain a steady temperature that *doesn't fluctuate more than five degrees within each twenty-four-hour period*. Monitor and track temperature periodically.	Maintain a *steady temperature of sixty-five degrees Fahrenheit* (plus or minus five degrees) with constant temperature monitoring and recording of results.
Maintain a steady relative humidity level with as little daily fluctuation as possible.	Maintain a steady relative humidity level that *doesn't fluctuate more than 5 percent within each twenty-four-hour period*. Monitor and track relative humidity periodically.	Maintain a *steady relative humidity level of 45 percent* (plus or minus five percent) with constant monitoring and recording of results.
Shelves should be constructed so they are at least four inches off the floor to ensure they are protected from minor flooding and twelve inches away from outside walls.	Steel shelving should be constructed so bottom shelves are at least four inches off the floor to ensure they are protected from minor flooding and twelve inches away from outside walls.	See Better section
Maintain a low light level, keeping lights turn off as much as possible and sunlight out of the storage area.	See Good section	See Good section No windows or unfiltered UV light in the storage area.
Smoke alarms should be installed in every storage area and on every level of the building; they should be routinely checked.	Fire alarm system directly connected to the local fire department.	Fire alarm system directly connected to the local fire department. Wet pipe sprinkler system installed.
Fire extinguishers should be placed in every storage area and routinely checked; staff should be trained in how to use them.	See Good section	Smoke and heat detectors installed appropriately in consultation with fire professionals
Conduct regular fire drills.	See Good section	See Good section
Seek inspection and input from the local fire department.	See Good section	See Good section
The area should be as clean as possible. No food, drink, trash, cleaning supplies, and so forth should be maintained in the storage area. All attract pests such as insects and rodents to the storage area.	Provide a separate, secure storage area for historical records, with limited access and no food, drink, plants, and so forth allowed.	See Better section
Monitor for pests.	See Good section	See Good section
Harmful chemicals not used in storage areas.	See Good section	See Good section Air ventilation system with filters installed.
Routine monitoring for flooding, water problems.	See Good section	Water detectors installed.

Tip: Have your facility inspected by your local fire department.

Cleaning and Housekeeping

Simple and regular housecleaning needs to be done to maintain a level of cleanliness in storage areas. This will help reduce problems with pests. Housecleaning should include damp mopping or vacuuming floors—preferably with a high-efficiency particulate arresting (HEPA) vacuum cleaner and dusting shelves, storage boxes, and exteriors of bound books with a clean, soft nontreated cloth or brush. *Do not* use cleaning products containing oil, chlorine, alum, peroxides, or ammonia. These products leave residues that are harmful to archival collections.

Storage Equipment for Archival Collections

The storage equipment that you use in your storage areas can also affect the preservation of your collections. Storage furniture can release gases that react in the presence of moisture and oxygen, creating damaging chemical reactions. This can be a serious problem in map cases, file drawers, locked bookcases, or exhibit cases. Historical materials stored in closed cabinets should always be protectively enclosed.

Shelving

If possible, use heavy, eighteen-gauge steel shelving with a baked enamel finish. Avoid wooden shelving and wooden materials around archival materials. Wood contains pitch, resin, and other acidic elements that can cause deterioration of historical records. If you must use wood, make sure that you seal it with latex paint, air-drying enamels, or moisture-cured (also called "moisture-borne") urethane.

Make sure the floor can handle the weight of fully loaded shelving. You don't want the floor to buckle or cave in! You can have an engineer or someone with expertise in building construction check the shelving and weight ratios for the floor area.

Shelving should have adequate support. Shelving should be bolted to adjacent units and to the floor so it is stable. Shelving should also have back and side braces and be adjustable. Air needs to circulate around collections so shelves should be twelve inches away from outside walls and have two inches of clearance between the bottom of the shelf and the top box on the next lower shelf. The bottom shelf should be elevated four to six inches from the floor to provide protection from minor flooding.

Filing Cabinets

Filing cabinets are not the best storage equipment for historical records. They are best used in reference areas for nonhistorical materials that are frequently accessed. If you must use filing cabinets to store historical materials, make sure that the records are supported by the file cabinet equipment or sturdy spacers. The records shouldn't be slumping or curling. Also make sure the cabinet finish is not chipping or peeling.

Equipment for Oversize Materials

Oversize materials can be awkward to handle and store. When housing large drawings and other rolled or sheet materials remember that drawers for oversize materials should be no more than two inches deep and that they should be filled only half full. Map cases should have flexible cloth dust covers. Oversized materials that are over 36 × 48 inches should generally be rolled *on*, not *in*, tubes and secured with acid free ribbon tied around acid-free paper strips to prevent the ties from cutting into the rolled documents.

Section III: Summary

Caring for your historical record collections involves both managing your collections and managing the environment that your collections are in. Your building and storage areas don't have to be part of a specially designed facility in order to provide adequate protection for your collections.

In this chapter, we have examined several aspects of the physical environment—from leaking roofs to UV levels to shelving. The outside shell of your building ultimately needs good routine maintenance and care in order to adequately protect your collections. The storage areas need to be the best that you can provide—and we have provided good, better, and best scenarios for you to consider. Do the best you can with what you have, and work to meet the "good" standard in order to provide at least the minimal amount of protection for your historical records collections.

Quiz

See the answers on page 323.

1. What is the first line of defense in protecting your archival collections?
2. What is one of the reasons storing archival collections in attics is bad?
3. What is one of the reasons storing archival collections in basements is bad?
4. If you have to store archival collections in a basement what is one of the things you can do to make the best of a bad situation?
5. What level of relative humidity should you maintain in archival collection storage areas?
6. Since damage caused by light to archival collections is a result of both the intensity and duration of exposure what should you do?

Notes

1. These cost estimates were valid as of December 2017.
2. Northeast Document Conservation Center, Preservation Leaflets, The Environment, "2.2 Monitoring Temperature and Relative Humidity," accessed March 2018. https://www.nedcc.org/free-resources/preservation-leaflets/2.-the-environment/2.2-monitoring-temperature-and-relative-humidity
3. Northeast Document Conservation Center, Preservation Leaflets, The Environment, "2.4 Protection from Light Damage," accessed March 2018. https://www.nedcc.org/free-resources/preservation-leaflets/2.-the-environment/2.4-protection-from-light-damage
4. Northeast Document Conservation Center, Preservation Leaflets, Emergency Management, "3.2 An Introduction to Fire Detection, Alarm, and Automatic Fire Sprinklers," accessed March 2018. https://www.nedcc.org/free-resources/preservation-leaflets/3.-emergency-management/3.2-an-introduction-to-fire-detection,-alarm,-and-automatic-fire-sprinklers
5. Northeast Document Conservation Center, Preservation Leaflets, The Environment, "2.1 Temperature, Relative Humidity, Light and Air Quality: Basic Guidelines for Preservation," accessed March 2018. https://www.nedcc.org/free-resources/preservation-leaflets/2.-the-environment/2.1-temperature,-relative-humidity,-light,-and-air-quality-basic-guidelines-for-preservation
6. CoOL, Conservation Online, "Integrated Pest Management: A Selected Bibliography for Collections Care," accessed March 2018. http://cool.conservation-us.org/byauth/jessup/ipm.html

Chapter 9

Security and Disaster Planning

Security and disaster planning are vital components of protecting the collections entrusted to your care. Security means that measures that are taken to address the physical safety of the building and the collections housed within it. Security includes the management of those collections and the management of those using the collections. Disaster planning identifies the types of disasters most likely to occur to your institution and how to best deal with the issues brought on by those disasters. Appendix T, the Disaster Plan Template, is the heart of the disaster planning section. There is an electronic version of this template you can download from the AASLH website at https://learn.aaslh.org/archivalbasics. I would encourage you to download this template so you can begin filling it out as you read this section. The chapter begins with section I discussing physical security, section II is devoted to collection and researcher management, and section III covers disaster planning. The chapter ends with a summary and a list of additional resources.

Section I: Physical Security

Your building, and in particular your collection storage areas, sometimes referred to as the stacks, must be secure during and after normal working hours. Security measures need to prevent unauthorized entrance to the building as well as unauthorized removal of collections from the building. You must be able to secure your collection storage areas independently of the building within which the collections are housed. There are six practical things to consider about the security of your facility:

1. Doors—They should be strong and well-constructed including their frames. Did you know that in most burglaries the door is broken down?
2. Locks—A lock is a "must" for records storage, reference, and archival workspaces. Deadbolt locks that have a bolt separate from the knob are vital.
3. Windows—They should always be locked and secured. Depending on your location, you may also want to consider gates and grills as an extra security precaution.
4. Alarms—These are recommended to detect after hours entry, although they may not be feasible for every program. If you don't have alarms, work with your local police to see if they will drive by your facility on a regular basis.
5. Keys—They should be carefully issued and tracked. If a key goes missing, the relevant lock should be changes and new keys issued.

6. Box labels—Believe it or not, box labels can actually be a security measure! Labeling the boxes with as little information as is necessary for staff to retrieve collections will make it much harder for an unauthorized person to find items of value. I know of one historic records program that labels boxes with just a number, no collection title or number. The collection boxes are given sequential numbers, the collection storage area starts with box 1 on shelf A and ends with box 1745 on shelf Q. Box 1423 is shelved between box 1422 and 1424 on shelf O. Some archival institutions label boxes with only the collection number and box number (i.e., collection 165, box 5). Many archival institutions label boxes with the collection name, number, and box number (i.e., Jones Family Papers, Collection 109, Box 1).

Do You Need A Security System?

Monitored security systems may be beyond the financial ability of many historical records programs. They are however, becoming more common and less expensive. If you have, or are planning to install, a security system, don't rely on it as your only security measure. Most thefts and vandalism of collections occur during working hours. A security system won't protect your facility and collections during the work day.

A basic security system monitors doors and windows and may protect interior areas using motion detectors. An electronic security system includes sensors, a control panel, and reporting devices. To ensure proper response to alarm triggers by a security system, it must be monitored twenty-four hours a day by a monitoring station. If you rely on a local alarm signal, you are relying on a neighbor or passerby to hear and respond to the alarm.

A quality security company will inspect your site and discuss your unique security needs. It should provide an evaluation of your premises, noting measures that could be taken to enhance security, including and beyond the scope of the monitoring system. Sales representatives should be knowledgeable and understand your unique needs. Companies often focus on nighttime protection, but if the evaluation is complete, it will also include your vulnerabilities during working hours.

Monitored security systems may be beyond your financial means, but strong doors and windows that are locked along with keys that are issued and tracked in accordance with procedures are steps that every institution can take.

Section II: Collection and Researcher Management

Collection and researcher management are measures taken to ensure that historical records don't walk out the door and disappear. Anyone—staff, researchers, maintenance and housekeeping staff, or passersby—could be the source of a security problem. Managing your collections well is a vital component of security. You won't know if something is missing from a collection if you don't know what you have and where it is!

Collection management activities that will increase the security of your collections include periodically inventorying all your collections and organizing your storage areas for quick and easy inspections. Staff should be able to quickly notice if a collection is missing or out of place. Boxes should be clearly labeled in obvious order, so missing items are easily noticed. Your institution should create procedures to check collections to make sure the collection is complete before researchers use them and to check them again after use to make sure nothing is missing. You should use call slips, sign-out sheets, and other records to track the use of collections. Collection use records are discussed in detail in Chapter 10, Reference. Never allow researchers unsupervised use of collections. Doing so invites mischief.

You should keep backup copies of all your finding aids as part of collection management activities. Finding aids provide detailed information about the collection that are helpful both to staff and researchers, but finding aids are at risk for theft, loss, and/or deterioration over time because of use. Finding aids, accession records, and collection use records prove your institution has legal ownership of the individual items that make up a collection. These records are crucial should you need to recover items that come up missing and are later found on the internet for sale.

Consider creating descriptions including images of particularly valuable items to help with identification and recovery if a theft occurs. These descriptions and images become part of the collection administrative records that are not available to the public. If possible, provide insurance coverage for particularly valuable items. You can also create copies of valuable items for use by researchers while the original items remain under controlled access. Researchers do not need to use an original autographed item or a priceless letter to understand their historical significance. Copies will suffice for research purposes.

Employee Theft

Unfortunately, even with good collection management practices, there are incidents of employee theft. There are some warning signs you should look for if you suspect staff theft. These include collections consistently in the wrong place, hidden collections, the same person reporting or finding missing materials, staff members unconcerned about materials reported missing, and/or inconsistent documentation and use records. Another warning sign is a staff member who consistently disregards established rules and procedures.

If you don't already have them, you should draft internal security regulations for your historical records program. These staff-related security regulations should include a statement about the importance of ensuring the security of the collections, a statement appointing a staff member in charge of security, rules for staff accessing collection storage areas, rules governing key distribution, rules for staff requesting and using collections for their own research, and information about existing security systems and procedures that detail what staff should do if there is a suspected or real security issue.

Researcher Management

Theft and vandalism by researchers is a problem for every archival institution. There are reported incidents of researchers stealing historical items from every type of archival program. There are many things you can do to prevent theft and vandalism, first among them is requiring researchers to register by presenting a valid photo identification card before using collections. No matter how small or understaffed your program may be, you must require researchers to sign in and you must keep a record of the materials they use. Many historical record programs create a file for each researcher including copies of their identification cards when they visited their facility, along with a list of the collections they used.

You should have a security and use policy for researchers. These policies must be followed as a condition for allowing researchers access to your collections. Circumstances may dictate specific rules for your institution but most all security and use policies include the following:

1. Researchers must register and present a photo ID to be granted access to collections.
2. Researchers must leave all personal belongings behind (usually in a locker) before they enter the research area. Researchers can take research materials (laptop

computers, notes, notebooks so forth and so on) into the research area with the understanding that these items will be inspected when they exit the area.

3. Researchers use only pencils while taking notes (it is easy to mark items accidently with pens).

4. Researchers can only use a limited number of items from a collection at one time.

5. Collection storage areas are closed to researchers; staff should retrieve the items and deliver them to the researcher.

The research area, where the researchers use collections, should have only one exit that requires researchers to walk past a reference desk or other staffed area to enter or leave the research area. Someone should always be in the research area to observe the researchers. As has been stated earlier, you must know what's in your collection so you can tell when something is missing. You must also use and retain call slips or use some other method of tracking what items researcher's used. If supervision of researchers isn't always possible, it is *vital* that collections are checked after being used.

Researcher security and use regulations should be publicly posted. I strongly encourage you to post them on your internet site. Researchers should be made *overtly* aware of your security and use policy, give them a copy of it, and, most important, don't allow exceptions to the policy.

Responding to Security Problems

Appoint someone on your staff security manager to be in charge of security issues. This person should be responsible for conducting assessments of existing security measures and making recommendations for any changes that need to be made. Your security manager should work with the local police department and your legal counsel to create procedures for handling security incidents.

Staff should be trained in procedures for dealing with security incidents. Be sure to contact your local police department and your legal counsel to help you understand the legal parameters of dealing with security incidents. You must clearly understand what your staff can lawfully do when a security incident happens. Staff should not take any action unless the incident was witnessed or material is proven missing. Having proof that items are missing means that the materials were inspected before *and* after use by a specific researcher and that the items were declared missing after the second inspection. At this point, invite the researcher into an office or another area with a second staff member present. Don't provoke, touch, or coerce the researcher. If the researcher agrees to be detained, contact the local police and await their arrival. If the researcher insists on leaving, one staff person should notify the authorities while a second staff member carefully escorts the individual out of the building (and records the license plate number of the researcher's automobile). As soon as the incident is over, document all the pertinent information about the incident and be prepared to give the police a copy of the documentation.

Most security incidents are noticed after the fact, making it harder to identify the perpetrator. In these cases, you should determine exactly what is missing, contact the police and your insurance company, and document all your actions thoroughly.

All your security and use policies and procedures must be written to reflect your own program's context, your staffing, your facility layout, and any existing security precautions. Security for historical records programs can ultimately be based on a very common sense approach. Sturdy, locked doors and windows, good collection management practices, and researcher registration and monitoring can go a long way to ensuring that your collections are safe and secure.

Section III: Disaster Planning

Natural disasters are a fact of life. From large, sometimes catastrophic events, like a hurricane or an earthquake, to smaller disasters, such as mold outbreaks or mild flooding, disasters put historical records at risk. People also cause disasters: theft, acts of violence, and terrorism are disasters for which you must be prepared.

Large or small, natural or man-made, emergencies put your program's staff and collections in danger. Some disasters may affect your whole collection, while others may affect only a part. Unfortunately, most historical records programs learn about the importance of planning for disasters only after the fact. An emergency does not have to become a disaster. Full-fledged disasters can often be avoided by recognizing and eliminating risks, and by preparing to respond effectively to emergencies.

Disasters occur every day. A pipe ruptures, a roof leaks, a fire starts. Disasters don't have to be large cataclysmic events in order to cause significant damage to property and historical records. You need to prevent the disasters you can (fix a leaky roof), and you need to plan for what you can't prevent. Disaster planning includes fixing known problems before they become a disaster, knowing how to respond when a disaster occurs, and knowing what to do after the disaster.

Fix What You Can and Prepare for the Rest: Make a Risk List

Can you prevent a disaster? Yes! Some disasters are completely preventable, such as incidents caused by leaky pipes, cracked windows, or damaged wiring. Use appendix S, the Risk List worksheet, to begin identifying potential risks to your historical records. As I discuss preventive planning, you can use it to fill in the risks that pertain to you. There are four steps to preventative planning:

Step 1: Identify hazards that could cause a disaster and get them fixed. Things like leaky roofs, pipes, broken windows, all the kinds of things discussed in chapter 8. Make a list of the problems you identify, and make plans to get them fixed. You can't prevent all disasters, but you can identify potential problems that may occur. Once you know the problems or risks, you can take steps to mitigate against and prepare for them.

Step 2: List the natural disasters that could affect you. You don't have to prepare for every disaster. You have to prepare for the disasters that could *realistically* happen to you. Consider your geographic location and what kinds of potential natural disasters could happen. These could include hurricanes, tornadoes, flooding, earthquakes, or forest fires.

Step 3: List the potential man-made disasters that could occur. These might include acts of terror, power outages, sprinkler discharges, or chemical spills.

Step 4: Prioritize your collections. If a disaster occurs, you should know which collections are the top priorities for staff to get out of harm's way. This can be a difficult judgment call; but when faced with a disaster what collections would you want to save first? Think in terms of a) what is your most historically significant collection, b) what are the collections that no other institutions have, and c) what are your most used collections? You may not have time to save all your collections—so which are most important? Doing this in advance is important. Staff may not think clearly during an incident and you do not want to make these decisions lightly.

Decrease Your Risks

Now that you've identified risks and prioritized collections, you can take action. Decide what needs to be done to eliminate or decrease the risks you've identified. Prioritize the actions and resolve them. You can't eliminate every risk, but you should eliminate what you can. You can't change the weather, but you can fix the roof!

Be Prepared!

The key to responding to disasters is to be ready for them. People faced with a disaster often don't think clearly, so the more prepared you are the better. There are several simple steps you can take that will help you when a disaster occurs.

To help you pull your preparedness lists together and begin creating your disaster plan, I have included a "Disaster Plan Template" as appendix T. Please read the template all the way through. It has blank checklists, but it also has important information about how to treat damaged materials. There is also an electronic version of this template you can download from the AASLH website at https://learn.aaslh.org/archivalbasics. You are free to modify and use this template as you wish.

As you work through the rest of this section, keep the checklist nearby and fill in the information that you already know. Later, fill in missing information. If some of the template doesn't apply to your situation, just leave it blank. Your disaster plan must reflect your current situation. When it's complete, you can delete the sections that don't apply, and you will have a solid foundation for a complete disaster response and recovery plan. Your disaster response and recovery plan is one of those documents that is never really done. Schedule time annually to review and revise it as needed. Your circumstances, the resources available to you, and your contacts will change over time.

Who To Call

When disasters occur, it is crucial that staff know and understand who is responsible for what. A simple and concise list of responsibilities is crucial. The list should identify

- Who is the senior decision maker?
- Who is the in-house security manager?
- Who interacts with fire, police, or other authorities?
- Who will serve as back up if someone is unavailable?
- Who should gather supplies?
- Who is responsible for salvage?
- Who is authorized to spend money?

The list should include names and phone numbers so the appropriate people can be contacted. You should update the list regularly. You can include this information on pages 251, 256, and 257 of appendix T or on pages 3, 7, and 8 of the downloaded disaster plan template. Prudence dictates that key staff members keep a copy of this list and your disaster plan at their home.

What Assistance Might Be Necessary?

You will need help when a disaster strikes. You will need a list of those individuals or companies that can help you along with their contact information and it is best if you take the time to create this list before a disaster occurs. This list may include contacts for everything from the local fire department to vendors who specialize in videotape recovery.

Some of these contacts will be local companies offering services everyone uses every day. These contacts will help you during the disaster and/or its immediate aftermath:

Police or sheriff	Fire department	Ambulance
Legal counsel	Computer emergency	Local emergency mgmt. agency
Janitorial services	Electrician	Plumber
Carpenter	Exterminator	Fumigation services
Locksmith	Electric company	Gas, telephone, water companies
Insurance company	Architect/builder	

Other contacts will be specialized vendors offering services specifically to the museum/archival community. These contacts will help you recover from a disaster:

Conservator	Document recovery/salvage
Computer recovery/salvage	Microfilm recovery/salvage
Videotape recovery/salvage	Freeze-dry company

Identifying Priority Collections

You have already defined your priority collections in the risk list. Now you should collect and record more detailed information about those collections and include them in your disaster plan. You should assign a priority to the collection, record the call number, location, size, and any notes. You can record this information on page 259 of appendix T or on page 9 of the downloaded disaster plan template.

What Do You Need?

There are some basic supplies that you should have on hand, or know where to get, in case of a disaster. All of these supplies are available at your local discount department store. Keep these supplies on hand and make sure staff knows where they are! Your disaster plan should indicate where these items are stored, or how staff could get access to them quickly. A supply checklist is found on pages 260 and 261 of appendix T or on pages 10 and 11 of the downloaded disaster template.

Disaster Equipment

Staff should also know where to find the equipment they may need to respond to a disaster. This equipment could include:

- Extra keys
- Fire extinguishers
- Cut-off valves for water, electricity, and gas

You should use page 253 of appendix T or page 4 of the downloaded disaster template for this information.

Why Do You Need Those Things?

Staff needs to know where your supplies are located, and they also need to understand what actions they should take to salvage collections. When you are preparing for a disaster, a key component is staff training. If you can attend a formal training session on disaster response, take the opportunity to do so. If you can't, there are lots of resources available for you to read.

Disaster Response: What Do We Do?

The first priority in an emergency is the safety of the staff and patrons. Staff need simple, straightforward information when disasters and emergencies occur. Your disaster plan should clearly and simply state what steps staff should take when responding to a disaster, including how to evacuate people from the facility.

The template disaster plan includes several emergency procedures sheets. These sheets don't focus on how to salvage collections; they cover how to immediately respond to ensure the safety of the people involved. These sheets can be used as part of your overall disaster plan. They can also be used as stand-alone documents, to be distributed to staff or posted as appropriate (note the overlap between security planning and disaster planning in these procedures).

Recovery

After a disaster, once everyone is safe and the authorities have told you it's safe to go inside, you can begin evaluating the damage and recovering material. Your disaster plan should outline appropriate steps for recovering your collections; and, if possible, your staff should be educated in recovery procedures.

The disaster plan template includes appropriate recovery operations for many different types of materials. Take a few minutes to read the *Recovery and Salvage of Materials* section of the template beginning on page 272 of appendix T or on page 22 of the downloaded Disaster Recovery Template. Pay particular attention to the sections that describe recovery of materials that you know you have in your collections.

You may have noticed a few things in these recovery instructions. When paper (*not* photographic paper) is wet, the best way to ensure recovery is to freeze it within forty-eight hours. It may sound strange, but it's true. Deep freezing is an effective way to stabilize collections for days or even months; it stops mold growth, ink running, dye transfer, and swelling. Damp and partially wet materials in a freezer will dry as the moisture changes directly from ice to vapor. A refrigerated truck may at least keep materials cool enough to prevent mold growth.

I would be very reluctant to use a household freezer for wet documents, as it can take up to eight months for materials to dry in these. Household freezers just don't get cold enough to facilitate drying. A household freezer is better than nothing and some institutions do advocate their use as a last resort, but it would have to be the last resort before I would use one.[1] If you have a small number of wet materials, you will usually be better off air-drying them with a fan than putting them in a household freezer.

Some materials such as photographs can be damaged by freezing, it is important to be familiar with recommended recovery procedures for specific types of materials.

Air-drying is the most common method of dealing with wet books and archival materials. It can be used to treat one item or many, but is most suitable for small numbers of damp or slightly wet books and documents. Air-drying is labor intensive and requires a great deal of space.

Don't handle or move anything until you know what is going to be done with it and where it should be moved. There is a lot to know about when you are working to recover materials. Staff education via training, reading, and practice are really important.

Throughout this section you have worked with a disaster plan template. At this point, you should have completed some sections of the template. I strongly encourage you to continue this process of disaster planning until the plan is complete and you have made it your own.

Additional Disaster Preparedness Resources

If you're looking for further information about disaster recovery, there are several high quality resources available:

- Library of Congress Emergency Management—https://www.loc.gov/preservation/emergprep/
- Northeast Document Conservation Center Preservation Pamphlets—https://www.nedcc.org/free-resources/preservation-leaflets/overview
- San Diego/Imperial County Libraries Disaster Response Network—Although designed specifically for libraries, most of their information applies to historical records disaster planning quite effectively—https://sites.google.com/site/sildrn/
- Conservation Online—A list of information resources, case studies, service providers, and a bibliography—http://cool.conservation-us.org/
- OHSHA's Emergency Preparedness site—https://www.osha.gov/SLTC/emergencypreparedness/gettingstarted.html
- FEMA Disaster Help site—https://www.fema.gov/help-after-disaster
- Dplan—the on-line disaster planning tool for cultural and civic institutions—http://www.dplan.org/

Summary

Making the most of the building that houses your collections is generally a study in common sense. Most historical records programs don't have a perfect facility or perfect policies and procedures. But you can make the most of what you have, fix obvious problems, and plan for security incidents and disasters.

Too many programs fail to recognize the risks their collections face—from theft, vandalism, disaster, to careless handling, or poor storage conditions. There are basic steps that you can take to lessen these risks.

Secure Your Collections

Good security can be put in place at minimal cost. With just a few dollars and some new rules, you can significantly improve the security of your collections.

- Install solid locks on doors and windows.
- Limit and keep track of who has keys to the facility.
- Ask the local police to drive by your facility routinely.
- Don't put too much information on your box labels—don't make it obvious what's inside!
- Require your users to register before using your collections.
- Supervise patrons as they use your unique historical records.
- Use and maintain call slips, or other forms of usage records so you know who has used your collections in case something comes up missing.
- Know what you have and where it should be.

Plan for Emergencies: They Can Happen to You

It's easy to think that emergencies and disasters happen to other people in other institutions. But the fact is, they can happen to any of us and any of our institutions at any time. As a caretaker of unique historical records, your ultimate responsibility is to keep those records safe from harm. In section III, you began to create your own disaster plan—essentially a compilation of many different kinds of lists that help you know how to respond when disaster strikes.

Continue putting this information together when you get "back to work." Then distribute it; post appropriate emergency response bulletins, and keep them up to date. If you ever have a disaster, make sure that when it's over, you evaluate how your plan worked and make any necessary changes.

Whether small or large, all programs that care for historical records must do what they can to ensure the preservation, security, and safety of the records in their care.

Note

1. The Library of Congress lists using household freezers for wet documents at, Library of Congress, Preservation, Emergency Response, Response and Recovery, What to do if Collections Get Wet, Freezing, "What to Freeze," accessed March 2018. https://www.loc.gov/preservation/emergprep/dry.html

Chapter 10

Reference

This chapter discusses providing reference services to researchers. Archives exist so that researchers can use the collections we acquire, describe, preserve, store, and manage. Is reference the most important thing an archivist does? I don't know, but I can say that the use case for archives, the argument used to get funding for archives, is that researchers use the collections in our care. The only reason to have archival collections is for researchers to use them.

In earlier chapters I discussed reference as it relates to description, detailing the contents of collections so that researchers can find what they want. I also covered reference as it relates to security, protecting collections while they are being used by researchers. Now I am going to go over assisting researchers to find the information they seek and creating the rules that govern that process.

This chapter is divided into four sections. Section I goes over registration, reference services, and writing your reference policy. Section II discusses how to provide reference services. Section III is a short introduction to copyright issues and their impact on reference. The chapter ends with section IV, a summary and quiz.

Section I: Reference Services

I have said that the underlying philosophical theme of archival work is that *archivists need to preserve the collections in our care while providing access to them*. Since the materials that are being accessed are unique historical records, you need to create comprehensive rules that govern how your collections are used. These rules ensure that the archival collections entrusted to your care are preserved while they are being used. The key document in this effort is your reference policy. Helping you create a good reference policy is the primary goal of this chapter.

Appendix U is a sample reference policy. The sample reference policy outlines the rules for using and accessing the historical records collections of the River Hills Archives. A reference policy includes

- Background information about your program, including hours of operation
- Who is entitled to access your collections
- Information about registration requirements
- Regulations for using the archives
- Information regarding copying

Before you begin to draft your own reference policy, you need to make some decisions about how you will let people access your archives including registration and what reference services you are going to offer. Reference services refers to those things you do to help researchers, things like photocopying and answering mail, phone, and email reference requests. It also covers the procedures that define how you provide reference services.

Access and Registration

Access in this context refers to granting entry into your archives and using its collections. In an archival institution open to the public, access should be provided on an equal basis to anyone who agrees to and abides by the rules and regulations of your program. Another way to think about it is that access is a privilege granted to those who follow your research policies. A private archival institution can limit access in any manner the institution choses.

Those archival institutions holding governmental records operate under a different set of rules dictated by public records law. However, these institutions still grant access to collections (records) based on the researchers following their research policies.

In an archival institution open to the public, all researchers should register before using the collections. Registration should include the researchers' name, address, and signature signifying that they agree to follow the rules and regulations of your program. Many programs require researchers to present a valid form of identification as well. As mentioned in chapter 9, registration is a security measure to help you identify those who might be involved in the loss of or damage to a collection. It is also a process that can help you identify peak usage days and times. This information will help you schedule staff and resources to best meet the needs of your researchers.

There are two forms that can be used as part of the registration process. A registration log, which details the information about a specific visit to the archives and a registration form which details the information about an individual researcher. You can use both forms or you can use one or the other.

A registration log is a quick list of who is using your archives on a particular date. The registration log can include any information you like. I always liked having some mention of the research topic in the log to give me an idea of which collections were being used by researchers. Some archival programs use a log without a registration form. If you decide to take this approach, you will need to include specific information about researchers in the log including address, phone number, email address, ID type, and the signature of the researcher. Keeping this much information in a log makes it over complicated and crowded. If you use both a log and a registration form, your research log might look like this:

Researcher Registration Log

Date:

Name:

Topic:

Time in:

Time out:

The registration form contains the contact information about an individual researcher, the rules governing the use of the archives, along with the researcher's signature. Use rules are a component of the reference policy. Appendix V is a Sample Registration Form, which can be downloaded from the AASLH website at https://learn.aaslh.org/archivalbasics. You are free to modify and use it as you see fit. If you chose to use a registration form without a registration log you will need to have the researchers fill out a new form every time they visit your archives.

Researchers should understand the registration process and the rules for using the collections. Many programs provide researchers with a copy of their reference policy including the use rules. They also post the policy and rules clearly, to ensure awareness and make enforcement of the policy easier. You should also post your fees and any conditions for making photocopies. It is helpful to post the registration process, the rules for using collections, fees, and any conditions for making photocopies on the website of your archives so that researchers are aware of these conditions for access before they visit your facility.

Research Services

Copying Records

You should determine your record copying policy and include it as part of your reference policy. If you have a photocopier or digital copier and want to be able to provide copies for your researchers, you will need to decide

- Are there limits on the number of requests researchers can make?
- Will you charge for copies? How much?
- Will you copy items that are copy restricted, fragile, or damaged?
- If you are using a digital copier what kinds of copies will be provided to the researcher? Will you give them paper only—or will you provide them with a copy of the digital file?
- Will you allow the public to make their own copies? I strongly caution you against this. Unique historical records need to be handled carefully and can be easily damaged by letting the public do their own copying.
- Will you allow the public to scan collection items with their own equipment? Again, I strongly caution against this for the same reasons stated above.
- Will you allow the public to take digital photos? If so, will you allow flash lighting? Recognize that this will have an impact on other researchers.

As examples of duplication policies—the Northern Kentucky University, Steely Archives Photocopying Policy—is attached as appendix W; the Mount Holyoke Photocopy and Digital Image Request policy is attached as appendix X, and the University of Illinois Archives Use and Reproduction Policy is attached as appendix Y.

Mail, Phone, and Email Reference Requests

The role of an archivist is to get researchers to the information they need via finding aids and catalogs, asking good reference interview questions to clarify their needs, and providing assistance as needed. Most staff in historical records programs don't have the time and resources to do research for the public and there is no obligation for them to do so. Still many historical records programs answer reference requests via mail, telephone, and email because some of the people who want to use their collections are not able to travel to their facilities to do so.

There are four options to meet the needs of researchers who cannot travel. First, you can make a list of those individuals who do research for hire and make that list widely available. Second, you can offer to do research as a service. Third, you can digitize your collections and mount them on the internet so researchers can access them remotely. Fourth, you can offer a combination of all these options. I think the fourth option is best, digitize those collections with wide demand, offer to do research for the remainder of you collections, and keep a list of researchers for hire. All these options require significant resources. What is the right answer for you? That decision needs to be made by taking into account the collections you hold, what researchers want from those collections, and the resources available to you.

If your program decides to do research as a service to your patrons there are some additional issues that need consideration. First, are you going to charge for these services? It is a commonly accepted business model to charge fees for research. Defining what those fees are can be challenging. If your program is providing copies of public records your state's public record laws may define what you are allowed to charge for copies. You can find out about your state's public records laws by contacting your state's archival program.[1] If you are providing copies of other records you can figure out the average time it takes to reply to a request and charge accordingly. The problem with this approach is that the ability to find information in collections varies from one collection to another. Some programs have an hourly rate for research. Other programs limit research requests to specific sets of records. In these cases they will send you a copy of a record for a fee provided you send them sufficient information to find the correct record in an index. There is no consensus on arriving at research fees.

If you do charge for research make sure that you notify researchers what the fee are, what research you will do, and how long it will take. The researcher should agree to this service arrangement before you actually begin the work. Remember, if you decide to answer research requests you must reply to them within a reasonable period of time. Answering research requests will be a significant drain on your resources and you may get more of them than you think you will. Consider offering research as a service very carefully before you commit to it.

Second, what are the limits to the research you provide? Some research requests may be quite straightforward, requiring you to pull and provide copies of particular records from specific collections. Other research requests can require time-consuming research and analysis. In some cases researchers will send you requests for multiple topics, i.e. send me all the information you have on the following list of 20 names. You need to state what kinds of research you will and will not do, the number of requests you will answer per individual correspondence, and provide the timeframes for replying to research requests in your reference policy.

Write Your Reference Policy

Now that you have defined the reference services you will provide you are ready to write your reference policy. If you already have a reference policy now is a good time to review it and consider any revisions that might be appropriate. Like all policies and procedures, your reference policy must reflect your program and situation. There is no one size fits all reference policy. To get started, see appendix Z the Reference Policy Template. The Reference Policy Template can be downloaded from the AASLH website at https://learn .aaslh.org/archivalbasics. You are free to modify and use it as you see fit.

You can complete your policy by filling in the blanks on the template. Be sure to read through the regulations section carefully and make appropriate revisions and additions that work for your program. You should also read through the copy section carefully to make sure that your own practices are adequately reflected.

Section II: Providing Reference Services

Creating a policy and good registration practices are just the first step in providing reference services to your users. Now that you have defined what services you are going to provide, how will you provide those services? Many archival programs have staff dedicated to serving researchers, referred to as reference staff. Reference staff are trained to handle researcher requests by consistently applying their reference policy to everyday situations. Ideally, reference staff should know your collections well and enjoy dealing with the public. Of the two, attitude is more important than knowledge; anyone can learn about your collections but if an individual doesn't like interacting with people, they will never do it well. If all your archival staff interact with researchers, make sure they are well versed in your reference policy.

Now that we have dealt with staff issues, what kind of physical environment do you need to successfully interact with researchers and what procedures will you create to guide your interaction with them?

Physical Environment

Every physical space is different and you will have to do the best with what you have. The physical space where people use your collections needs to include

- A desk or space for registering users
- Facilities for users to leave their belongings while they use the collections
- Desks or flat work surfaces with adequate lighting to allow users to work with the collections and take notes. Ideally, these should be in full view of the reference staff member responsible for supervising the use of your program's collections
- Access to reference materials including dictionaries, atlases, and other frequently used, but not unique, materials
- Access to your catalogs and finding aids
- The recognition that most if not all researchers will want to bring a portable computer or some digital device into the research area. Besides allowing sufficient room for these devices, will you supply electrical outlets for them? Will you provide an internet or wireless connection? If you provide internet or wireless connectivity, remind reference staff it is not their job to provide technical support to researchers. The institution has met its obligation to the researchers by providing an internet connection that works.

Figure 10.1. Ohio University Robert E. and Jean R. Mahn Center for Archives and Special Collections reading room. Notice how each table has an internet connection in the center. Not every archival reading room is as nice as this one!
Photo by Laurie Gemmill Arp, courtesy of Ohio University Libraries

Interacting with Researchers

The first thing reference staff should do when researchers visit your facility is to greet them and get them registered. First-time researchers may need an explanation of why registration is necessary, direction to where to leave their belongings, and other basic information about your facilities. Some of the people coming into your archives will know nothing about an archives and because their only experiences with a similar institution will be a public library, they will be surprised and perhaps offended by your security procedures. In the vast majority of cases, they will willingly abide by your security procedures if you take the time to explain to them that archival collections are one-of-a-kind items and that you are tasked with preserving and providing access to them. Most people are reasonable once they understand why archival collections are different from those items held at a public library.

New researchers will also need an explanation of your collections and information about how to find what they are looking for. So you will need to tell them about your reference materials, finding aids and tools, and about the procedures they need to use if they want to look at a particular collection. If you find that you are explaining the same things over and over, you might consider creating handouts that cover these kinds of basic information. The information covered in handouts should also be posted on your website. Handouts will save you time and help your users. They can be distributed during registration.

Once the researchers are registered and understand your facilities, your role is to help them find what they are looking for. The key to providing good reference service is to listen carefully and know your collections. Some researchers will know exactly what they want to find (for example, Anne Smith's death certificate from March 23, 1930), while others may have more general research questions. You will need to work more with a new researcher than you will a more experienced researcher.

Your role is to match the researcher to the appropriate collections. To do this, you will need to listen carefully and ask researchers follow-up questions to determine exactly what they are looking for. Then use your knowledge of your collections and your finding aids and tools to point researchers in the right direction.

Calling Collections

Ideally, your historical records collections will not be directly accessible by researchers. In other words, researchers can't just go to a shelf and get the items from whatever collection they want to use. Instead, researchers should fill out a call slip and staff will retrieve the items or boxes from the collection they want to use for them.

Call Slips

A call slip is just a simple form that researchers fill out in order to request that some particular material be called from the stacks and brought to them to use. Appendix AA is a sample call slip. It can be downloaded from the AASLH website at https://learn.aaslh .org/archivalbasics. You are free to modify and use it as you see fit.

Researchers should have access to call slips in order to indicate to staff exactly what collections they want to look at. Call slips generally ask them to provide

- The unique collection number or call number, as given in finding aids or catalogs
- The particular box number(s), volume number, or other distinct unit of the collection being requested
- The author or creator of the collection
- The title of the collection
- User's name
- Today's date
- The number of the chair or table where the researcher is sitting, if your seating is numbered

Call slips may also contain the name of the reference staff member providing access to and inspecting the collection, a note on the physical condition of the collection, and a place for staff to make notes. The note section is generally used for jotting down the location of the requested materials in the collection storage area.

Once collection items have been retrieved from the collections storage area, reference staff should provide collection items to the researcher one at a time (i.e., one folder at a time or one box at a time depending on the collection). Reference staff must inspect collection items before giving them to the researcher for use. Besides checking the collection to make sure all the items are present, reference staff should check the physical condition of the collection. If staff feel that the physical condition of the collection is such that letting a researcher use it would harm it, they must have the authority to deny access to the collection. If this happens, staff should do what they can to meet the needs of the researcher, but their overriding concern, their highest priority, is the safety and preservation of the collection. Collections taken out of service should be sent to conservation to be repaired so that they can be returned to service as soon as possible.

Restricted Information

Make sure that reference staff doesn't allow access to restricted information. There are two kinds of restricted information: information that the creator of the collection has restricted access to and information that access to is restricted by law.

Sometimes access to sensitive information is closed by the creator of a collection. Hopefully, the restriction was defined, both which information is restricted and what the duration of the restriction is, in the legal instrument transferred the collection to the archives. Your finding aids should clearly state that they contain restricted materials. If this is the case, make sure reference staff check for restricted materials before they grant access to a collection.

There are two federal laws that restrict access to information containing health or educational information. If you see anything in archival records concerning health information or specific student education records you need to determine if that information is protected under HIPAA or FERPA regulations.

The Health Insurance Portability and Accountability Act of 1996 (HIPAA) (45 CFR 164) "gives you rights over your health information and sets rules and limits on who can look at and receive your health information."[2] The Family Educational Rights and Privacy Act (FERPA) (34 CFR Part 99) "protects the privacy of student education records . . . Generally, schools must have written permission from the parent or eligible student in order to release any information from a student's education record."[3]

Figuring out if the archival records in your care fall under HIPAA or FERPA regulations or other laws can be complicated to say the least. If you have access to legal counsel, they should be brought into review the information in question. The Society of American Archivists has a couple of good sources of information on these matters, Menzi L Behrnd-Klodt's *Navigating Legal Issues in Archives*[4] and *Rights in the Digital Era*[5] are worth having.

Some Things to Consider

You should not allow researchers to retrieve or reshelf unique historical records from your collection storage area. Using a call slip will help you understand which materials are being used and when they were used. Staff can retrieve requested records based on the call slip. File call slips in date order and keep them on hand. Call slips will provide evidence of who used what collection and when they used it in the event you find that you have missing or damaged items from a collection.

Replace valuable items with photocopies or microfilm copies whenever possible. This was covered in chapter 9, but it bears repeating: do not let researchers use original items that have substantial monetary value. Doing so increases the likelihood that items from your collections will walk out the door.

Consider whether or not you will allow users to access collections that are not processed. As stated earlier I strongly caution against this. You do not know what is in an unprocessed collection, so you will not know if portions of the collection are taken. You also do not know if there is sensitive information in the collection that should not be made available to the public. If you decide to allow access to unprocessed materials, make sure users understand the difficulties they may encounter in using unprocessed material; and make sure that they know to keep the records in the existing order.

You need to treat all your researchers the same. Consistency is important in keeping control over your research area and keeping your researchers happy. No one should be treated better or worse than anyone else. This means you should create and maintain a staff manual that documents the decisions, policies, and procedures used for dealing with researchers and that the guidance is followed. Keep the manual up to date and organized and make sure reference staff have easy access to it so they can consult it as needed.

Collect standard reference materials when you can, such as dictionaries, atlases, local histories, and other publications related to your collections. If you are looking for reference materials, but aren't sure what you need, contact other libraries, archives, or museums in your area. They should be able to tell you what resources are the most helpful; and they might even have old or duplicate copies that they would be willing to give you. You can also ask researchers for a list of resources they would find helpful.

If you have researchers that are working on local histories, family histories, or other items that relate to your collections and community, ask them if they would consider donating a copy to your archives. Doing so will help other researchers and it will gain your archives a supporter. Nothing endears a researcher to an archives like saying we want a copy of your work for others to use. It validates their passion and work.

Refer researchers to other libraries or organizations with related materials, other reference tools, or different collections that could help them with their research. Keep the addresses and phone numbers of these kinds of organizations available for quick reference. Researchers appreciate these kinds of "tips."

Good Reference Practice—It's a Matter of Security!

Providing good service to researchers is one of the primary functions of archivists. Good reference practices lead to more than happy users; they lead to a more secure environment for your collections.

Your reference policies and procedures will assure that your collections are used responsibly and maintained for years to come. Make sure that your staff and your researchers understand that reference policies *must* be followed in order to keep collections safe.

Retain your registration forms or logs and your call slips for several years after they have been created in order to be sure you can retrace who used a collection in case something comes up missing.

Additional Resources

- Pugh, Mary Jo. 2005. *Providing Reference Services for Archives and Manuscripts.* Archival Fundamental Series II. Society of American Archivists ISBN: 1-931666-12-1
- Hunter, Gregory. 2003. *Developing and Maintaining Practical Archives: A How to Do Manual,* Second Edition. Neal-Schuman Publishers, Inc. ASIN: B01181LKC6
- Theimer, Kate. Ed. 2014. *Reference and Access: Innovative Practices for Archives and Special Collections.* Rowman & Littlefield. ISBN 978-0-8108-9091-6

Section III: Copyright

I briefly mentioned copyright in the chapter 4 section covering instruments of transfer. I am going to go over copyright in more detail now because of its effect on reference staff and researchers. I am not going over copyright issues in great depth. I am not a copyright expert and any concerns you might have about copyright should be addressed by your legal counsel. Having said that, you need some understanding of copyright so that you can inform reference staff and your researchers about the copyright issues that affect them.

Copyright is "a form of intellectual property law, protect[ing] original works of authorship."[6] Copyright protections are called for in the U.S. Constitution, defined in Title 17 of the United State Code and regulated by Title 37 of the Code of Federal Regulations. The Constitution defines copyright as "securing for limited times to authors and inventors the exclusive right to the respective writing and discoveries." Copyright protections were deemed important enough to include in the constitution because they "promote the progress of science and the useful arts."[7] The U.S. Copyright Office, which administers copyright law, is a department of the Library of Congress.

Copyright gives the copyright owners the exclusive right to copy their work, distribute copies, or create derivative copies of their work among other things. It also gives copyright owners the ability to authorize others to exercise their exclusive copyright rights. Copyright applies to literary, musical, dramatic, choreographic, pictorial, graphical, sculptural, motion picture, sound recording, and architectural works. Those categories have been interpreted very broadly. Essentially any original form of expression that is fixed on stable media can be protected by copyright.

How long copyright protections last is not always easy to figure out. According to the U.S. Copyright Office Circular 15a, "Different standards apply depending on whether federal statutory copyright protection was secured before or on or after January 1, 1978, the date the current law—the Copyright Act of 1976—took effect. In addition, several amendments enacted since January 1, 1978, affect duration."[8] As a general rule, for works created after January 1, 1978, copyright protection lasts for the life of the author plus an additional seventy years. Circular 15a also states that "all works published in the United States before January 1, 1923, are in the public domain," meaning that there is no copyright protection for these works. There is no copyright on public records. The Cornell University Library Copyright Information Center puts out a great chart on the "Copyright Term and the Public Domain in the United States"[9] that lists the length of copyright for many works.

Copyright can be easily transferred to heirs or to other entities. U.S. Copyright Office Circular 1, Copyright Basics states the following:

> Any or all of the copyright owner's exclusive rights, or parts of those rights, can be transferred. The transfer, however, generally must be made in writing and signed by the owner of the rights conveyed or the owner's authorized agent. Transferring a right on a nonexclusive basis does not require a written agreement. You can bequeath a copyright by will or pass it along as personal property.[10]

The difficulty for archivists and researchers is determining who holds copyright, whether they are alive or dead, and if they have made arrangements for the transfer or maintenance of copyright.

Copyright is a concern for archivists because if a researcher plans on publishing their research in any manner and they quote from archival material they must determine who holds the copyright of that material so they can get authorization to quote it. If a researcher does not get authorization to quote from a copyrighted work, he or she can be sued for copyright infringement, which is the use of a copyrighted work without permission.

Never assume that your organization holds copyright, even if it owns the materials. If at all possible you need to find out from the donor who holds the copyright on the materials being donated and keep accurate records of copyright information on the materials that you receive. As stated in chapter 4, when acquiring records from donors, make sure copyright is addressed within the deed of gift or other transfer instrument.

In your reference practices, make sure that it is clear in all policies, correspondence, and interactions with researchers that it is their responsibility to determine the copyright holder and to obtain clearance to publish copyrighted materials. Most archives mark photocopies and photographic prints with a statement that copies have been provided for research purposes only and that it is the researcher's responsibility to determine who holds the copyright and to get the right to publish any copyrighted material. Note that the Northern Kentucky University, Steely Archives Photocopying Policy attached as appendix V, the Mount Holyoke Photocopy and Digital Image Request policy attached as appendix W, and the University of Illinois Archives Use and Reproduction Policy attached as appendix X, all address copyright issues.

Copyright law is a complex and confusing subject and it is currently undergoing revision due to the changes in the way we create, share, and publish content. If you have copyright concerns, you should consult with your legal counsel or other legal practitioners specializing in copyright law.

Two good sources for additional information on copyright are the copyright site of the U.S. Government—https://www.copyright.gov—and the Stanford University Copyright and Fair Use site—https://fairuse.stanford.edu/overview.

Section IV: Summary

Your historical records program protects and preserves historical materials and makes them available for use. No matter how small your program is, you must incorporate good reference policies and procedures into it.

Good references policies and practices assure that your researchers' needs are met, but they do much more than that. They assure that your collections are accessed in ways that protect them from dangers such as theft, vandalism, and even human mistakes.

Creating a good reference policy that accommodates your own situation and facilities is vital. Letting your researches know what the rules are, and explaining to them *why* the rules are necessary, is also important.

Quality reference service allows for the protection of the collections while making sure that researchers find what they want, get access to what they need, and, ultimately, have a successful research experience.

Quiz

See the answers on page 324.

1. Is access to your collections a right or a privilege?
2. Which is more important—access or preservation?
3. Is offering research as a service, fulfilling written, phone, or email research requests, something you must do?
4. An archive can exist without providing reference services—true or false?
5. What are the keys to providing good reference services?
6. Why should you inspect a collection before giving it to a researcher?
7. Should you allow researchers to make their own copies of archival collections?
8. Whose responsibility is it to obtain clearance to publish copyrighted materials?
   A) the researcher   B) the historic records program

Notes

1. Council of State Archivists, "Directory of State Archives," accessed January 2018. https://www.statearchivists.org/connect/resources-state/

2. U.S. Dept. of Health and Human Services, HIPAA, accessed September 2018. https://www.hhs.gov/hipaa/index.html

3. U.S. Dept. of Education, Law and Guidance, General, Family Educational Rights and Privacy Act (FERPA), accessed September 2018. https://www2.ed.gov/policy/gen/guid/fpco/ferpa/index.html

4. Menzi L. Behrnd-Klodt, 2008. *Navigating Legal Issues in Archives*, Chicago: Society of American Archivists. ISBN: 1-931666-28-8

5. Menzi L. Behrnd-Klodt and Christopher Prom eds. 2015. *Rights in the Digital Era*, Chicago: Society of American Archivists. ISBN: 1-931666-74-1

6. Copyright.Gov, "Copyright in General," accessed January 2018. https://www.copyright.gov/help/faq/faq-general.html#what

7. National Archives, "U.S. Constitution," Article 1, Section 8, accessed January 2018. https://www.archives.gov/founding-docs/constitution-transcript

8. Copyright.Gov, "Duration of Copyright," Pg. 1, accessed January 2018. https://www.copyright.gov/circs/circ15a.pdf

9. Cornell University Library, Copyright Information Center, "Copyright Term and Public Domain in the United States," accessed March 2018. https://copyright.cornell.edu/publicdomain

10. Copyright.Gov, "Copyright Basics," Pg. 3, accessed January 2018. https://www.copyright.gov/circs/circ01.pdf

Chapter 11

Outreach

In this chapter, I am going to go over outreach, those activities designed to promote archival programs and the use of their collections. Archivists believe that people will fully support historic records programs if they understand what archives do and the nature and importance of their collections. Outreach activities designed to advertise archival programs and their collections are the result of this belief. There is no doubt that effective outreach activities increase the use and funding of archival programs.

Topics in this chapter include knowing your audience, designing efforts to reach that audience, low-cost outreach activities, and extending outreach by using the internet and exhibits. I have also included short sections on fundraising and grant writing in this chapter. Fundraising and grant writing are specialized forms of outreach focused on obtaining funds for your program. In many fundraising activities, you are trying to reach the same audience (or a subsection of it) that you did for your promotional outreach activities. When you submit a grant application, you are reaching out to a specific entity—a grant funder.

The chapter is divided into four sections. Section I covers outreach activities including digital outreach: actions you take via the internet. Section II is a short discussion of exhibits and exhibit loans. Section III deals with fund raising and grant writing. Each of these three sections ends with a short summary. Section IV is the chapter summary and quiz.

Section I: Outreach

Know Your Audience

You have acquired, arranged, described, and preserved some terrific historical records. Now how do you get the word out so people know what you have? Who do you get the word out to? Who is your audience? Who are the people that would find your collections useful?

The audience for your archival program was discussed in chapter 2 when you drafted your collection policy. Go back and take a look at how you defined your audience in that exercise. Are you happy with what you came up with? Take some time to go over your registration slips and registration logs if you kept them. What are people researching at your archives? Are your researchers doing family history or are they doing academic research? Are the people using your collections who you thought they would be? Are you not reaching the researchers you thought you would? Does the definition of your audience need to be revised? Knowing your audience is an important part of knowing how to connect with them and what they need.

Now consider both your audience and your collections. Look at your call slips. Which collections are being used? Do you have important collections that are not being used? Do you have records that would be particularly interesting to a specific group of people? Census records that genealogists could use? Photograph collections that school groups could use? Map collections that owners of historic houses would find useful? Which collections deserve more use, more exposure? These are the types of collections you should target for outreach activities.

What kinds of people would be interested in your collections? How can you get the word out about your collections to these particular groups? Outreach should be done thoughtfully, so that you are sure to reach out to the appropriate group of people about the collections they are interested in. A local group of antique car collectors wouldn't find a lecture about "Using Records and Photographs to Restore Your Historic Home" particularly relevant, but they might be very interested to read a column in their newsletter about the photograph collections of local automobile races held in the 1940s.

Any outreach activities that you create need to be designed so they reach an intended audience. Sometimes you may want to reach out to a broad audience by using an article in your local newspaper or announcements at your local public library. Other times, you will want to focus on specific groups and specific collections. In these cases, you will be evaluating both your collections and your audience, then matching them up and getting the word out appropriately.

Outreach activities can range from exhibits and seminars, to tours of the archives, to creating simple brochures, or publishing a book about local history. Keep in mind that each time a researcher enters your facility you are reaching out to them by showing them the usefulness and value of your program and its collections.

Designing Your Outreach Activities

As you consider an outreach program, ask yourself these questions:

1. Does the outreach activity support and enhance the mission of your program? Small programs with very limited time and resources have to fit outreach into all the other aspects of archival work. Thus making sure that outreach activities support the program's fundamental mission is vital—you don't have time to work on activities that are peripheral to your main activities.
2. What are the needs of your researchers and how can you best meet them? What collections are used the most? Creating a brochure explaining how these collections are organized and their background will help researchers and cut back on the reference work you have to do. You can also ask your researchers, in person or using a formal poll, what kind of help they need, including which of your collections need better or different finding aids.
3. What resources do you have for outreach? Outreach activities can be time consuming, and some (although certainly not all) can be expensive. What resources can you call on? Are there people or organizations that would be willing to donate time and expertise in designing and printing brochures? Are there organizations that could donate supplies? Are there local foundations that could provide funding? Be creative: don't try to do it all yourself.

Low-Cost Outreach Activities

There are many outreach activities that you can use to attract attention to your program for little cost. Before getting started consider selecting someone to be your outreach coordinator. This individual should be excited and enthusiastic about your program and its collections. They should like interacting with people, be able to write and speak well, and they should be eager to talk about your program and the importance of your collections. Your outreach coordinator should start small, and see what works and what doesn't. The outreach coordinator can develop larger more complex outreach programs once they have some experience and have had some successes.

Before trying any outreach activity make sure that the researchers in your facility are comfortable, informed, and have a good experience using your collections. The best outreach is word of mouth. Make sure that researchers speak well of your archives. Do everything you can to ensure that they tell others about how well your archives is run and how good their research experience was at your facility. To do this, ask yourself these questions:

1. Is your facility user-friendly?
2. Is your facility clean and pleasing to be in?
3. Does your reference staff interact positively with users?
4. Are your finding aids are organized and understandable?
5. Are your reference tools easily accessible?
6. Do you have signs posted so it's easy for users to navigate your building?
7. Do you have signs that include your hours of operation?
8. Do you provide samples of forms that researchers may need to fill out?
9. Do you have a handout that explains the rules that researchers need to follow?

Many archival institutions ask researchers to fill out an exit survey identifying what went well and what didn't go well during their research visit. These surveys are a great way of identifying the strengths and weaknesses of your reference services and they give researchers a voice, a way to help you improve the reference experience at your institution. If researchers have a reasonable complaint about your archives, make sure it is addressed as soon as possible. The worst thing you can do is ignore survey feedback.

If researchers don't find what they are looking for in your collections, try to point them in the right direction by referring them to another program that might be able to help them—don't turn them away! The most basic form of outreach is making sure that the researchers using your collections are comfortable, informed, find what they need, and have a good experience at your facility.

Play the Role of Community Ambassador

Your outreach coordinator is your program's representative and ambassador. Whenever possible they should invite people to visit your archives, including local government officials, your own governing or oversight board, and members of your community. It is important that your historic records program is involved and visible within your community. The outreach coordinator should attend community events, especially those related to your program's mission. They should give talks to local groups and schools explaining what you do and encouraging them to visit. In fact, they should talk to anyone who will listen! You might consider newspaper columns or articles, or interviews on local radio stations, in order to get people aware of and interested in your program.

The kinds of community activities the outreach coordinator could participate in or create are limited only by their imagination. Examples include offering to help work on community celebrations and create displays or publications for those events, working with reference staff to organize workshops for researchers on specific topics of interest, holding an open house, running a film night centered around a historic film while displaying collections that relate to the topic of the film, or conducting a photography or writing contest. The best outreach events highlight the strengths of your program's collections paired with the interests of your community. Be inventive—and don't be afraid to fail. It is better to try and fail than not try at all.

Look for opportunities to write in local groups' newsletters, school newsletters, or the local newspaper. Write a short "this week in history" column, for example, or consider writing a column highlighting a different collection every month. Exhibits of your historical materials are a common and excellent outreach tool. Exhibits are discussed later in this chapter.

Work with other cultural and historic groups in your area, like the local library, museum, school, or other historical records programs. Combining your efforts will help all of you and will provide more resources for outreach efforts. Will the library give you some free exhibit space if you are willing to do an hour-long "introduction to family history" workshop for them? Perhaps you can work with the library to create a brochure that highlights common collections. Working with the cultural and historic organizations in your area creates goodwill with them and within your community. It is much better to be seen as a team player in your community than a snobbish institution that is difficult to deal with.

Working with the Media

Be willing to work with the local media. Newspapers, radio, and television all provide opportunities for your program to get the word out about its collections to a wide audience. Knowing how to work with the media, and being comfortable doing it, can be daunting.

Two good resources available that you can use to learn more about working with the media are:

1. The Museum Marketing Tips website[1] has a variety of links and information available for helping museum and other cultural organizations work with the media. It includes a section devoted to "Advertising and Public Relations," with links to many useful resources, including templates for press releases, information about creating good public service announcements, and even information on how to create effective road signs!
2. The Society of American Archivists publication, "Many Happy Returns: Advocacy and the Development of Archives,"[2] edited by Larry J. Hackman. This manual presents practical advice on how to find and relate to various publics: how to better serve the client in person, launch a fundraising campaign, work with media, market programs, organize programs around historical events, train and successfully use volunteers, and avoid the most common public relations errors by planning.

One core media related tool is the press release. Press releases are a key method of officially getting your message out and making announcements to your community. Press releases are an official act by your institution, so there should be a policy or protocol defining who reviews, authorizes and releases press notices. Appendix AB is a Sample Press Release template, which can also be downloaded from the AASLH website at https://learn.aaslh.org/archivalbasics. You are free to modify and use it as you see fit.

Digital Outreach

Digital outreach is comprised of three different tool sets: collection tools designed to get information about your collection out to a wider audience, Internet tools created so you can get information about your historic records program out to a wider audience, and, lastly, social media tools, the uses of which are still evolving.

Collection tools are essentially catalog records describing your collections that are made available to a wide community via searchable databases. These tools rely on a cataloging standard called MARC (Machine Readable Cataloging). MARC is a standard way of creating cataloging records, also called bibliographic records.

By providing MARC catalog records to large, collaborative databases, researchers throughout the United States and around the world will have access to information about your archival collections. Researchers will know where to find your unique collections and be able to contact your organization to use the material for their research. The number of researchers using your collections will grow due to the increased exposure of your collections through these databases.

If you have an online public access catalog (OPAC), you probably already use MARC to create your catalog records. If your MARC records are stored only in your local online system, you should consider utilizing OCLC's[3] (Online Computer Library Center) World-Cat. WorldCat is "the most comprehensive database about library information in the world."[4] OCLC maintains this database using MARC records submitted from a variety of organizations. Using WorldCat ensures that your MARC records are made available to a worldwide audience who can discover your collections via this large collaborative and searchable database.

If you don't use MARC and don't have an online public access catalog, you can use another service that is run by the Library of Congress in order to get the word out about your collections. Called the National Union Catalog of Manuscript Collections (NU-CMC—pronounced "nuck-muck"), it is a free-of-charge cooperative cataloging program available to repositories located in the United States and its territories. The repository must admit researchers and must lack the capability of entering its own manuscript cataloging into OCLC's database. The NUCMC home page is at https://www.loc.gov/coll/nucmc/index.html.

NUCMC uses information or data you provide on your archival collections to prepare a catalog record using the MARC format for inclusion in OCLC's databases. The team does not arrange and describe or write finding aids for your collections nor do they advise on the arrangement process.

There are other collection tools like ArchiveGrid that bring information about collections and institutions together online. ArchiveGrid has "over 5 million records describing archival materials, bringing together information about historical documents, personal papers, family histories, and more. With over 1,000 different archival institutions represented, ArchiveGrid helps researchers looking for primary source materials held in archives, libraries, museums and historical societies."[5] ArchiveGrid uses MARC records copied from WorldCat.

In some ways the ultimate collections tool is the encoded archival description (EAD). EAD enables you to create a computer readable version of your entire finding aid that can be posted and searched online. EAD is a XML standard for encoding finding aids. XML is similar to HTML, the coding language used to create websites. The EAD standard[6] is supported and maintained by a partnership between the Society of American Archivists and the Library of Congress.[7] Creating EAD finding aids can be difficult, but there are lots of tutorials and tools on the internet to help you. Not every collection is worthy of the effort that it takes to create an EAD finding aid, but some are. If you are lucky enough to have such a collection, try creating an EAD finding aid.

Internet Tools

There are a number of communication tools available on the internet that institutions can use. Creating a website for your institution is a good place to start. There are lots of companies that will create a website for you for a little cost, or provide you with templates that will let you design your own website for very little. Tools to design websites are also very cheap and relatively easy to use. The tools are so easy that it takes very little technical skill to design a website. Anyone can do it.

Your first website should start with the basics, posting information about where your institution is, what the hours and the nature of your collections are. This kind of website is called a brochure site. As time goes on and you add more and more information about your institution, the site will become more helpful to your researchers. Posting information about any special events you are hosting and connecting to your community and researchers is a great use of a website.

As your institution becomes more comfortable posting information on the website, consider posting information about your collections and reference policies to the site so your users will have a better idea of what your collections are and the level of service they can expect when they visit your archive. You can also post copies of the finding aids to your most popular collections and expand that out as time allows. If you have an online public access catalog (OPAC), you can connect copies of finding aids to the bibliographic entries of those collections.

If you have digitized collections or portions of them you can provide access to these files via your internet site. Digital projects are a great way to create enthusiasm about specific collections and/or your archives. Many researchers now expect collections to be digitized and made available to them via the internet. Chapter 12 discusses the growing importance of digital records. Chapter 13 discusses how to create and run digital projects.

Examples of archival websites abound: the Library of Congress is a great site to emulate (https://loc.gov). Other great sites include the City of Providence (RI) City Archives (http://www.providenceri.gov/cityarchives), the Baltimore City (MD) Archives (https://baltimorecityhistory.net), the Dufferin County (Ontario) Museum and Archives (http://www.dufferinmuseum.com/Research/ResourcesGuidelines.aspx), and the Handel and Haydn Society Archives of Boston (https://handelandhaydn.org/archives) to name but a few.

Social Media Tools

There are lots of social media tools and sites that are worth looking at. Creating a Facebook page for your institution is an easy option to consider. The Brooklyn Museum (https://www.brooklynmuseum.org) uses many of these tools—Twitter, YouTube, Facebook, blogs, and Instagram to name a few. They also use crowdsourcing, using the internet to ask users to "tag" collections or items with descriptive terms (metadata). Crowdsourcing is a fascinating use of the internet and an example of what can be done with a little imagination.[8] Be bold—don't be afraid of trying new social media tools to get the word out about your institution.

Using social media tools must be done with care, a post can go wrong very quickly. When you use social media tools officially on behalf of your institution, you have an obligation to your institution to use these tools in an efficient and responsible manner. Consider revising the policies or protocols that define reviewing, authorizing, and releasing press notices to cover using social media tools. The social media policy or protocol should not be too cumbersome. You want to be nimble, but you also want to have more than one person making the decisions about using social media.

Outreach Summary

Outreach to your audience doesn't have to be expensive and overly time consuming. Outreach should be a part of your overall historical records program. If you have never done outreach activities before, start with activities that are small in scale and simple— creating brochures, writing a press release, or working as part of a committee for a community event.

No matter how simple or elaborate your outreach efforts are, getting the word out about the unique resources your historical records collections offer the community is an important task that should not be overlooked.

A few good additional outreach resources include the following:

- Dearstyne, Bruce W. 2015. *Leading the Historical Enterprise: Strategic Creativity, Planning and Advocacy for the Digital Age.* Rowman & Littlefield. ISBN: 978-0-7591-2399-1
- Freeman Finch, Elsie. 1994. *Advocating Archives: An Introduction to Public Relations for Archivists.* Rowman & Littlefield. ISBN: 978-0-8108-4773-6
- Hackman, Larry J. Ed. 2011. *Many Happy Returns: Advocacy and the Development of Archives.* Society of American Archivists. ISBN: 1-931666-37-7
- Koontz, Christie and Mon, Lorri. 2014. *Marketing and Social Media: A Guide for Libraries, Archives, and Museums.* Rowman & Littlefield. ISBN: 978-0-8108-9080-0
- Purcell, Aaron. 2015. *Donors and Archives: A Guidebook for Successful Programs.* Rowman & Littlefield. ISBN: 978-0-8108-9323-8
- Theimer, Kate. Ed. 2015. *Educational Programs: Innovative Practices for Archives and Special Collections.* Rowman & Littlefield. ISBN: 978-1-4422-4952-3
- Theimer, Kate. Ed. 2014. *Outreach: Innovative Practices for Archives and Special Collections.* Rowman & Littlefield. ISBN: 978-0-8108-9097-8

Section II: Exhibits and Loans

Exhibits are a great opportunity to allow people to see your historic record collections. Exhibits are the main activity of museums, but are also used by archival programs. Although exhibits will never be the main activity of your historic records program, they will most likely be an activity that you will occasionally need to do. When you do exhibits, you need to be aware of the significant security and preservation-related issues inherent in them.

Loaning materials is an activity often directly related to exhibits. Occasionally programs are asked to loan their records to another organization so that they can be exhibited with similar or related collections. Again, you need to be fully aware of the significant security and preservation challenges these situations create.

Exhibits

The purpose of most exhibits is to educate people and get them interested in doing additional research in a particular topic or collection. An archival exhibit entices people to use archival collections while exposing them to interesting historical facts or individuals. To do this, you need to present an archival item or items along with interesting facts about them that put them into historical context. You need to tell a compelling story with historical facts using items from your collections as illustrations. The best exhibits catch your eye and interest. The kinds of collection items you want to use for exhibits are those that made you say to yourself, "Wow, that is cool," (or something similar) the first time you saw them. Exhibits advertise your archives and its collections.

No matter how large or small your exhibit, there are always preservation considerations that need to be addressed. Often these considerations are overlooked in the planning and design of the exhibit. Whenever possible, use copies of original records for exhibit purposes. Digital copiers can make facsimiles that are virtually identical to the original; and high quality copying services are available in most areas. Copying can even be used to improve the quality of photographic images by using digital imaging tools such as Photoshop. Using a copy for an exhibit means that you do not have to worry about security and preservation concerns. Original materials should be placed in exhibits under special conditions and only when absolutely necessary.

There will be situations when the original sheet materials, such as photographs and loose-page documents, must be displayed. In these cases the items must be protected. There are four simple rules that must be followed when exhibiting original paper-based materials:

1. Display originals on a short-term basis.
2. Keep light levels at a minimum.
3. UV light is particularly damaging to paper documents, so make sure that measures are taken to guard against it.
4. Exhibit cases and frames should be enclosed, locked, sealed, and made out of materials that will not create gases that damage documents. Metal is better than wood.

Light

We have already discussed the damage light can cause to historical records. Exhibiting original records makes light exposure inevitable. However, there are some steps you can take to keep exposure (and therefore damage) to a minimum.

- Cover any windows in the exhibit areas with blinds, shades, or curtains.
- Install UV filters on windows or on exhibit cases.
- Filtering capacity should be greater than 90 percent.
- Assume that natural light, fluorescent, and tungsten-halogen light sources give off unacceptable levels of UV and that UV filters need to be in place.
- Turn off the lights when visitors aren't in the room.
- Put cloth covers over the cases during nonworking hours.

For more information on the harmful effects of light during exhibits, see the Library of Congress Collections Care section, Limiting Light Damage from Display/Exhibition[9] or the Northeast Document Conservation Center (NEDCC) preservation pamphlet, "2.4 Protection from Light Damage."[10]

Figure 11.1.   Exhibit at the Ohio University Robert E. and Jean R. Mahn Center for Archives and Special Collections. Notice how there is no direct light in the exhibit case.

Photo by Laurie Gemmill Arp, courtesy of Ohio University Libraries

Exhibit Cases

Paper-based materials must be exhibited in cases. Cases provide protection against the public touching the items, changes in temperature and humidity, and can help you control exposure to light. Creating or purchasing good display cases can be costly, but these costs are mitigated by the cases being used for multiple displays over many years.

Cases can be sealed using silica gel. This seal allows you to control the relative humidity within the exhibit case. Creating a stable environment for the items on display by sealing the display cases can be beneficial. It can also be harmful if the case is made out of materials that create gases containing acids. In a sealed case, these gases have no escape so they create a micro environment that is very harmful to the items on display. It is important that display cases are made of materials that do not create gases or of materials that can be treated to limit gases. The best choice is to use inert materials to create exhibit cases: materials like coated steel, anodized aluminum, Plexiglas, or glass boxes (with frames on the outside of the case).

Making display cases out of inert materials can be expensive and difficult. Display cases can be made out of wood, but they must be treated to reduce gaseous emissions. Do not treat or seal wood display cases with oil based sealants and paints. Acrylic and latex paints will *not* adequately seal the wood. The best choice is to treat wood with two-part epoxy paints and sealants, which need to be mixed and are somewhat difficult to use.

Some woods are better than others for display cases because they produce fewer harmful gases. Stay away from oak. While it is a very popular choice for furniture, including cases, it is very acidic. The best wood for display cases are poplar, basswood, and true African mahogany.

The NEDCC Preservation pamphlet, "2.5 Protecting Paper and Book Collections during Exhibits,"[11] states that you should "try to avoid plywood and wood composites which are made with adhesives containing formaldehyde that result in the creation of acid. If you are using these materials try to use:

- Exterior plywood bonded with exterior glue (a phenol formaldehyde adhesive). Plywood that has an APA (American Plywood Association) stamp on it only uses phenol formaldehyde adhesives.
- Particle board, such as Medite II.
- Plywood faced with Kraft paper, such as MDO (medium-density overlay) and HDO (high-density overlay).

Regardless of which wood used, you should not place collections items directly on a wood surface. Use a barrier material, such as Plexiglas or acid-free, lignin-free, buffered cardboard on which to place the display items. Acid-free paper is not thick enough to create a sufficient barrier.

Make sure that the climate, temperature, and humidity are appropriate for the materials being exhibited. You should monitor temperature and humidity in the exhibit area and take appropriate steps to assure that it is the best it can be. We discussed environmental control for historic records in chapter 6.

Placing Materials within Exhibit Cases

Sheet materials should be attached to pieces of acid-free, lignin-free, buffered board, or other archival material that has been cut just slightly larger than the document itself. This "mount" provides a barrier between the document and the exhibit case and provides support for the object when it is moved. You should attach the item to the mount using archival quality corner supports or edge supports—neither of these options requires adhesive being applied to the item itself.

NEDCC has two publications specifically about mounting documents for exhibits. The first is preservation pamphlet "4.0 Matting and Framing for Art and Artifacts of Paper."[12] The second is preservation pamphlet "7.4 How to Do Your Own Matting and Hinging."[13]

Books and Bound Volumes

Bound volumes should be displayed horizontally, or at a mild angle. Do not prop them upright! If an open volume is displayed, it shouldn't be laid out completely flat, but left to open only as far as the binding will allow. If the pages don't remain open on their own, you can use strips of polyester film closed with double-sided tape placed around each side of the open book.

If possible, use a book cradle or wedge, or even supports made from folded museum board, to assure that the volume is opened only as far as it does naturally. Finally, turn the pages every few days to reduce exposure to light. When you turn pages, turn many pages, not just a couple.

Loans

Exhibiting historical records is an important way to raise awareness; however, it must be done thoughtfully and with preservation in mind. This is even more important if your materials are going to be exhibited on loan, in a facility that is not your own, and in an environment you do not control.

Lending materials is common practice for some programs, and infrequent in others. In either situation, your program should have a standard loan agreement form that delineates the conditions of the loan. You may also want to consider a loan policy statement that governs the loaning practices of your organization.

It is common practice to insure the items being loaned. There are two parts to insuring items for loan. First, as the lender, your organization should create a report detailing the condition of the item being loaned including images prior to the items leaving your facility. Second, you need to determine the insurance value of the items being loaned. The organization hosting the exhibit should insure the items during the loan period including transportation to and from the exhibit space. Proof of such insurance should be required before the loan is made.

Documenting Loans

A loan policy details the processes and requirements involved in loaning material for exhibition purposes. See appendix AC, "Sample Loan of Documents for Exhibit." This template is very generic; you can download it from the AASLH website at https://learn .aaslh.org/archivalbasics to modify and use as you see fit.

Be aware that the documentation of your loan agreement is a legal contract. As such, the template you use needs to be reviewed by your legal counsel. Any loan agreements should be approved and signed by the appropriate governing boards and signing authorities before the loan is official.

Exhibits and Loans Summary

Exhibiting and loaning your historical records is a great way to extend your outreach to larger audiences. However, as with any access-oriented activity, there is an inherent tension between the preservation of the materials and the use of them. You're going to need to control the amount of light materials are exposed to and the amount of handling they receive.

Because exhibits can cause serious preservation problems, the best choice is to always exhibit high-quality copies of your materials. When this isn't an option, you must ensure that preservation concerns are taken into account and that the exhibit environment is as conducive to preservation as possible.

Section III: Fundraising and Grant Writing

Now that you have made your way through the basics of caring for historical records collections, you may have identified several areas where you need to make improvements. You may need to purchase smoke alarms and fire extinguishers for your storage area, you may need to attend some training on disaster response, or you may need some funding to upgrade your storage equipment. Your current budget may not allow for these kinds of activities and you are thinking, "This is a good idea, but how are we going to get the money?" No matter how large or small your historic records program is, raising funds to support archival work is always a challenge.

There are several ways to get the money you need for your historic records program. If your program sits within a larger organization, you can make your case that you need an increase in your budget. If your program stands alone, you will need to think of ways you can raise money. In either case, fundraising and grant writing are two good ways to raise money.

Define What You Need

Before even thinking about how you will get the funding you need, you should clearly define what you need funding for and how much funding you need. You need to be able to state your case for funding clearly and concisely. Think in terms of a needs statement—what do you need, why do you need it, how much will it cost, and why is it important?

When you have your needs statement for funding defined, clearly thought out, and articulated, you can begin to think about how to raise money to fund it. If you are part of a larger organization, your first step will most likely be to find out whether or not more funding will be available in your program's budget. Larger organizations may also be able to call on the services of a development staff—people whose job responsibilities include researching and identifying funders, writing grant proposals, and meeting with potential donors. You need to work with these people, if you are lucky enough to have them!

Many historical records programs don't have large parent organizations with development departments. In these cases, it will be the staff and volunteers who work on fundraising efforts including writing grant proposals that get funded.

Fundraising

Fundraising activities range from the simple to the complex, from displaying a poster that asks for donations for a specific purpose to telephone campaigns, from bake sales (or book sales) to silent auctions. Fundraising is a process that requires creativity and ingenuity. What works in one place may not work in another. Regardless of what kind of fundraiser you are trying to do, there are several steps you need to take to be successful:

- Set a goal—how much money do you need to raise? A fundraiser without a goal is like an arrow without a target. This is part of your needs statement so you should have this amount already defined.
- Develop a plan—the more complex your fundraiser is, the more important planning it well will be. Understand who is in charge of what. You might put your outreach coordinator in charge of overseeing the entire fundraiser, or they might be tasked with supervising only a portion of the event.
- Create a schedule—again, more complex fundraisers need a schedule developed so that you are sure that everything gets done in the right order and on time.
- Select the right fundraiser—one that your group can and will participate in and support.
- Do one fundraiser at a time—doing many fundraisers does not always mean raising more money. Doing a few fundraisers and doing them well will often produce better results.
- Create enthusiasm and excitement—you are raising money because you believe in your cause and you want others to believe, too. Show enthusiasm in what you do—it's contagious!
- Your fundraiser is a "mini" business; treat it like a business. Make good decisions and use good accounting practices. Create and keep good records of money going in and money going out. Just a hint of impropriety, even the smallest financial scandal, will ruin your fundraising efforts for a long time.

Fundraiser Ideas

There are many unique and interesting ideas for fundraisers. Here are a few of my favorites to get your creative thoughts started about potential fundraisers for your program:

- Mother's Day flower sale
- Bake sale
- Saint Patrick's Day raffle
- Dinners
- Walking tours of historic homes
- Concerts
- Fairs—Christmas, Easter, spring, summer, fall
- Sales of special items—Christmas ornaments

Remember, the best fundraisers are fun and interesting and related to your collections, be creative!

Applying for Grants

When you apply for grant funding, you write a grant proposal that defines what you will do with the funding if you get it. The proposal is then submitted to a grant funder for consideration, if they like your proposal they give you funding. Grant writing is a time-consuming and detail-oriented process. How you write a grant proposal is based on the requirements of the funder. The main steps in developing a grant proposal are research, writing, and submission to the funder. Before you start writing a grant, make sure you have identified the funding source and understand their requirements thoroughly.

Research

Research the project you want to do. Gather appropriate statistics to document need and look at professional literature to learn more about what others are doing and saying about your area of need. The more you know before you start writing, the better. Again think in terms of a needs statement: what do you need, why do you need it, how much will it cost, and why is it important? You should also think about how you prove that you met the need for your project. How do you define and prove that your project was a success?

If you've never written a grant proposal before, you should also do some research about how to write a proposal. Your local library should have books available on this topic, and there are numerous websites that offer helpful grant writing information.

You also need to research your funding options. There are two types of grant funders: local funders who may not need a long or detailed grant submission and regional, state, national, or international funders, who will probably require a very detailed grant submission. In general, the more money you want, the more detailed the grant submission requirements. Regardless of how big or small the funding entity is, your project needs to match the grant funders focus and interests.

Local Funders

Your best bet for finding funding may not be the federal government or large funders; but your own local foundations, organizations, or corporations. There are very often local, community grant programs that you can apply to for funding.

How do you find local funders? Ask around, read the newspaper, go to the library, and do some research. Establish relationships with these local organizations—ask them if they have archival materials that they would like to donate or would like assistance with; take key people out to lunch; put them on your newsletter mailing list. All these simple steps help you raise awareness about your program and put you in a better position to apply for funding; or ask for a donation if they don't have a grant program.

Asking individuals who visit your facility for funding is one fundraising technique. Consider sending out an annual letter to those who visit or regularly benefit from your institution asking them to make a small donation. The success of this kind of fundraising rests on the experience of those who visited your facility. If they had a good experience, you will raise money; if not, you will not. Cultivating relationships with wealthy individuals or companies for larger donations to your historic records program can lead to sustainable funding for your program but involves substantial time and effort. Be transparent and pleasant when creating these relationships. You do not want to come across as predatory. A strong, clear message about the intended use of the funds is important for both techniques.

Regional, State, National, or International Funders

If you are looking for a regional, state, national, or international funding entity, start by asking your state archives, state library, regional historical association, or state historical records advisory board[14] about grant-funding sources. They should be able to point you to such sources.

Grant submissions for these kinds of funders are competitive. In most cases, the funding entity will have a defined amount of funding to give out. Proposals will be evaluated against each other using the funders' requirements as the measuring stick. The proposals that best fit the requirements get funded.

In most cases, these kinds of grant funders will tell you explicitly what they want in a grant submission and how they want them written. If so, your task will be to match your collections, skills, and perhaps technical abilities to the funder's requirements. I strongly advise you to look at the grant funder requirements carefully. If possible, set up a meeting or call with the grant funder to outline your project and ask them for whatever advice they can give you. In some cases, the funder will tell you if you have a chance of getting funded including how to make your proposal more competitive. Ask if you can submit a grant proposal for their review. You can also ask for copies of grant submissions that have been funded so you can see how they were written.

Be careful when you write a grant proposal. You want to get your proposal funded, so you may commit to doing a lot of work to get funding, to offer the funder the sun, the moon, and the stars to get the money. The problems begin when you get the funding and you have to produce the sun, the moon, and the stars. A grant submission is basically a contract between you and the funder—you have to produce what you say you will or you may be forced to return the funding or part of it.

Writing a grant proposal always takes longer than you think it will. Make sure you know when the proposal needs to be submitted when you schedule time for writing it—and give yourself some extra time just in case. Remember that the management of your organization and perhaps your comptroller may need to review and sign off on the proposal before it is sent out. Give them time to review the proposal and give yourself some time to make any edits they suggest. You do not want to be running around the day the proposal is due looking for signatures, collating pages, making last-minute edits, and driving to the post office as it closes. Take my word for it!

Writing a Proposal

Grant proposals are divided into several elements. The standard elements found in most proposals are these:

- Cover letter—An introduction to your organization, the reason for the proposal, and amount requested.
- Abstract—A clear summary of the proposal. Not an introduction, but a summary that encompasses all the key points. The abstract is best written after the entire proposal is complete.
- Statement of need—The statement of need is often the most important part of the proposal. It answers the "why" question—why should we fund this proposal? Why should we be interested in it?
- Objectives—Objectives answer the "what" question. What are you going to accomplish in order to meet your stated need? Objectives should be stated clearly and limited in number (no more than six). Think in terms of how you will define success. What do you need to do to be successful?
- Methodology/work plan—This section explains how and when you are going to meet your objectives.
- Qualifications (institutional and staff)—In order to make your case, you need to show that you have the appropriate qualifications within your staff and within

your organization. You want the funder to have confidence in your ability to accomplish the project you propose.

- Budget—Your budget should cover appropriate expenses for the nature of the project, including personnel, overhead, equipment, supplies, travel, and miscellaneous. Budgets should be well thought through—don't pad the budget, yet make sure that it is adequate. Proofread your budget multiple times before you send it in.
- Evaluation—Many proposals require you to include an evaluation component in your project. This is a way for you to measure and demonstrate that you met the objectives you set out to achieve. How do you prove that the project was successful?
- Sustainability—Many proposals also ask you to demonstrate a commitment to sustaining the project that has been started with grant funding. If possible, show that you can include the maintenance costs of the grant in your operating budget. If you cannot do this, you need to think about your next grant or other sources of funding to bear the maintenance costs of the grant going forward.

Submission

Once your proposal is written, edited, proofed, and finalized, it should be submitted. Many funders have specific guidelines for how proposals should be submitted—for example, they must be postmarked by a certain date; there must be ten copies plus the original submitted; they must not be bound, only paper-clipped. Some funders may require you to use a specific website to submit your proposal. Whatever the method of submission, pay attention to the details of the process. Make sure that the appropriate forms are filled out and the appropriate signatures are on the proposal. Success in grant writing is often in the details!

Additional Grant Writing Resources?

Obviously there is much more to be said about each one of these sections of a grant proposal. If you are interested in pursuing grant funding, you will need much more information about how to write an effective proposal. There are lots of resources on grant writing, here are just a few:

- Bauer, David G. *How to Evaluate and Improve Your Grants Effort*. Westport, CT: Oryx Press, 2001.
- Bauer, David G. *The "How To" Grants Manual*. Phoenix, AZ: Oryx Press, 1999.
- Golden, Susan L. *Successful Grantsmanship*. San Francisco, CA: Jossey-Bass, Inc., 1997.
- Karsh, Ellen and Fox, Arlen Sue. *The Only Grant Writing Book You Will Ever Need*, Fourth Edition. Basic Books. 2014.
- O'Neal-McElratch, Toni. *Winning Grants Step by Step: The Complete Workbook for Planning, Developing, and Writing Successful Proposals*, 4th Edition. Jossey-Bass. 2014.
- Smith, Nancy and Works, E. *The Complete Book of Grant Writing*. Sourcebooks Inc. 2012.
- See the American Grant Writers Association Inc. "Grant Writing for Non-profit Organizations" http://www.agwa.us/nonprofitgrantwriting
- See the Catalog of Federal Domestic Assistance—https://www.cfda.gov/
- See the Grant Writing Tools for Non-profit Organizations—http://www.np guides.org/

- See the Foundation Center, Proposal Writing Short Course—http://foundation-center.org/getstarted/tutorials/shortcourse/

Fundraising Summary

Archival activities, from accessioning to preservation, should be part of your program's overall budget. However, there will be times when it's necessary to find additional funds. That is when grant writing and fundraising skills come in handy.

Creative fundraising and good grant writing can help you purchase new equipment, process collections, or build a new facility. Although some archivists don't think of these activities as crucial to the preservation of historical records, the reality is that preservation and access cost money. Money that often has to be raised by those who care for the records. Whether or not you're an expert grant writer or fundraiser, these are vital activities that help us ensure our collections are cared for.

Section IV: Chapter Summary

Outreach, exhibits, loans, fundraising, and grant writing are secondary tasks for archivists, compared to acquiring, describing, preserving, managing, and providing reference services to historic collections. But these secondary activities separate good archival programs from great archival programs. They may also help your historic records program survive during the lean years and, make no mistake, for cultural and historic organizations, most years are lean years! Archival programs ignore outreach and related activities at their peril.

There are many worthy organizations and causes trying to raise money, so make sure your fundraising activities stand out. To do so they have to be fun, educational and interesting. If you embrace outreach activities you and your program will be rewarded.

Quiz

See the answers on page 324.

1. How can you find out what collections researchers are using?
2. What is the most basic form of outreach?
3. What is the primary role of an outreach coordinator?
4. What is a press release?
5. What is a MARC record?
6. What are collection tools?
7. What are the two things you need to worry about when creating an exhibit?
8. Before you start fundraising what do you need to figure out?
9. The best fundraisers are?
10. What must you know before writing a grant?

Notes

1. Museum Marketing Info., accessed January 2018. http://www.museummarketing.info/
2. Society of American Archivists Bookstore, "Many Happy Returns: Advocacy and the Development of Archives," accessed January 2018. http://saa.archivists.org/store/many-happy-returns-advocacy-and-the-development-of-archives/2024/

3. OCLC, "Advancing our Shared Mission," accessed January 2018. http://www.oclc.org

4. OCLC, "WorldCat Discovery," accessed January 2018. https://www.oclc.org/en/worldcat.html

5. ArchiveGrid, About ArchiveGrid, accessed March 2018. https://beta.worldcat.org/archivegrid/about

6. Encoded Archival Description, Official Site, accessed March 2018. https://www.loc.gov/ead/

7. Library of Congress, Librarians, Archivists, Finding Aids, accessed March 2018. https://www.loc.gov/rr/ead/

8. See MW2013: Museums and the Web 2013, The Annual Conference of Museums and the Web, April 17–20 2013, Portland OR, "Digital Humanities and Crowdsourcing: An Exploration," accessed January 2018. https://mw2013.museumsandtheweb.com/paper/digital-humanities-and-crowdsourcing-an-exploration-4/ Or Wikipedia, "Crowdsourcing," accessed January 2018. https://en.wikipedia.org/wiki/Crowdsourcing

9. Library of Congress, Preservation, Collections Care, "Limiting Light Damage from Display/Exhibition," accessed January 2018. https://www.loc.gov/preservation/care/light.html

10. Northeast Document Conservation Center, Preservation Pamphlet, "2.4 Protection from Light," accessed January 2018. https://www.nedcc.org/free-resources/preservation-leaflets/2.-the-environment/2.4-protection-from-light-damage

11. Northeast Document Conservation Center, Preservation Pamphlet, "2.5 Protecting Paper and Book Collections during Exhibition," accessed January 2018. https://www.nedcc.org/free-resources/preservation-leaflets/2.-the-environment/2.5-protecting-paper-and-book-collections-during-exhibition

12. Northeast Document Conservation Center, Preservation Pamphlet, Storage and Handling, "4.0 Matting and Framing for Art and Artifacts on Paper," accessed January 2018. https://www.nedcc.org/free-resources/preservation-leaflets/4.-storage-and-handling/4.10-matting-and-framing-for-art-and-artifacts-on-paper

13. Northeast Document Conservation Center, Preservation Pamphlet, Conservation Procedures, "7.4 How to Do Your Own Matting and Hinging," accessed January 2018. https://www.nedcc.org/free-resources/preservation-leaflets/7.-conservation-procedures/7.4-how-to-do-your-own-matting-and-hinging

14. Council of State Archivists, "Directory of State Archives," accessed January 2018. https://www.statearchivists.org/connect/resources-state/

Chapter 12

Digital Records

The goal of this chapter is to get you started thinking about collecting digital records by introducing you to the issues involved with acquiring, storing, managing, preserving, and making them available to researchers. To do that, I will define some of the major terms, issues, theories, and cover the processes and resources needed to preserve and make digital records available to researchers. I will also point you to some resources[1] for further information on digital records and their preservation. I will not recommend specific solutions to you, although I will define the steps you have to take to collect, maintain, preserve, and make digital records available to researchers. Most of all I want to encourage you to start collecting digital records.

There are three reasons I am not making specific recommendations about digital records to you. First, anything I recommend about how to archive digital records would be based on an assumed set of resources. This severely limits the value of any recommendations because your resources are unique. Second, the tools and techniques designed to archive digital records change constantly. This means that any recommendations I make about how to do things will be out of date six months after I make them. Lastly, managing and preserving digital records is an on-going process. You need to take a continuous series of actions to monitor and address the health of the digital records in your care. This process is called "digital curation," and to do it well, you need to keep up with the advancements in the field of digital preservation. Recommendations from me will not help you do that.

I have enlisted the help of three electronic record archivists and one electronic records manager to assist me in writing this chapter. Veronica Martzahl, from the Massachusetts State Archives; Nick Connizzo, from the Vermont State Archives; Allen Ramsey, of the Connecticut State Archives; and Jennifer Seymour have all volunteered their time and expertise to review and comment on the drafts of this chapter. I was also fortunate to have an old friend, Cal Lee, professor at the University of North Carolina School of Information and Library Science, SAA Fellow, and current editor of the *American Archivist* review parts of this chapter and offer his comments. I very much appreciate their help and the help of the American Association of State and Local History (AASLH) and the Council of State Archivists (CoSA). With all this help, any and all errors or omissions in this chapter and in this book are entirely my fault.

I have broken this chapter down into seven sections. In section I, I will define some basic terms and discuss the differences between analog or nondigital records and digital records. Section II is a review of some of the main theories supporting digital preservation.

In section III, I will review the changes that are needed in your collections policy to accession digital records. Section IV discusses the appraisal of digital records. Section V defines the processes you need to preform to archive digital records. In section VI, I go over the resources needed to archive digital records. The chapter ends with section VII, a summary, a quiz, and a list of some of the digital preservation resources that are available to you.

Section I: Introduction to Digital Records

In the past I used the term *electronic records* when I talked about electronic files. Others prefer to use the terms *digital assets, digital materials, digital objects*, or *digital records*. What all these terms have in common is that they refer to an electronic file (or files) that must be interpreted by a computer application and rendered by a machine so that a human can view and understand the information in the file.

The Glossary of the Society of American Archivists defines *electronic or digital records* as "Data or information that has been captured and fixed for storage and manipulation in an automated system and that requires the use of the system to render it intelligible by a person."[2] In chapter one, records were defined as documents in any form containing information created by an individual or organization during the course of their activities. Records offer evidence of activities and relationships. Digital records are the electronic versions of physical records. *Digital record* is the term I will use throughout this chapter. I use the term *record* here in the broadest possible way; there are no content limits to the kinds of digital information you take into your archives. When I talk about nondigital records, I will use the term *analog records*, meaning records in any physical format—paper records, microfilm, maps, photographs; anything transcribed on nondigital media.

> *Digital record*—a record that needs to be interpreted by a computer application and rendered by a machine so that a human can view and understand it.

Born Digital versus Digitized

There are two kinds of digital records: those born digital and those that are converted (reformatted) from an analog to a digital record. Born digital records, also known as "native digital records," are just what you think they are: digital files created on some form of machine. Increasingly, all our information and records are born digital. Very little new information is created on paper and converted to a digital record.

Reformatted or converted digital records are the result of scanning information from an analog source to create a digital copy of that source. This process is generally referred to as "digitization," and it will be covered in chapter 13.

Metadata

Metadata is a term used constantly when discussing digital records. Do not let this technical sounding term scare you. The simple definition of metadata is "data about data," or information about an information resource. A good example of metadata is the bibliographic records that you use to search for resources in your local library. Title, author, date of publication, publisher, and IBSN number are all metadata about a book; information about an information resource. There are lots of different kinds of metadata. I am going to focus on three types in this chapter. Administrative metadata that relates simple facts about a record; descriptive metadata, which describes the record and its contents; and preservation metadata that describes the steps that were taken to preserve the record.

In some ways, the more metadata you have, the better, assuming that the metadata you have is correct. If you don't have enough administrative metadata, you don't know what you have or where it came from. If you don't have enough descriptive metadata, researchers may not be able to find or understand what you have. If you don't have enough preservation metadata, you may not be able to prove the reliability and/or authenticity of the record. Reliability meaning, is the record what it claims to be? Can I have faith that the record is what it says it is? Authenticity is proven reliability over time. Can I still have faith in the evidentiary value of the record after twenty years of maintenance? Reliability and authenticity are the goals of digital preservation. If you cannot prove that a digital record is reliable and authentic, there are very few reasons to keep it. Metadata is the primary tool used to establish and maintain reliability and authenticity.

Metadata can be defined by a standard or it can be undefined, created as needed with no standard. As examples of standard metadata, the value for metadata field Y is author, or the value for metadata field X is date published. Standard metadata can also have pre-defined values, you pick the value from a list of options presented to you. To continue the library book example, the current metadata standard for bibliographic records is the Resource Description and Access standard (RDA), published in 2010.[3] Library catalogers use RDA to create metadata records about items located in their libraries using the definitions of metadata fields found in that standard.

> *Metadata*—data about data, information about an information resource.

The vast majority of this chapter is about digital curation, actions taken to safeguard digital records. The salient differences between analog and digital records are how they are managed and preserved. However, the philosophical theme of archival work—archivists need to preserve the collections in our care while providing access to them—is as valid for digital records as much as for analog records. Do not overlook access concerns just because you are dealing with digital records. Full-text search does not mean that descriptive metadata has no importance to digital records. Without good descriptive metadata, neither you nor researchers will find the digital records you seek. Nothing is as lost as one digital record among 100,000 similar digital records. Descriptive metadata is just as important for digital records as it is for analog records.

Digital Curation

Digital preservation, along with the actions I have described as archiving digital records, are more accurately referred to as "digital curation." Wikipedia defines digital curation as "the selection, preservation, maintenance, collection and archiving of digital assets."[4] Maintenance, the on-going set of actions taken to ensure that one has access to digital records over time, is the essence, the heart of digital curation.

Digital curation requires continuous monitoring and active preservation, whereas preservation of analog records can be done just in time or as needed. As an example, a paper record from 1898 will be brown and brittle because of the acid content, but you can still read and understand that record. Provided the correct preservation techniques and care are used, the 1898 record can be saved. That is not the case with a digital record from ten years ago. If you do not have the correct device to read the media upon which the digital record is imprinted (for example, a CD drive to read the disc upon which the record resides), you cannot read it. If the electronic (digital) imprint on the disc is damaged by the ravages of time, or by proximity to a magnet, or the disc itself is physically damaged, you cannot read it. If you do not have the correct computer hardware and software to interpret the digital record,

> *Digital curation*—the selection, collection, maintenance, preservation and archiving of digital records.

you cannot read it. The need to overcome digital imprint vulnerabilities, media imper-manence, and the necessity of having the correct hardware and software to read a digital record means that the need to plan and take digital preservation actions are much more pressing than is the case for analog records.

Dealing with digital preservation issues takes effort, expertise, technical resources, and funding. But Rome was not built in a day, and you can start your digital curation program small and build it as you gain expertise and technical resources. The important step is to get started gathering the resources and expertise needed to deal with the digital records that are coming your way.

What Are the Differences between Digital and Analog Records?

On a philosophical level, there is no difference between a digital and an analog record. A paper birth certificate and a digital birth certificate have the same value as evidence, provided you can prove both are authentic. On a practical level, there are dramatic dif-ferences between digital and analog records. Digital records require the correct hardware and software to read them, the digital imprint resides on media (discs, tapes, etc.) with short lifespans, and the digital imprint itself is susceptible to corruption from a variety of sources. Digital records are easily changed with little or no evidence of modification. Analog records reside on media that is relatively stable; they can be read with the naked eye, or in the case of microfilm, with a light and a magnification device. Analog records can be modified but there is usually evidence of modification and we have a lot of experi-ence detecting fake documents.

The biggest difference between analog and digital records is the speed with which digital records become unreadable because of hardware and software obsolescence. Nothing like this exists in analog records. The hardware and software needed to view and use digital records has about a five-year lifespan. After ten years, the hardware and software needed to view and use a digital record is two generations old. After twenty years, finding the hardware and software to view and use a digital record is exceedingly difficult. This speed of obsolescence drives the timeframe within which one needs to take digital preservation actions. It also means that you need to monitor the "heath" of digital records. You need to check on them to make sure the digital imprint is still readable and that the hardware and software needed to use them are still available. Digital records can experience preservation problems very quickly with little or no warning. One day they are fine, the next they are gone.

Should You Attempt Digital Curation?

Given the costs and difficulties of digital curation, one must ask the question, does our historic records program need to collect digital records? Before you answer that ques-tion, think about the world we live in. Every record I have created or used in the last ten years has been digital. I would be willing to bet that the records you created operating your historic records program during the last ten years were also created digitally. In the time that I worked as a records manager, if an analog record was needed by anyone in the corporation, it was digitized and sent to them as a digital record. In today's world almost all records are created digitally. This means that if your historical program is to continue into the future, if we as archivists are going to document the history of the twenty-first century, we have to accession, store, manage, preserve, and provide access to digital records. Historic records programs have to operate digital curation programs if they expect to survive.

If you find the idea of digital curation daunting, if you have fears that you or your institution cannot successfully attempt digital curation, do not feel alone. Every archivist that I talked to in the last twenty-five years was concerned about digital curation. They feared that they or their institution could not deal with digital records for a variety of reasons, including lack of expertise or lack of resources. Many archival institutions initially refused to accession digital records. I understand the concerns about doing digital curation, but in my opinion, there is no choice. If our archival institutions are to continue, if we are to record the history of the twenty-first century, we must preserve and make digital records available for research.

The reality of this change, the importance of digital records, and the need to do digital curation is being felt in archival institutions and libraries throughout the U.S. and the world. Federal archivists and large institutions were the first to attempt digital curation. Some of these institutions started their digital programs in the 1960s. Midlevel archival institutions, state archives, and various cultural institutions started their digital programs over the last thirty years or so. Libraries holding archival records led by institutions like OCLC and the Research Library Group (RLG) started working together to start digital programs in the mid-1990s. Smaller archival institutions will need to start their digital curation programs during the next ten years. We have no choice. We must collect, preserve, and make digital records available to our researchers to fulfill our duty as historic records programs. We will not be able to tell the story, the history of the twenty-first century, without digital records.

Are you and your institution ready to start digital curation? If the answer is no, take heart: you can start getting ready. The best way to learn anything is to do it, so get started. Regardless of your current level of readiness, your program needs to start learning about and doing digital curation now.

During the course of this chapter, I am going to tell you that you need to do this and that to manage digital records. All those things are true, but you do not have to do everything at once. No institution can go from not accessioning digital records to having a digital curatorial program in a year, or even three years. Take small steps and rejoice in small victories—all you have to do is get started. The most important step in your digital curation program is the first step, getting started.

Partnerships

If you are not ready to accession digital record collections or you do not have the technical means to deal with a particular type of digital collection, you will need to refer those collections to an institution that can accession them. This means that you should start talking with those institutions that do digital curation in your area. While you are talking to these institutions, take the opportunity to discuss creating a digital curation partnership with them. The partnership can be formal or informal, and the level of the partnership can vary from being able to ask for advice on digital issues to forming a joint digital repository. The more you can share digital curation expertise and expenses with another institution or group of institutions, the better off you are. Digital curation is a responsibility that all institutions holding digital records share. No one, no institution can or should bear this burden alone. The library and archival communities are very open to sharing and creating partnerships, so don't be shy about getting to know your neighbor archival institutions and asking for help. At minimum, you want to have local resources to consult with on digital curation issues. The state archives of your state is a great place to start looking for help. They should have a digital curation program and they should know the digital curation programs in your area.

Section II: Theory

You need to understand some archival theory to successfully deal with digital curation issues. I have kept this section to a minimum by covering only two aspects of archival theory. First, what makes a record? What attributes do we need to see in a record regardless of what medium the record is in? Second, given that the physical nature of digital records is so different than analog records, how does a digital archive function? What does the model digital archive look like?

The Pittsburgh Project

When archivists started thinking about how to preserve digital records they found that they needed to define the attributes of a record. Another way of putting this is to ask yourself, what do I need to see to believe that a record is authentic, that it is valid? The first major research project to investigate digital records was "The Functional Requirements for Evidence in Recordkeeping" by the School of Informational Sciences at the University of Pittsburgh. This project (a.k.a. "the Pittsburgh Project") ran from 1993 to 1996 and was funded by the National Historic Publications and Records Commission.[5] In an ironic twist of fate, the portion of the University of Pittsburgh's website that held the reports of the project were lost in 2002. Much of the website and the project reports were recovered using the Internet Archives' Wayback Machine later that year.[6]

There were many findings from the Pittsburgh Project and the University of British Columbia's InterPARES[7] project that independently considered related digital preservation issues. At the risk of oversimplifying these findings, I will say that for practitioners, the key findings boil down to five concepts that have become the foundation of digital curation: reliability, authenticity, context, content, and structure.

Reliability and Authenticity

Reliability is defined as, is the record what it purports to be? Can I have faith in the record, is it real? Can I believe it? Was it created as it claims it was? Will the record be accepted as evidence in court?[8] To be accepted as evidence in court, "the proponent [the party introducing the record] must produce evidence sufficient to support a finding that the item is what the proponent claims it is.[9] Can you prove that the record was reliably created? If not there is little reason to accession it.

Authenticity is proven reliability over time. Can I still have faith in the record? Can I still believe the record after all the time and preservation actions that have been taken on it?

Reliability—is this record what it says it is? Can I have faith that this record is real? Will this record be accepted as evidence in a court?

Authenticity—proven reliability over time. Can I still believe this record?

Context, Content, and Structure

Context is closely related to reliability. What were the circumstances surrounding the creation of this digital record? What system created it? What is the provenance[10] of the record? Context helps prove reliability. What associations or connections does the record have? Is it an attachment to an email? Context helps prove reliability. Content meaning what is the substance of the record? Is there a digital imprint that tells us something? Finally, structure: Is the content arranged in the same manner as it was when the digital record was created? Without structure, it can be difficult to make sense of the content. If you have one line or string of characters without any break, it is almost impossible to understand the content. A record must have context, content, and structure to be a record. If you don't have context, you don't have reliability. If you don't have content, there is nothing to be reliable. If you don't have structure, it is difficult or impossible to understand the content.

A dollar bill is a good example of context, content, and structure. The context of the dollar bill is that it is printed by the U.S. government. If that context is questionable, if the ink or paper is not correct, if you think the bill was counterfeited, it is worthless. If the content of the bill cannot be seen, if the bill is so washed out or faint that you cannot tell what kind of bill it is, it is worthless. If the structure of the bill is wrong, if the banner, "The United States of America," is at the bottom of the bill and not at the top the bill, it is counterfeit and, therefore, worthless. Without context, content, and structure, you have nothing.

Context—what were the circumstances surrounding the creation of this record? What system created it, what is provenance of the record?

Content—is there something there, what is substance of the record?

Structure—how is the content of the record arranged? How is the content presented?

There are lots of different ways of proving that a digital record has reliability, authenticity, context, content, and structure. The nature of the digital record, how it was created and maintained, will determine your ability to prove its reliability, authenticity, context, content, and structure. The better you can prove the reliability, authenticity, context, content, and structure of a digital record the more convincing that record is.

As discussed earlier creating and maintaining metadata is how archivists prove reliability, authenticity, context, content, and structure. It is crucial that you create and maintain information about who created the digital records and how they were created along with information about the chain of custody of that record (how and when responsibility for the record was transferred) and what has been done to preserve it. Providing proof by metadata of the records survival through time is how you prove reliability and authenticity.

The Open Archival Information System Reference Model

Now that we have an idea of the attributes of the digital records that we are trying to preserve, what kind of system is needed to hold these records and their metadata? The Open Archival Information System (OAIS) Reference Model, published in 2002 by the Consultative Committee for Space Data Systems (CCSDS), has become the internationally approved model of a digital archive (a.k.a., a digital repository). By model I mean an intellectual construct defining what actions or functions must be taken (requirements) and what roles and responsibilities must be fulfilled by an organization to act as a digital archive. OAIS was approved as an ISO (International Organization for Standards) standard in 2002 and a revised version was published as ISO standard 14721:2012 in 2012.[11] A standard is an approved model. If your institution meets the standard, it meets the requirements, roles, and responsibilities defined in the model. Since standards are defined, whether or not your institution meets the standard can be judged.

Functions of the OAIS Model

The OAIS model defines the functions or services that need to be performed by a digital archive. These functions are ingest (accessioning), archival storage, data management, preservation planning, access, and administration. These functions should seem familiar to you; they are the same high-level functions you perform when you archive analog records. You do the same things to digital records that you do to analog records—just in different ways.

Archival services in the OAIS model are supported by computer and network services referred to as common services. Common services ensure that the network and computers operate as intended. Some functions take more time, attention, and budget than others, but no function is more important than the others. All the functions must be performed for a digital archive (and an analog archive) to be successful.

Ingest is the same process as accessioning analog records. The digital records are received from the creators with the information about how the records were created, information about the transfer of the records (chain of custody information), and proof that the records are complete and uncorrupted, along with descriptive information about the digital record. Information collected during the ingest process is called the submission information package or SIP. Some SIP metadata may be common to all the records in an accession.

The archival storage function handles the long-term storage and maintenance of the digital records. To do this, the archival storage function defines how the digital records will be held (online, near-line, and/or off-line)[12] and in what format the digital record will be held. Archival storage function also handles media migration. Media migration is copying the digital record from one physical media source to another.[13] Examples of physical media sources include computer hard drives, floppy discs, USB thumb drives, flash drives, zip discs, tape, tape cartridges, CDs—anything that can hold a digital imprint. The archival storage function also defines what kind of disaster recovery plan[14] will be used by the archive. A disaster recovery plan details how the data will be backed up (copied) for use in case of an emergency.

Media migration—Copying a digital record from one physical media source to another.

The archival storage function uses the Archival Information Package or AIP. This includes the digital record itself and all the metadata about how the record is rendered (displayed), any constraints on access rights, media refreshment, format migration actions, and any other preservation actions taken on the digital record.

Format migration means changing the file structure from one file type or format to another[15]—from one hardware or software configuration to another. As an example, changing a text document from a Microsoft Word file type (.doc) to a standardized Portable Document File/Archive (.pdf/a), which is easier to preserve.[16]

Format migration—Changing a digital file structure from one file type or format to another; changing a digital file from one hardware or software configuration to another.

The AIP metadata is linked to the digital record. One of the most important pieces of metadata in the AIP is the fixity check. Fixity checks are also part of the AIP metadata. Fixity[17] refers to the physical state of the digital record as it was received, meaning digital record A is made up of X number of digital bits arranged in a specific manner. A fixity check is based on the number and arrangement of the digital record's bits. It is created when you run a checksum algorithm, a mathematic equation on a digital record. The output of this mathematical process is a string of characters, typically a 32-bit hash.[18] Every time you run the same checksum algorithm on a digital record, you should get an identical output. If the output is different, the bits of the digital record or their arrangement has changed. A fixity check gives you a way to prove that the digital record you ingested (accessioned) has not changed over time. If it has changed, you have a preservation problem. This sounds like a complicated process, but it is not. You can purchase a checksum application for less than thirty-five dollars; some are free. You can run the checksum application on a large number of records using an automated process, have the outputs recorded, and get automated alerts if any of the hash outputs have changed.[19]

A fixity check should be run on every digital record you bring into your archive. If possible, you should run a fixity check on the records while they are in the donor's custody so you can prove that what you got from the donor is what is in your archive. You should also run fixity checks periodically on a percentage of the files in your digital archive as a way to monitor their health. Practices vary, I ran a fixity check randomly on 10 percent of the files in the digital archives I was responsible for on an annual basis. I chose 10 percent because my institution's quality-control procedures were based on samples of 10 percent. Fixity checks give you the ability to prove authenticity over time.

The data management function is responsible for descriptive metadata and the database systems that provides information to researchers so they can find the digital records they want access to from the archive. Data management also handles the creation of use and maintenance reports from these databases.

Preservation planning is the ongoing process of keeping up to date with advances in the digital preservation field and the creation of long-term preservation strategies to implement those advancements. Preservation planning also reviews the overall operations of the digital archive and makes policy recommendations and revisions to the administration as needed.

Access deals with the researchers using the digital archive. It is the public face of the digital archive responsible for access policies, how the researchers search digital records, and what metadata is given to them along with the digital records they request. If the digital archive has an online presence, access would be in charge of creating and maintaining that site.

The set of metadata given to researchers along with the digital record is called the dissemination information package or DIP. Like the AIP metadata, the DIP metadata is attached to the digital record itself. The contents of the DIP may differ from that held by the archival storage function. As an example, the DIP may provide the researcher with a PDF version of a Word document held in archival storage. Researchers do not need, want, or are entitled to all the metadata associated with the digital records they request from the digital archive. The DIP defines what metadata they are provided.

Administration is responsible for the operations of the digital archive, including coordinating the interactions of the functions. Administration settles any disagreements between functions and prioritizes the activities of the digital archive. Administration also implements policies and decides how funding will be spent.

OAIS Takeaways

What should small organizations take from the OAIS model? First, the goal of your digital curation program should be that all the functions describes in the model are performed in some manner. The functions do not necessarily have to be separate or named, and they do not have to all be performed when you start your program—but the goal of your digital curation program is to perform all the functions. At some point you have to bring digital records into your archive, you have to store and care for those records, you have to describe those records so you and your researchers know what you have, you have to plan to preserve the records, you have to make the records available to researchers, and you have to administer the operations of all those functions.

There are two other things that stand out to me from the OAIS model. The first is preservation planning. It is vitally important that a digital archive staff keep informed of the changes that take place in digital preservation techniques and practices so that they can implement those changes as needed. Digital curation is a lifelong learning process.

Second is the importance of metadata and the recognition that there are different kinds of metadata. If you are going to accession, preserve, and make digital records available to researchers, you have to be able to intake, create, and associate metadata with specific digital records. Your ability to create and associate metadata to digital records needs to be unlimited, since you cannot predict the nature or quantity of the metadata you will need. You don't have to group your metadata into SIPs, AIPs, and DIPs, but it is important to understand that the metadata you bring in or create when you accession a digital record is separate from the metadata that is created as part of storing and persevering that digital record, and that the metadata you provide researchers is a subset of all the metadata you have.

I cannot define all the specific metadata you need to collect or create, as circumstances play a big part in determining what metadata you need. At minimum you need metadata that

1. Creates a specific unique identifier for each digital record at the item level, along with the ability to link individual digital records to a collection.
2. Details the provenance of the record, who created it, where it came from, date and method of transfer along with any specifics about hardware or software needed to use (render) the record. This metadata can be created at the collection rather than item level.
3. Describes the content of the digital records and the collection within which they reside. This metadata can be created solely at the collection level if the contents of the individual digital items can be searched.
4. Document fixity check information including the date and values of all fixity checks performed. It is vitally important that you create and update fixity checks. They are the primary means of proving the reliability and authenticity of your digital records.
5. Details any preservation actions you take; for example, the refreshment of the media the digital record resides on or the migration of the digital record from one format to another.

The more valid metadata you create and keep, the better. Having said that, I understand that the creation of metadata takes effort. Like everything else in archives, metadata is a balancing act. Do you have enough metadata to preserve and prove the reliability and authenticity of the digital records in your care versus are you spending too much time creating metadata and therefore ingesting too few digital records? The circumstances you are in; the value of the digital records you ingest; the hardware, software, and staff available; your budget; and the needs of your researchers will define the metadata you need.

Section III: Revising Your Collections Policy

Once you have made the decision to accept digital records into your archive, you will need to revise your collections policy to accommodate them. The collection focus, topics, time periods, and mission statement of your archives is not changing because you want to ingest digital records. What is different is that the creators of the digital records, be they donors, institutions, or public entities, need to understand that you need more latitude to preserve digital records than is the case with analog records. One of the primary difference between analog and digital records is that the concept of an original record, or a record as an artifact does not apply to digital records. The lack of a digital "original record" and the need to take numerous and much different preservation actions on digital records means that the archives must have the freedom to manage digital records as they see fit. This freedom to act needs to be stated in your collections policy and included in your transfer instruments, your deeds of gift, record of transfer, or deeds of sale.

Archivists need to take four actions to preserve digital records that are unlike anything we do with analog records. First is the need to continually refresh the electronic imprint of the digital record by recopying it to whatever media it is on (i.e., tape, hard drive, CD, DVD, or whatever) or by recopying it onto a different media—media migration. Second is the need to migrate the digital record from one hardware or software configuration to another to ensure future compatibility—format migration. Third is the need to augment the digital record with metadata as needed. Last is the need to have total control over which digital records you preserve and the ability to delete any records that lack historic value.

The ability to delete at will is particularly important when ingesting something like a collection of email where only a small portion of it, say 15 percent, has historic value. You will not have the time to evaluate individual emails, but you can use methods like sorting or the inclusion of key words or phrases to identify which files may have historic value versus those that do not.

File Formats

You should limit the file formats[20] of the digital records you collect and define those formats in your collections policy. The format of a file dictates which application can read the file. As examples, the .doc file format is used by Microsoft (MS) Word, .pdf and .pdf/a are used by a PDF reader, .wpd is used by Corel WordPerfect, .mdb is a database file used by MS Access, and .mov is used by the Apple Quicktime digital video application. File Extentions.org[21] has a good up-to-date list of file extensions and the applications that use them.

Every file format has its own set of preservation issues. Proprietary, dated, or rarely used file formats will have more and more difficult preservation issues than open or common file formats. Proprietary file formats are "formats of a company, organization, or individual that contains data that is ordered and stored . . . such that the decoding and interpretation of this stored data is only easily accomplished with particular software or hardware that the company itself has developed."[22]

File format—the standard way that information is encoded for storage in a computer file. It specifies how bits are used to encode information in a digital storage medium. File formats are tied to programs, meaning programs will only read (use) specified formats.

If you collect files with proprietary formats, you are at the mercy of the vendor. You have to use their software and/or hardware to view those files. If the vendor chooses to no longer support the version of their program that you have, you may have no way of getting help with that application. If the vendor raises the price on their applications, you have to pay that price if you want to view their files on the latest version of the software. Using proprietary formats locks you into specific software and/or hardware and limits your ability to migrate the files.

The fewer file formats you try to preserve, the better, because the fewer preservation plans you have to create and implement the better. Some archival institutions will define a preservation file format for different file types: one for documents, another for images, and another for video files, so on and so forth. Then they will move as many files as possible into those formats to minimize their digital preservation issues. An example of a file format that is easy to preserve is .pdf/a, which was created to preserve digital documents. An example of a file format that is difficult to preserve is .ddz, a proprietary file format read only by the daydreamer engine of the fever-dreamer application used to create computer games.[23] The Library of Congress has created a Recommended Format Statement to "maximize the chances for survival and continued accessibility of creative content well into the future."[24] That statement covers both analog and digital formats. I strongly urge you to consult this document when making decisions about which file formats to bring into your archives.

Again, take small steps when you first get your digital curation program started. Take very few formats until you gain some confidence, expertise, and resources. The good thing is that most people and institutions use common formats—learn how to deal with them first.

Section IV: Digital Appraisal

Every archival institution faces resource issues. No archives has enough funding to collect, preserve, and make available all the collections offered to it. Digital curation resources are even more scarce because they are so difficult to come by. This means archivists have to be very prudent about how those resources are used.

There are three aspects of digital records that have to be considered before you spend your limited resources on them. First, do they have enduring historical value? Second, can the institution being offered the records afford to preserve them? Third, do the digital records have to be preserved digitally? Can the historical information in them be preserved and made available in an analog form? The third question is controversial. Before getting to it, lets consider digital appraisal.

Enduring Historical Value

In chapter 3, we talked about appraisal in terms of "does the collection being offered to you fit the terms of your collections policy?" That approach is fine for a basic understanding of appraisal, but there are more things to consider than just "does it fit my collections policy?" Archivists need to consider whether the collection (or items) has historic value and how much will it cost to preserve the collection. The bottom line appraisal question is this, is this collection worth the resources we need to invest in it to preserve and make it available to researchers?" Can we as an archival institution afford this collection?

These can be very difficult questions to answer. That is why many archival institutions use a board of trustees committee, often called the collections committee, to ratify appraisal decisions. Collections committees focus on the budgetary issues of appraisal decisions. Committee members will examine the appraisal recommendations of the archivist in charge and vote to accept or reject collections or in some cases individual items. Those archival programs that collect the records of their parent institution use a different method of appraisal connected to their record management practices. These record scheduling practices have a separate but equally rigorous review process.

Appraisal recommendations made by archivists are based on answering the two questions mentioned above. First, does the collection/item have historic value, and second, can we afford to preserve this collection? To answer the historic value question archivists have to uncover detailed information about the collection. Is the collection or item genuine? Is it credible? How long a time frame does the collection cover? Does the collection or item support the accepted view of history or does it tell us something we did not know? Does it increase our understanding of history? We touched on those questions in appraisal scorecard provided in chapter 3. The questions concerning credibility are reflected in sections II and IV of the appraisal scorecard. The questions concerning historical significance are reflected in sections I and III.

The historic value question can be a difficult one to answer and archivists will disagree on it more times than not. I consulted with my colleagues on the historic value question whenever possible. The more complex the collection, the more archivists I talked to. It is always better to get additional educated opinions on historic value. Another archivist will not have the same frame of reference that you do, so they will often see something you do not. Getting other opinions on appraisal decisions is a best practice.

Can We Afford to Preserve This Collection?

Next is the preservation question—can we afford to preserve this collection/item? This is an easier question to answer with analog collections, because unless they had exceptional preservation issues, the answer was usually yes. This is a more difficult question to answer for digital collections. You have to ask technical questions about preservation, the first of which is "do we have the ability to read the physical media that holds the digital records?" If you don't have the correct hardware to read the media, can the digital records be transferred to your archives by another means? Assuming the digital records can be safely transferred to you, what is the size of the collection? Do you have enough storage space in your digital archive to hold the collection? You asked similar storage space questions when filling out the appraisal scorecard for analog records.

The next issue concerns file formats. Can you preserve the digital record in its original digital file format? As stated in the previous section, the Library of Congress Recommended Format Statement[25] is a good reference point for this discussion. I would be very reluctant to bring a proprietary format into a digital archive, especially dated, obscure, proprietary formats. If you decide to bring a proprietary format into your digital archive, one of your first tasks should be migrating those records into a nonproprietary preservation format.

You also have to verify the reliability and authenticity of the digital records before you accept them. Can you prove who or what created them, how they were created, and how they were maintained? The reliability and authenticity of the digital records directly affects their historical value. If their reliability and authenticity is questioned, their historical value is suspect. Hillary Clinton's email captured off the server maintained by her staff has historical merit. Hillary Clinton's email as published by WikiLeaks has little or no merit as evidence of what Ms. Clinton did or did not do because their authenticity cannot be established. Hillary Clinton's email as published by WikiLeaks might be evidence of Russian meddling, but it has little merit as evidence of what Hillary did or did not do.

Do We Have to Keep the Records in Digital Form?

Another question you must ask is this: Do we have to keep this information/record in digital form? This seems like a simple question given that digital records are what our users want, but it is not because of the cost and difficulties of digital curation. Some digital records are almost useless in analog formats; databases and spreadsheets lose their usefulness if they cannot be queried (manipulated). The records of digital mapping applications known as geographic information systems (GIS) has to be read (rendered) by specific applications to have any value. Search, and in some cases, full-text search makes finding what you want from digital records much easier than manually searching analog records. The point here is that if a record (or information) has to be kept in digital form to be useful, then do so.

There are cases where you might keep a digital collection as an analog collection. As I said earlier, this is a controversial subject. I have said throughout this book that very little in archives is totally right or totally wrong. The right answer to many archival questions depends on the circumstances you find yourself in, circumstances including the specifics of the individual records or collection, expertise, funding, and the other resources that may or may not be available to you and your institution. Depending on your circumstances, you might consider preserving some digital records as analog records. The kinds of digital records you might preserve as analog records include simple text documents, meaning documents without imbedded links to other information resources, or small email collections. Especially those email collections where the only email of historical significance is a limited series of exchanges between a few entities.

Email is essentially correspondence, so the first question you must ask yourself is do these emails have historic value? Answering this question will have to be done at the collection (aggregate) level. Archivists do not have the time to examine individual emails for historic value. Assuming that the email is correspondence you think has merit as historic records because of the topics covered or the significance of those sending or receiving the email, the next step is to delete those emails that do not have merit. You can sort email, or run key word or phrase queries on it so that worthless email, be it unsolicited "junk" email, private email, duplicate email, or email of little or no consequence, can be identified and deleted from the email that you are going to preserve. If possible, ask the creator of the email to run the sorts and queries and delete worthless email before you accession it. They will have a good idea of which sorts and key words or phrases will identify email of no value.

Next you must ask if the email has to be preserved in a digital format? Is it absolutely essential that researchers have the ability to manipulate, query (search), sort, and view the records in digital form to use them? It will always be easier to search (query) email in electronic form—but is it completely necessary to do so? How necessary is it for the researchers to see the email folder hierarchy or view header information? Can the email collection be used in analog form?

If the answer to this question is yes, the email can be printed out and preserved as paper. Indexes can be created to paper versions of email that make it accessible by printing out different sorts of the email. These simple indexes may be all that researchers need to use the collection. If you are considering printing out email think about what you are going to do with email attachments and header information. Attachments need to be printed out and linked with the email they are part of. Header information can be printed with the text of emails. Preserving email by printing is a last resort, it is not a simple or adequate solution—consider it very carefully before proceeding.

For some small institutions that need to archive limited email collections, printing it out and creating paper indexes is an option, but it should always be the option of last resort. I strongly urge you to use this option sparingly. I would also urge you to keep a copy of the email in digital form. None of us know what the future may bring; the answers to many digital preservation problems may be just around the corner. Perhaps one day you will be able to deal with the email in a digital form.

If you are convinced that an email collection must be kept in electronic form, the next step you need to take is migrating the email out of the email application format into a format that can be easily preserved. Email systems are not records keeping or preservations systems. They do not have the functionality you need to preserve and access the email files over the long term. Regardless of what application you keep the email in, it must be preserved in a stable format. Microsoft updates Outlook so often that keeping email in the .msg or .pst formats (or whatever format Microsoft is using) is not a viable long-term option. The other commercial email systems have similar format issues. Some of the more stable formats you can consider moving email into include .pdf/a, .rtf (rich text format), or .txt.

Section V: What Must You Do to Archive Digital Records?

Institutions collecting digital records have a responsibility to the creators of those records, to researchers, and to the archival community to do all that they can to manage and preserve the records well. That means they (you) need to have a basic level of digital curation competency. Digital curation competency requires four things:

- Knowing what to do (functionality)
- Knowing how to do it (expertise)
- The hardware needed to store and make digital records available
- The software needed to manage and preserve digital records

Expertise may be the most crucial component of a digital curation program. I don't think anyone will ever have enough expertise to confidently manage and preserve digital records. Having said that, you should not stop from collecting and preserving digital records just because you think you do not have enough expertise. None of us will reach digital curation perfection. There are too many digital records with historic value to collect to leave digital curation to just those institutions that think themselves worthy of digital curation. The needs of history are too compelling to let a compulsion for perfection deter anyone from starting a digital curation program.

In this section I am going to cover what you need to do to manage and preserve digital records. In the next section, I will discuss the hardware, software, and expertise needed to do those things, to preform those functions.

The archival community has defined digital curation competency in several different ways. OCLC created a set of high level requirements for a "trusted digital repository" based on the OAIS model along with a process to certify institutions that meet those requirements. That process has become an ISO standard.[26] The Council of State Archivists created a model of competency called the State Electronic Records Preservation (SERP) Framework, which covers program/policy matters as well as technical issues.[27] The National Digital Stewardship Alliance,[28] a library consortium launched by the Library of Congress, has their own model of digital competency called "Levels of Digital Preservation."[29]

I am going to define a more basic level of digital curation competency that fits the audience this book serves: volunteer archivists. As you start your digital curation programs, I urge you to constantly seek to reach higher levels of digital curation competency. CoSA's SERP framework and the NDSA's Levels of Digital Preservation are good sets of tools for you to use to measure the progress of your digital curation program.

Notice that I have not said anything about how you preform digital curation functions. You have the option of doing these steps yourself, by creating and operating your own digital repository. You also have the option of paying a vendor to use their software and hardware to manage and preserve the digital records you collect. Regardless of how you implement digital curation functions, the following things have to be done to collect, manage, preserve, and make digital records available to users. These functions will sound familiar to you as they are taken from the OAIS model discussed earlier in this chapter.

Ingest

First you need to ingest the records into your digital repository. Before you begin the ingest process, ask the creator of the records to not delete their copy of the records until you have confirmed that the records have been successfully ingested into your digital archive.

Things can go wrong during transfer and ingest. Things can go wrong during transfer and ingest. Working off a copy of the records for ingest is an easy precaution to take.

As you start the ingest process, you must gather or create the metadata that establishes the reliability of the records. Think in terms of who created the record, why was it created, and how was it created. You also need to describe the content of the collection. This metadata can be applied at the collection level rather than at the item level provided the individual items have persistent links to the collection. This topic was touched on earlier in the *OAIS Takeaways* section (see pg. 150).

As part of the ingest process, you have to run a virus scan on the digital records to ensure that you do not bring a virus into your storage network and digital repository. This is vitally important; you cannot risk infecting your digital archive by overlooking this step. Since cybersecurity tools and attacks are constantly evolving, I recommend that you get the best virus scan tool you can and that you update it regularly.

You also need to check the health of the digital records you ingest. This is a two-step process comprised of checking the digital record for corruption and running a checksum to create the initial fixity check.[30] Checking a digital record for corruption means validating that the digital record is whole, that it can be opened and used by whatever application the file format is designed for. The initial fixity check will give you a baseline that you can refer to to check the health of the digital record over time. If you are ingesting a large number of records you can do a 10 percent quality control check for corruption. However, every record will need a fixity check.

Managing the Records

Now that you have ingested the digital records, you need to manage them. You have to take the actions necessary to ensure their existence and authenticity. These actions fall into three broad categories. First, actions to ensure that the digital records remain viable as digital imprints or bit streams. This means recopying the digital records on the media upon which they are held or recopying them to a different media source. These actions are often referred to as refreshment plans. Second, actions to ensure the digital records survive hardware/software failures, human errors, and/or disasters. These actions are often referred to as disaster recovery or backup plans. Finally, actions taken to ensure the security of the digital records in your care. Security actions include cybersecurity measures taken to ensure that outside entities do not penetrate your system and destroy the records, and actions designed to prevent a malicious actor inside your organization harming the digital records in your care.

Refreshment

Digital records are imprinted on to physical media, whether it is a 3.5-inch floppy disc, a CD, a computer tape, or a computer hard drive. Each of these media types has a different life span, meaning there is no guarantee that the digital imprint will persist on that media past that time period.[31] The bit stream can deteriorate to the point where it cannot be read by the application. Media life spans are not exact. In some ways this makes the problem worse since you never know exactly when you will lose the ability to read digital records. What we do know is that every digital medium will fail at some point. This means we have to plan to recopy the digital records from one media type to another on a periodic basis. If you do not recopy the digital records from one media type to another you will lose access to them. All refreshment actions should be documented by creating metadata that describes the actions.

Backups

You must create multiple copies (backups)[32] of the digital records in your care to guard against application failures, catastrophic events (fire, floods, etc.), and/or human error. This is standard practice followed by every information technology (IT) organization. There are several different kinds of backups, but I am only going to discuss full and differential backups. A full backup is a complete copy of the digital records and all metadata. A differential backup stores anything that has been changed since the last full backup. Most IT organizations create backup schedules where differential backups are created on a reoccurring basis, say twice a week, and full backups are created less often; once or twice a month. Backups can be stored in different places, on a different server, in a different building, or in a different location. The farther away the backup is geographically from the use copy of the digital record, the safer you are. Generally speaking, the more copies you have of your digital holdings and the more physically distant they are from your institution, the safer they are. Backup information should be kept as system documentation.

Cybersecurity

The need to protect your digital holdings from internal and external threats is undeniable. Cybersecurity threats and the tools to defeat them evolve at a breakneck pace, so my comments are going to be very basic. At minimum you need a firewall[33] to protect your holdings from external threats. Get the best firewall you can and make sure it is updated as needed.

There are lots of cybersecurity tools and firms out there whose business it is to help you, so get the best cybersecurity advice you can. Most information on cybersecurity is very technical. CNET[34] "publishes reviews, news, articles, blogs, podcasts and videos on technology and consumer electronics."[35] CNET doesn't focus on cybersecurity, but the cybersecurity content it does have is easy to understand. CISO publishes "Security Advisories and Alerts"[36] for their products that are more technical and helpful to IT staff.

If you operate servers, make sure that server application patches provided by the vendor are installed as soon as possible. Patches repair cybersecurity vulnerabilities and installing them is a server administration task that must not be overlooked. I would also keep copies of all digital holdings, including any web pages that you have on a separate server. This copy of your digital holdings is for cybersecurity/preservations purposes and is separate from backup copies of your holdings. This topic is covered in more depth in the digital preservation section.

Internal threats to your digital holdings are the result of both human error and malicious intent. The best way to safeguard your holdings from internal threats is to have a well-defined and strictly adhered to set of roles and responsibilities. You need to create a set of checks and balances so that one individual acting alone cannot delete or harm your digital holdings. As an example, if an archivist is tasked with deleting email that has no value from a collection, he or she tags the emails that needs to be deleted. The archival supervisor would review the tagged emails and authorize their deletion to the system administrator. The system administrator is the only person who has the actual ability to delete the emails from the digital repository. Each of those three people has a role and the capability to preform only that role. Audit trails detailed in audit logs document who did what and when it was done. Audit trails are created automatically in many digital archiving applications or can be created manually in spreadsheets. Creating and implementing separate roles and responsibilities and documenting them by audit trails is cumbersome. In some ways, separating roles and responsibilities among staff is designed to slow the pace of activity. Don't let frustration with your ability to complete tasks in a timely manner seduce you in taking roles and responsibility short cuts, you will only endanger your digital holdings by doing so.

Metadata

Creating and preserving metadata to ensure the reliability of the digital records in your care is an important part of maintenance. You must document the actions you take on the digital records. In many cases you will be taking the same actions on all the items in a collection, so you need the ability to make bulk metadata changes or additions. Actions that need to be documented by metadata include

- Making a different version of the digital record for preservation and/or access purposes
- How different versions of records were created and what quality control checks were taken to ensure there were no differences between versions
- Preforming periodic fixity checks on the digital records
- Revising or editing collection or item descriptive information
- Moving the digital records from one storage type to another
- Migrating file formats

Any and all actions that you take on the digital records while they are in your care must be documented. Whatever actions you take on the digital records should also include an audit trail—documentation of who did what and when they did it that cannot be edited.

Preservation Planning

Digital preservation planning requires four steps. First you must keep a preservation copy of your digital holdings as insurance. Second, you must define a digital preservation strategy that defines what you are going to do to preserve your digital holdings. Third, you must take the actions called for in your strategy. Lastly, you must keep current with advances in digital preservation practices so that you can modify your strategy as needed,

The first step in preservation planning is keeping a second complete copy of all your digital holdings (records, metadata, and web pages) for preservation purposes. Most digital archivists create a redundant copy of their digital holdings separate from backup copies and keep it off site where it is only accessed under very strict conditions.[37] This preservation copy of your digital archive should be isolated from all internet connections or be behind the most robust firewall you can afford. The preservation copy of your digital holdings is only used to create a copy of a digital record and metadata should the use copy of that record become damaged in some manner. Access to the preservation copy of your digital holdings should be very tightly controlled. The preservation copy of your digital holdings is your last safeguard, your protection from all digital evil; be vigilant in protecting it.

The second part of any digital preservation plan is defining your digital preservation strategy and outlining the actions you will and will not take to preserve the digital records in your care. Part of this strategy concerns file formats. You need to decide which formats you will accept into your digital repository and what steps you will take to preserve those formats. You also need to define your preferred digital preservation formats and when you will move (migrate) different file formats into your preferred preservation formats.[38] As stated earlier, moving files from one format to another is called format migration.

Format migration is defined as "a set of organized tasks designed to achieve the periodic transfer of digital materials from one hardware/software configuration to another."[39] Format migration is one of the two digital preservation options widely adopted at this time. The other being emulation, creating interfaces that enable old applications to run on new hardware, and software. Emulation is covered a bit later. Your preservation strategy may call for you to preserve some formats by migration and others by emulation.

Format migration is a labor intensive process that demands documentation, quality control checks, and making decisions about the look and functionality of the digital record. When you move a record from one format to another, it may change how the record looks when it is viewed (rendered), and it may change how it can be used. How much change in the look and functionality of a record can be tolerated before it is no longer reliable and authentic? Subtle changes in the look and functionality of a record due to one migration might be acceptable, but what happens when you make small changes every time you migrate a record and you migrate it five times? Migrating records is a huge task that requires careful planning, testing, quality control checks, and deliberative decision making.

Emulation creates a software interface to enable new software and/or hardware to run old operating systems and applications. Emulation started in computer gaming because people wanted to be able to run old applications like PAC-MAN on new computers. Emulation has become standard IT practice. On the plus side, emulation allows you to keep the look and functionality of the original digital record. Because of this, there are those that say that emulation is the best digital preservation strategy available.[40] On the minus side, emulation can be very difficult and expensive. It is not feasible for most archival institutions to create emulators so we must reply on commercially available emulators. This can be a real problem because digital preservation is not high on the agenda of commercial IT vendors. Having said that, there are emulators out there and they are a good option for some formats.

There are other digital preservation options, the most popular of which are creating a computer museum. Collecting and maintaining the hardware and software necessary to render the digital records you accession is not a viable preservation strategy in the opinion of most people. Having said that it can be an important intermediate step in preserving some digital records. In some cases it may be the only feasible measure you can take while you wait on a better technological solution like an emulator to come your way. Collecting and maintaining old hardware and software should not be dismissed out of hand.

Once you have defined and implemented your digital preservation strategy, your next task is keeping informed of advances in digital curation practices so that you can revise your digital preservation strategy as needed. The types of digital records offered to your archives will change over time. Both the purpose of the records and their technical makeup will change. Who among us saw the importance and prevalence of social media ten years ago? Keeping up with these changes in technology means that digital curation requires a commitment to life-long learning.

The best way to keep informed of advances in digital curation practices is to join one or more of the state, regional, or national archival organizations. These organizations hold annual meetings or conferences in which digital curation topics are discussed in program sessions. The Society of American Archivists (SAA) manages a "Directory of Archival Organizations for the United State and Canada" with links to all the appropriate websites;[41] find one or more of these organizations you like and join them.

Email discussion groups called listservs are another great way to keep informed of digital curation topics. SAA operates discussion lists open to all.[42] CoSA runs the Electronic Records Listserv for the "topical exchange among electronic records archivists."[43] Listserv messages can be received in a digest, where you get all the messages from one day in a single email. I would suggest getting the digest form. It is easy to scan for topics of interest, and you are not bothered by messages hitting your inbox throughout the day. There will always be some fluff in a list, but there will be real gems as well. Lists are always a good use of your time. Other resources for archival continuing education are listed in section VI.

Reference Services

Providing reference services for the digital records you collect and preserve is the reason your digital archives exists. Reference services for digital records is much different from the reference services provided for analog records, so your reference polices will need to be revised to accommodate these differences. Before getting into the details of reference policy revisions, I want to stress the underlying philosophical theme of archival work: *as archivists, we need to preserve the collections in our care while providing access to them.* You cannot provide access to an item in a collection if such access threatens the preservation and/or security of that item. Balancing access and preservation is the essence of archival work, one without the other or favoring one over the other is unacceptable.

To make the revisions to your reference policy, you need to answer some basic questions about how you will provide access to your digital records. These questions include the following:

- Are you going to provide in-house access to your digital collections?
- Are you going to provide online access to your digital collections?
- Are you going to provide research services to digital records for off-site researchers via mail or email requests?
- If you provide search services for your digital collection, how much search, how much work are you willing to do?
- Which metadata elements are you going to use for search?
- Which metadata elements are you going to provide researchers?
- What metadata elements will you make available to researchers if they ask for evidence of the reliability and authenticity of your digital records?
- How will you make copies of your digital records available to researchers? Will they download records off your site? Will you send them copies of records on CDs or some other physical media? Will you load records onto internet sites for researchers, sites like Dropbox, One Drive, Google Drive, and so forth and so on?
- Will you copy records on media supplied by researchers? I would strongly advise against this as a cybersecurity measure unless they give you brand new media in unopened boxes. You risk infecting your system by connecting to used media sources that have not be scanned for viruses.
- What format will you make available to researchers; the original format, the preservation format, an access format, or all the above, if requested?

Once these questions have been answered, you can revise your collections policy to accommodate digital records. You may need to revise your reference policies later based on your experiences implementing those policies.

Deciding to make your digital collections available online may seem like an easy decision, but creating a web presence for your digital records that is user friendly is anything but easy. You need to build a website that lists information about your digital collections and facilitates searching those collections. If you decide to create an online presence for your digital records, you need to recognize that doing so takes significant digital resources. Since these are often the same resources you need for digital curation, make sure you have enough resources to accomplish both these tasks.

Section VI: What Resources Do You Need to Archive Digital Records?

What expertise, hardware, and software do you need to collect, store, manage, preserve, and make digital records available to researchers? These are difficult questions to answer because you will always want more expertise, hardware, and software than you have. I believe you have to have an application or access to an application that stores your digital records and the metadata associated with them that can generate copies of the digital records with selected metadata for researchers. The hardware and expertise you need depend on the application you choose and the volume of digital records you expect to accession.

Software

The software application you choose for your digital archive must be able to perform functions that are called requirements in software design and assessment documents. Rather than define all the requirements needed for a digital archive here, I will just mention what I think are the major requirements that you must have:

- The application must hold digital records in any format.
- The application must have a persistent link between digital records and the metadata associated with those records.
- The application must accommodate unlimited structured and unstructured metadata.
- The application must accommodate multiple digital records sharing the same metadata. As an example, a Word document and the PDF version of that document must share the same descriptive metadata, while also having metadata that applies to each of the separate formats.
- The application must have the ability to display (render) digital records.
- The application must be able to export copies of digital records along with selected metadata associated with those records.

Requirements can include functions you must have, those you want to have, and those you would like to have. As an example, the Department of Defense (DoD) 5015.2 "Electronic Records Management Software Application Design Criteria Standard"[44] in use since 1994 lists the federal requirements for an electronic record keeping application. While DoD 5015.2 applications are not designed specifically as digital archives, they can act as one.

Notice that I did not include the automated implementation of preservation plans in the list of digital archive application "must-have" requirements listed above. While there are digital archive applications that can take automated preservation actions on designated files, such applications are costly. This is changing, so be aware that digital archive applications with this capability exist and that they may be an option for you. Right now it is much more likely that small historical institutions will acquire applications that force them to take preservation actions manually.

Applications that can act as a digital archive fall into two broad categories: commercial applications and open-source applications. Commercial applications, where you buy software and the support for it are a good option for small institutions. Open source software is free, but support installing it, using it, and fixing problems is not. In some cases, you are expected to join the open source software "community" created to support the software. Some of these communities have dues and some ask for your participation in upgrading the software, or a combination of both. While open source communities can be very helpful, you may need server level expertise to install and use open source software. This level of expertise is beyond what average computer users have, but it is not at all uncommon. Open source software can be a viable option for small institutions.

Most commercial and open-source applications can also be used as hosted services, also known as software as a service (SAS). Software as a service means that your digital records and their metadata will be housed on the host's servers and you pay for access to their hosting application in a variety of ways. Charges for SAS can be per volume, per function, or a combination thereof. Using SAS is a good option for small institutions. If you chose this option, make sure the vendor meets or is at least familiar with the Trusted Digital Repository requirements.[45] Review the SAS contract carefully with input from your legal counsel. Some SAS vendors make it very difficult to take digital records and metadata (a.k.a. data) out of their application.

There are a number of commercial digital archiving applications available for use including:

- Archive it—https://archive-it.org
- Archivematica—https://www.archivematica.org/en
- CONTENTdm—http://www.oclc.org/en/contentdm.html
- Libnova—http://www.libnova.com/en
- Preservica—http://preservica.com/about-us
- Applications that meet the DoD 5015.2 standard. You can visit the site of the Joint Interoperability Test Command to see what applications meet DoD 5015.2 at http://jitc.fhu.disa.mil/projects/rma/reg.aspx

Open source software suites that can act as a digital archive include:

- DSpace—http://www.dspace.org
- Fedora Repository—http://fedorarepository.org
- Islandora (a Fedora interface)—https://islandora.ca[46]

There are also software tools available to help you manage your digital records within the applications that hold them. Two of the best places I know of to find these tools are the Council of State Archivists (CoSA) Program for Electronic Records, Training, Tools, and Standards (PERTTS) Portal[47] and the Archives Association of British Columbia's (AABC) Archivist's Toolkit.[48] LYRASIS references both these sites from their Preservation Services site.[49]

Hardware

If you decide to operate a digital archive application at your location, the hardware you needed to do so will be part of the application requirements. The hardware falls into two groups: the server needed to run the application and work stations used to access the application on the server.

Generally speaking, you need a RAID[50] server with as much processor speed/capability and storage space as you can afford. RAID stands for redundant array of independent disks. This configuration of disks creates reliable data stores by using multiple general-purpose computer hard disk drives. There are different RAID levels; RAID 5 uses distributed parity so that if one hard disk fails you can replace it without losing any data. RAID is the network storage configuration in common use today. That will change. What you need from future network storage applications is a guarantee that should a portion of the storage solution fail, that portion can be replaced without the loss of any of your data.

The amount of storage space you need for your digital collections is a tough questions to answer. If you think your digital collections will take 50 gigs of space, I would advocate that you get 150 gigs of storage space. You will always need more storage than you think you will and you will need room to grow. More important, than how much storage space you get is making sure that it is easy to add additional storage space to your server without reconfiguring your application.

The more RAM (random access memory) the better. RAM enables applications to operate at high speed and to preform multiple operations simultaneously. When you are waiting on applications to load or to run operations, you are experiencing the need for more RAM. Most of the applications I have seen require at least 1 gig of RAM. If you are going to use a system via hosted services, you will still need a very capable computer to act as your terminal. The crucial hardware needed for hosted services is your internet connection, the faster the connection the better your access to services. Remember, if your application is going to be connected to the internet, you will need firewall protection.

Work stations are computers linked to the server by a network. Work stations can be used by archivists to ingest and manage the records held in the server or they can be used by the public to access copies of records and metadata held in the server. Archival work stations will need almost server level amounts of RAM, access to network storage devices, and fast network connections. These work stations will be used by archivists to run complex queries, create and revise metadata, and make bulk metadata changes.

Work stations used in your reading room by the public will need much less technical capability than those used by staff. These work stations can have small amounts of RAM, no internet connections, and no access to storage space. Their only task is to access your digital archives application on the server and run simple queries. Work station requirements will vary according to the application and user needs and should be included in the application documentation.

Expertise

Defining the expertise needed to collect, manage, preserve, and make digital records available to users is difficult. It is important to recognize that you and your institution will gain expertise as time goes on. You do not need all the expertise mentioned here to get started with digital curation. If you are going to run your digital archives application and/or a website at your institution, you will need staff with server level IT skills. By this I mean someone proficient in the operating system used by your servers. This person (or people) needs to be able to install and delete applications, configure user accounts, create and manage storage areas, and configure RAID levels. They need to be able to create and implement backup plans and procedures. They also need the ability to understand cybersecurity threats and implement the tools necessary to defeats those threats. At minimum, they need to be able to install firewalls and scan for threats. Server level IT skills are fairly common. IT skills are needed to a much lesser extent if you use hosted services (software as a service)—which is one of its greatest benefits. I am not going to bother to list IT training opportunities because there are so many and they are generally specific to a region. I will say that Microsoft offers some training for free.[51]

Regardless of server expertise, someone in your institution has to be proficient in the application that you are using to manage your digital records at the tactical or operational level. Application proficiency comes from using the application. Experience created by this on the job training can be augmented by vendor classes if they offer them, but nothing beats actually using the application. The tasks you need be able to perform in the application include

- Setting up and deleting user accounts with varying levels of capabilities
- Adding new records including importing records and metadata
- Creating structured and unstructured metadata
- The ability to make bulk metadata changes
- Creating record templates that include mandatory and optional metadata fields
- Creating and running complex queries and reports
- The ability to run checksum queries and cybersecurity scans

At a strategic level, someone in your institution needs to be able to research digital preservation trends and issues. This individual needs to be able to identify new digital preservation tools appropriate for your institution and advocate for their adoption. This individual also needs to take the lead in managing and revising your digital preservation plan.

Creating digital management and preservation expertise is of great interest to archival institutions and related professional associations. Besides joining archival organizations, attending conferences, and participating in Listservs, your digital curation staff should be aware of and use the educational offerings of CoSA, SAA, and ARMA, as appropriate.

CoSA, the Council of State Archivists, created the State Electronic Records Initiative (SERI) to help the states create electronic records programs and train staff for those programs. The SERI Educational Webinars Recordings and Materials[52] range from recording of presentations to presentation slide decks to PDFs. SERI also offers self-directed training modules on a variety of topics including authentication, file duplication, metadata, and format conversion.[53] These educational materials are free and available to the public. CoSA and the state archives in your state are natural allies for small institutions starting digital preservation programs. If I were starting a digital curation program, they would be among the first people I would contact.

The Society of American Archivists (SAA) has a "Digital Archives Specialist (DAS) Curriculum and Certificate Program, designed to provide you with the information and tools you need to manage the demands of born-digital records."[54] SAA serves professional archivists, most of whom have master's degrees in history or library and information science, or both. This means SAA's educational offerings assume a high level of competence, are well designed, and can be expensive. Check the SAA website for their continuing education offerings,[55] and check their bookstore for publications on all archival topics.[56] The SAA bookstore is a great resource for all archivists.

ARMA, the Association of Records Managers and Administrators, has many educational opportunities on digital record issues. These offerings focus on the maintenance of digital records rather than on preservation. See their online learning section for a complete list of their courses.[57] ARMA also has a great bookstore with numerous publications of interest.[58]

In addition to these resources and those listed later in this chapter, you can search the web for digital preservation sites and educational offerings. They are too numerous to mention; they change constantly and their quality ranges from great to questionable. I would check the entity offering the course before I invested my time and money in it. Some software vendors offer educational opportunities as an enticement to use their products. These offerings may not be what you expect. I would check them carefully before committing to take them. There is no shortage of digital maintenance and preservation resources.

Section VII: Summary

There are a few things you have to do to collect, maintain, preserve, and make digital records available to users. You have to:

- Document the provenance of the digital records you ingest.
- Make sure you're ingesting digital records that are uncorrupted and that are free of viruses that could harm your digital archive.
- Monitor the health of your digital records.
- Protect your digital records from external and internal threats.
- Document and take actions on your digital records to preserve them.
- Make your digital records available to users.

Collecting, managing, preserving, and making digital records available to researchers is more difficult than it is for analog records. The expertise, software, and hardware needed to perform these task digitally is considerable. The difficulties of digital curation are very clear to me as they are to every archivist I have ever talked to. Many archivists, many institutions, and many of you may be intimidated by these difficulties, but they must be overcome. Reality is forcing all archivists and all historic records programs to collect, manage, preserve, and make digital records available to our researchers. If we want to document the history of the twenty-first century, we must collect, manage, preserve, and make digital records available to researchers.

I have spent much of this chapter detailing all the things you have to do to implement digital curation. It was not my intent to scare you or make you think that you should not attempt digital curation. Quite the contrary. I think every historic records program should start a digital curation program. Nothing beats on the job training. Just get started; experience will tell you what you need to do. The only thing you have to do is to make the institutional commitment to do digital curation the best that you can. History is depending on you, your efforts, and the commitment of your institution.

Digital Records: Partial List of Resources

Archive it
   Commercial digital archiving application: https://archive-it.org/

Archivematica
   Commercial digital archiving application: https://www.archivematica.org/en/

Association of Records Managers and Administrators (ARMA)
   Online learning section: http://www.arma.org/page/OnlineLearning

Australian digital resources:

- National Archives of Australia Digital Information and Records New South Wales, Digital Records Preservation Policy: https://www.records.nsw.gov.au/record keeping/rules/policies/digital-records-preservation
- New South Wales Digital Records Preservation Policy: https://www.records.nsw .gov.au/recordkeeping/rules/policies/digital-records-preservation
- South Australia Digital Records Management: https://government.archives.sa.gov .au/content/digital-records-management

Cal Lee

Cal is a professor at the University of North Carolina School of Information and Library Science. His work is high end and cutting edge, but don't be intimidated. Cal has a very practical side; he worked in the trenches as an electronic records archivist for the Kansas State Archives and he is very approachable.

- Documents authored: https://ils.unc.edu/callee/
- Electronic Recordkeeping Resources: https://ils.unc.edu/callee/ermlinks/

CISO

Aimed at IT professionals, Security Advisories and Alerts: https://tools.cisco.com/ security/center/publicationListing.

CoOL

Conservation on Line, Electronic Records: http://cool.conservation-us.org/bytopic/ electronic-records/

CNET

Technological publication: https://www.cnet.com/topics/security/

Council of State Archivists (CoSA)

One of the best collections of digital record resources out there. Very nice stuff, continuously added to. It is my first go-to resource.

- Electronic Records Listserv: https://www.statearchivists.org/connect/listservs/
- Electronic Records Education and Training: https://www.statearchivists.org/ electronic-records/education-training/
- Resource Center: https://www.statearchivists.org/resource-center/resource -library/
- Self-Directed Training Modules: https://www.statearchivists.org/electronic -records/education-training/self-directed-training-modules/
- State Electronic Records Initiative (SERI) Educational Webinar Recordings and Materials: https://www.statearchivists.org/electronic-records/education-train ing/seri-educational-webinars/seri-educational-webinar-recordings-materials/

Department of Defense (DoD)

- DoD 5015.2 "Electronic Records Management Software Application Design Criteria Standard: http://jitc.fhu.disa.mil/projects/rma/downloads/p50152stdapr07.pdf
- Joint Interoperability Test Command (list of applications that meet DoD 5015.2): http://jitc.fhu.disa.mil/projects/rma/reg.aspx (to see what applications meet DoD 5015.2)

D-Space

Open source repository software: http://www.dspace.org/

File Extentions.org
   https://www.file-extensions.org/

Fedora
   Open source repository platform: http://fedorarepository.org/

Islandora
   A Fedora interface: https://islandora.ca/

InterPARES
   Archival research project: http://www.interpares.org/

Internet Archives
   Wayback Machine: https://en.wikipedia.org/wiki/Wayback_Machine

Libnova
   Commercial digital archiving application: http://www.libnova.com/en/

Library of Congress
   Hard to find a better resource.

   • Levels of Digital Preservation: http://www.digitalpreservation.gov:8081/ndsa/activities/levels.html
   • PDF/A for Long-Term Preservation: https://www.loc.gov/preservation/digital/formats/fdd/fdd000318.shtml
   • Preserving Your Digital Memories: http://digitalpreservation.gov/personal archiving/
   • National Digital Stewardship Alliance, a consortium of organizations supported by the Library of Congress committed to the long-term preservation of digital information: http://www.digitalpreservation.gov:8081/ndsa/about.html
   • Recommended Formats Statement: http://www.loc.gov/preservation/resources/rfs/
   • Sustainability of Digital Formats: https://www.loc.gov/preservation/digital/formats/index.shtml

LOCKSS
   Lots of Copies Keeps Stuff Safe, open source digital preservation tools: https://www.lockss.org/

Microsoft Training
   https://www.microsoft.com/en-us/learning/training.aspx

National Archives and Records Administration (NARA)
   Always a good resource.

   • Toolkit for Managing Electronic Records: https://www.archives.gov/records-mgmt/toolkit#list
   • Electronic Records Management Guidance: https://www.archives.gov/records-mgmt/initiatives/erm-guidance.html
   • Email Management: https://www.archives.gov/records-mgmt/email-mgmt
   • Strategy for Preserving Digital Archival Materials: https://www.archives.gov/preservation/electronic-records.html

OCLC
   One of the leaders in the library community

- CONTENTdm, commercial digital archiving application: http://www.oclc.org/en/contentdm.html
- Demystifying Born Digital: https://www.oclc.org/research/themes/research-collections/borndigital.html).
- Resource Description and Access standard (RDA): https://www.oclc.org/en/rda/about.html)
- The Open Archival Information System (OAIS) Reference Model Introductory Guide (2nd Edition): http://www.dpconline.org/docman/technology-watch-reports/1359-dpctw14-02/file
- Trusted Digital Repository: https://www.oclc.org/content/dam/research/activities/trustedrep/repositories.pdf

Preservica
Commercial digital archiving application: http://preservica.com/about-us/

Recommendation for Space Data System Practices Reference Model for an Open Archival Information System CCSDS 650.0-M-2 Magenta Book:
https://public.ccsds.org/pubs/650x0m2.pdf

Society of American Archivists
Great educational resources, great bookstore.

- Archives and Archivists Listserv: https://www2.archivists.org/listservs
- Book store: https://saa.archivists.org/Scripts/4Disapi.dll/4DCGI/store/storeFront.html?Action=Store
- Digital Archives Specialist (DAS) Curriculum and Certificate Program: https://www2.archivists.org/prof-education/das
- Directory of Archival Organizations for the United State and Canada: https://www2.archivi

Quiz

See the answers on page 324.

1. Is there a difference between a digital record and an analog or nondigital record?
2. What are the two kinds of digital records?
3. What is metadata?
4. What is digital curation?
5. What is the most important step of digital curation?
6. What is reliability?
7. What is authenticity?
8. What are the three attributes of a record?
9. What does a fixity check do?
10. What is the first step in preservation planning?

Notes

1. The Library of Congress is a great place to start learning about digital preservation. See Personal Archiving, "Preserving Your Digital Memories," accessed February 2018. http://digitalpreservation.gov/personalarchiving/

2. Society of American Archivists, Glossary, "Electronic Record," accessed February 2018. http://www2.archivists.org/glossary/terms/e/electronic-record

3. OCLC, About RDA, accessed February 2018. https://www.oclc.org/en/rda/about.html

4. Wikipedia, "Digital Curation," accessed February 2018. https://en.wikipedia.org/wiki/Digital_curation

5. The National Historical Publications and Records Commission (NHPRC), a statutory body affiliated with the National Archives and Records Administration (NARA). NHPRC supports a wide range of activities to preserve, publish, and encourage the use of documentary sources, created in every medium ranging from quill pen to computer, relating to the history of the United States. National Archives, National Historic Publications and Records Commission, "About NHPRC," accessed February 2018. https://www.archives.gov/nhprc/about

6. The Wayback Machine is a digital archive of the World Wide Web and other information on the Internet created by the Internet Archive, a nonprofit organization, based in San Francisco, California. The Internet Archive launched the Wayback Machine in October 2001. Wikipedia, "Wayback Machine," accessed February 2018. https://en.wikipedia.org/wiki/Wayback_Machine

7. The International Research on Permanent Authentic Records in Electronic Systems (Inter-PARES) aims at developing the knowledge essential to the long-term preservation of authentic records created and/or maintained in digital form. It provides the basis for standards, policies, strategies, and plans of action capable of ensuring the longevity of such material and the ability of its users to trust its authenticity. "InterPARES Project," accessed February 2018. http://www.interpares.org/

8. For more on reliability and authenticity see Duranti, Luciana. "Reliability and Authenticity: Concepts and Implications." *Archivaraia, The Journal of the Association of Canadian Archivists* no. 39, Spring 1995

9. Federal Rules of Evidence, Rule 901, section (a).

10. As you may recall, provenance refers to the practice of keeping groups of records together based on who created them. Information about the creator of the records is the provenance of the records.

11. You can purchase the OAIS standard from ISO at https://www.iso.org/standard/57284.html for CHF 198—about $204.00 dollars. If you don't want to purchase the standard, you can get "The Open Archival Information System (OAIS) Reference Model Introductory Guide (2nd Edition)," which describes OAIS by Brian Lavoie from OCLC for free at http://www.dpconline.org/docman/technology-watch-reports/1359-dpctw14-02/file. You can also get the "Recommendation for Space Data System Practices Reference Model for an Open Archival Information System CCSDS 650.0-M-2 Magenta Book" dated June 2012 for free at https://public.ccsds.org/pubs/650x0m2.pdf. This document became ISO standard 14721:2012.

12. "Online" indicates a state of connectivity [available via a network], while "offline" indicates a disconnected state [from the network]—Wikipedia, "Online and Offline," accessed February 2018. https://en.wikipedia.org/wiki/Online_and_offline. Near-line refers to something like a data bank, where a tape, cartridge, or other device holding data can be connected to the network via an automated process or very quickly.

13. Society of American Archivists, Glossary, accessed February 2018. https://www2.archivists.org/glossary/terms/m/media-migration, "The process of converting data from one type of storage material to another to ensure continued access to the information as the material becomes obsolete or degrades over time. Media migration does not alter the bitstream. Examples of media migration include copying files from 5.25 floppy disks to 3.5 floppy discs to CD to DVD."

14. A disaster recovery plan (DRP) is a documented process or set of procedures to recover and protect a business IT infrastructure in the event of a disaster. Wikipedia, "Disaster Recovery Plan," accessed February 2018. https://en.wikipedia.org/wiki/Disaster_recovery_plan

15. Society of American Archivists, Glossary, accessed February 2018. https://www2.archivists.org/glossary/terms/f/format-migration. "The process of converting a data from an obsolete structure to a new structure to counter software obsolescence. Format migration may involve changes in the internal structure of a data file to keep pace with changing application versions . . . [or] changes from one application to another, such as Word to WordPerfect . . ."

16. PDF/A is an ISO-standardized version of the Portable Document Format (PDF) created for use in the archiving and long-term preservation of electronic documents. PDF/A differs from

PDF by prohibiting features ill-suited to long-term archiving, such as font linking (as opposed to font embedding) and encryption. The ISO requirements for PDF/A file viewers include color management guidelines, support for embedded fonts, and a user interface for reading embedded annotations. For more information see Wikipedia, "PDF/A," accessed February 2018. https://en.wikipedia.org/wiki/PDF/A and the Sustainability of Digital Formats: Planning for Library of Congress Collections "PDF/A, PDF for Long-Term Preservation" accessed February 2018 at https://www.loc.gov/preservation/digital/formats/fdd/fdd000318.shtml

17. File Fixity is a digital preservation term referring to the property of a digital file being fixed, or unchanged. Fixity checking is the process of verifying that a digital record has not been altered or corrupted. Wikipedia, "File Fixity," accessed February 2018. https://en.wikipedia.org/wiki/File_Fixity

18. There are different checksum algorithms out there. I used an MD5 algorithm, which is now somewhat dated. An MD5 algorithm will probably work fine for your institution, but you might want to do some research on checksum algorithms before you commit to one. Your needs and the changes in technology may offer you better options than an MD5 algorithm by the time you read this book. One of those options might be the SHA-2 algorithm created by the NSA.

19. For more information on checksums see the Council of State Archivists (CoSA) resource site, accessed February 2018. https://www.statearchivists.org/resource-center/resource-library/?keyword=checksum

20. A file format is a standard way that information is encoded for storage in a computer file. It specifies how bits are used to encode information in a digital storage medium. File formats may be either proprietary or free and may be either unpublished or open. Wikipedia, "File Format," accessed February 2018. https://en.wikipedia.org/wiki/File_format

21. File Extentions.org, "The Source for File Extensions Information," accessed February 2018. https://www.file-extensions.org/

22. Wikipedia, "Proprietary Format," accessed February 2018. https://en.wikipedia.org/wiki/Proprietary_format

23. Wikipedia, "List of file formats," accessed February 2018. https://en.wikipedia.org/wiki/List_of_file_formats

24. Library of Congress "Recommended Formats Statement," accessed February 2018. https://www.loc.gov/preservation/resources/rfs/

25. Library of Congress "Recommended Formats Statement," accessed February 2018. https://www.loc.gov/preservation/resources/rfs/

26. In March 2000 RLG (Research Library Group) and OCLC began a collaboration to establish the attributes of a digital repository for research organizations. Those organizations that met these attributes would be certified as a "Trusted Digital Repository," accessed February 2018. http://www.oclc.org/content/dam/research/activities/trustedrep/repositories.pdf. This work has become as ISO standard, "ISO 16363," accessed February 2018. https://www.crl.edu/archiving-preservation/digital-archives/metrics-assessing-and-certifying/iso16363

27. CoSA, Electronic Records, Program for Electronic Records Training, Tools, and Standards, "SERP Framework" accessed February 2018. https://www.statearchivists.org/pertts/serp-framework

28. The NDSA "is a consortium of organizations that are committed to the long-term preservation of digital information . . . [whose mission] is to establish, maintain, and advance the capacity to preserve our nation's digital resources for the benefit of present and future generations." Library of Congress, Digital Preservation, National Digital Stewardship Alliance, "About," accessed February 2018. http://www.digitalpreservation.gov:8081/ndsa/about.html

29. Library of Congress, Digital Preservation, National Digital Stewardship Alliance, "Levels of Digital Preservation," accessed February 2018. http://www.digitalpreservation.gov:8081/ndsa/activities/levels.html

30. Fixity checks are discussed in depth on pg. 16

31. Library of Congress, Personal Digital Archiving Series, "How Long Will Digital Storage Media Last," accessed February 2018. http://digitalpreservation.gov/personalarchiving/documents/media_durability.pdf

For CDs see the NIST/Library of Congress "Optical Disc Longevity Study," accessed February 2018. http://www.loc.gov/preservation/resources/rt/NIST_LC_OpticalDiscLongevity.pdf

For other media sources see "Digital Archaeology: Rescuing Neglected and Damaged Data Resources," accessed February 2018. http://www.ukoln.ac.uk/services/elib/papers/supporting/pdf/old-p2.pdf

32. In information technology, a backup, or the process of backing up, refers to the copying and archiving of computer data so it may be used to *restore* the original after a data loss event. Wikipedia, "Backup," accessed February 2018. https://en.wikipedia.org/wiki/Backup

33. A network security system that monitors and controls the incoming and outgoing network traffic based on predetermined security rules. A firewall typically establishes a barrier between a trusted, secure internal network and another outside network. Wikipedia, "Firewall (Computing)," accessed February 2018. https://en.wikipedia.org/wiki/Firewall_(computing)

34. CNET, accessed February 2018. https://www.cnet.com/

35. Wikipedia, CNET, accessed February 2018. https://en.wikipedia.org/wiki/CNET

36. CISCO, CISCO Security, CISCO Security Advisories and Alerts, accessed February 2018. https://tools.cisco.com/security/center/publicationListing.x

37. A "dark archive" see SAA, Glossary, "Dark Archive," accessed February 2018. https://www2.archivists.org/glossary/terms/d/dark-archives

38. File formats were discussed in Section 3, pg. 22 and section 4, pg. 25.

39. "Preserving Digital Information Report of the Task Force on Archiving of Digital Information commissioned by the Commission on Preservation and Access and the Research Libraries Group, May 1996," accessed February 2018. https://www.clir.org/pubs/reports/pub63/

40. Jeff Rothenberg, "Digital Preservation Summary," April 4, 2003, accessed February 2018. http://www.nationalarchives.gov.uk/documents/rothenberg.pdf

41. SAA, Directory of Archival Organizations for the United States and Canada, accessed February 2018. https://www2.archivists.org/assoc-orgs/directory

42. SAA, Email Discussion Lists, accessed February 2018. https://www2.archivists.org/listservs

43. CoSA Listserv, accessed February 2018. https://www.statearchivists.org/connect/listservs/

44. "Electronic Records Management Software Application Design Criteria Standard," April 25 2007, accessed February 2018. http://jitc.fhu.disa.mil/projects/rma/downloads/p50152stdapr07.pdf

45. "Trusted Digital Repository," accessed February 2018. http://www.oclc.org/content/dam/research/activities/trustedrep/repositories.pdf. This work has become an ISO standard, "ISO 16363," accessed February 2018. https://www.crl.edu/archiving-preservation/digital-archives/metrics-assessing-and-certifying/iso16363.

46. In the spirit of full disclosure my wife works for Lyasis (https://www.lyrasis.org/Pages/Main.aspx), which has ties to both Fedora and Islandora.

47. Council of State Archivists, Resource Center, accessed February 2018. https://www.statearchivists.org/resource-center/resource-library/

48. Archives Association of British Columbia, "The AABC Archivists Toolkit: Digital Preservation Management," accessed February 2018. http://aabc.ca/resources/archivists-toolkit/electronic-records/

49. Lyrasis, "Digital Preservation Services," accessed February 2018. https://www.lyrasis.org/services/Pages/Digital-and-Preservation-Services.aspx

50. Wikipedia, "Standard Raid Levels," accessed February 2018. https://en.wikipedia.org/wiki/Standard_RAID_levels

51. Microsoft, "Find the Right IT Training: Online and In-person," accessed February 2018. https://www.microsoft.com/en-us/learning/training.aspx

52. CoSA, Electronic Records, Program for Electronic Records Training, Tools, and Standards, "Educational Webinars," accessed February 2018. https://www.statearchivists.org/pertts/education-training/seri-educational-webinars/seri-educational-webinar-recordings-materials. If directed to the main Educational page, follow the links in the left hand bar.

53. CoSA, Electronic Records, Program for Electronic Records Training, Tools, and Standards, "Self-directed Training Modules" accessed February 2018. https://www.statearchivists.org/

pertts/education-training/self-directed-training-modules/—/—If directed to the main Educational page, follow the links in the left hand bar.

54. Society of American Archivists, "Digital Archives Specialist Curriculum and Certificate Program," accessed February 2018. https://www2.archivists.org/prof-education/das

55. Society of American Archivists, "Continuing Education," accessed February 2018. https://www2.archivists.org/prof-education/continuing-education

56. Society of American Archivists, "SAA Bookstore," accessed February 2018. https://saa.archivists.org/Scripts/4Disapi.dll/4DCGI/store/storeFront.html?Action=Store

57. ARMA, "On-line Learning," accessed February 2018. http://www.arma.org/page/Online Learning

58. ARMA, "ARMA On-line Store: Publications," accessed February 2018. https://www.arma.org/store/ListProducts.aspx?catid=636275

Chapter 13

Digitization

The goal of this chapter is to give you the information needed to plan and implement a simple text digitization project. To do this, I am going to define digitization and some of its terms, discuss project planning, and the processes and resources needed for digitization. I chose to focus on the digitization of documents (text) in this chapter because it and the digitization of photographs are the most common type of digitization projects for smaller archival institutions. Digitizing text may require some special steps and the use of different software. At the same time, the planning, processes, and technologies used to digitize text are basically the same for digitizing other nondigital sources—maps, photographs, microfilm, film stock, and the rest. If you are considering digitizing something other than text, the differences you will encounter may include the type of scanner used, and will include the file formats and metadata used to enable search. The resources I point you to include information on the digitization of these other media sources.

My descriptions of project planning and digitization processes are going to be brief. I will not go into detail about the digitization process because there are numerous digitization resources available via the internet and in print that cover this subject. Instead, I will go over the basic concepts and point you to the best of the digitization resources. In most cases, I will give you multiple resources on each topic as opinions on technical matters vary.

The chapter is divided into five sections. The first section is an introduction to digitization and some of its terms. Section II discusses project planning. Section III goes over the hardware and software resources needed for digitization. The fourth section reviews digitization processes and workflows. The chapter ends with section V, a summary and a quiz to test your understanding of digitization and a list of digitization resources.

There are five steps in the digitization process. First, you plan your digitization project by deciding what you want to digitize (selection), how you are going to digitize those items (the format, resolution, metadata, and output standards), and how you are going to make the results of the project available to your users (access). Next, you create a plan of work and gather the equipment and expertise together needed to meet those goals. Another way of saying this is that you decide what you are going to do, get the equipment to do it, define who is going to do it, and how it is going to be done. Third, you do the work. Fourth, you review the results of your work, make it available to your users, and revise your plan of work based on feedback from your users as needed. The final step is the long-term maintenance of the project, the continual modifications to metadata, and the migration of the project files to updated platforms as needed.

Digitization as an Access Tool

Digitization projects are access projects. They are done to increase the use of records by making digital copies of those records available to a wider audience, in most cases, via the internet.[1]

Digitization is not a preservation tool, but it does have implications for preservation. The original analog item is seldom if ever used for access once a digital copy (surrogate) has been created for access purposes. In the vast majority of cases, institutions do not digitize items to preserve them. They digitize items to make them available to those who cannot or do not wish to visit the institution to use the items in their original analog form.

Digitization projects are popular because people like having access to digital information resources. Digital surrogates (digital copies) can be viewed on the electronic devices that we use every day, including smartphones. Digital surrogates are much easier to transport than the original paper versions. They can be shared as email attachments, and in some cases their contents can be copied into other documents or used to start new documents. As I said earlier, in the last ten years that I worked as a records manager, if a nondigital item or record was needed by anyone in the corporation, it was digitized and used as a digital copy. No one wanted to use an original paper copy of anything.

Section I: Terms

Digitization is a technical process, so the terms used to define and describe that process are technical. I have done my best to define the terms in this section as simply and clearly as I can, but they are technical terms and as such reading about them and understanding them can be tedious. Make no mistake, if you are going to do digitization projects, you need to understand these terms.

The Society of American Archivists defines digitization as "the process of transforming analog material [nondigital items] into binary electronic (digital) form, especially for storage and use in a computer."[2] When you digitize a document or photograph, you place the original analog item on the plate of a scanner, close the cover, and start the software to create a digital image of the item. That digital image can be adjusted, cleaned up, and enhanced to a limited extent by software as needed. Metadata, information about the item, can be linked to the image and the image can be made available to your users via a database that is searched using the metadata you created to describe the image.

Digitization—the process of creating a digital image from an analog item.

If you have a digital image of text, you can transform the image into a digital document whose text can be searched by running optical character recognition (OCR) software on it. OCR software looks at the image and assigns what it thinks is the correct letter to each character in the image. This creates a text version of the image. OCR software can create a Word or PDF document from an image. How well OCR works (its confidence rate) depends on the quality of the image and the characters. If you scan documents created in the last twenty years or so using modern fonts (character sets) and letter sizes (10 or 12 points), you can get great results. If you scan documents that are yellowed with age with dated fonts and small letters (8 point or less), you can get bad results. OCR will not work well, if at all, on handwritten documents. You must run OCR on images to enable full text search.

Optical character recognition (OCR) software converts images of text into machine readable text—text that can be copied or searched.

Images are the foundation of all digitization projects, so we need to be able to talk about them in exact terms using technical specifications. There are three technical specifications used when discussing images: resolution, bit depth, and compression.

Resolution and Bit Depth

Digital image quality is defined by resolution and bit depth. Resolution is the number of pixels per inch (PPI) or dots per inch (DPI) in an image. PPI and DPI are generally used interchangeably. The more pixels or dots per inch the finer the image. An 8 × 10 image at 200 PPI will have 3,200,000 pixels (1600 pixels × 2000 pixels). The higher the PPI (or DPI), the bigger the file size of the image.

Bit depth or tonal resolution defines the number of black and white shades in an image or the number of colors used in a color image. A grayscale image with 8-bit depth will have 256 shades of black and white. A color image with 8-bit depth will have 256 levels of color. A 16-bit depth grayscale image will have 65,536 shades of black and white, a 16-bit color image will have 65,536 levels of color. An 8-bit depth image is sufficient for most documents including color documents.[3]

PPI and DPI—PPI is pixels per inch or dots per inch in an image. The more PPI or DPI you have the finer the detail in the image.

Bit depth—the number of shades used in a black and white image or the number of colors used in a color image. A grayscale image with 8-bit depth in one channel will have 256 shades of black and white. A color image with 8-bit depth in three channels will have 256 different colors.

Compression

Because image file sizes can be large, some file formats use a mathematic process using algorithms to compress the files into smaller sizes for storage. There are two kinds of compression: lossy and lossless. A file format using lossless compression "allows the original data to be perfectly reconstructed from the compressed data."[4] File formats using lossy compression will keep only some of the shades of grey in a grayscale image and some of the colors used in a color image. Images using lossy file formats will lose fidelity over time. Lossless file formats include but are not limited to TIFF, PNG, a specific type of JPEG2000, and PDF/A. Lossy file formats include but are not limited to JPEG, PGF, and DjVu. Archivists strongly prefer image file formats using lossless compression to ensure that the digital images replicate the originals as closely as possible.

Master and Derivative Copies

Digitization is a commitment of labor and resources and it creates stress on the items being scanned, so you only want to digitize an item once. This means that you want to create a master digital copy at high resolution that can be preserved and used to create use copies in varying resolution rates. Digital use copies are referred to as derivative copies. Derivative copies can range from 64 DPI thumbnail images to high resolution images with 600 DPI.

The Federal Agency Digitization Guidelines Initiative (FADGI) document, "Raster Still Images for Digitization: A Comparison of File Formats,"[5] is a great source of information on TIFF, JPEG2000, JPEG, PNG, PDF, PDF/A, and GeoPDF file formats. It compares and contrasts the strengths and weakness of each of these file formats in a table that can be difficult to read because of its size. Reviewing this table is a great first step in deciding what file format to use for your master digital copy.

The specifications for master copies vary with the type of material being digitized. NARA's "Technical Guidelines for Digitizing Archival Materials for Electronic Access: Creation of Production Master Files—Raster Images"[6] dated June 2004, is one of the foundational documents of the digitization process. It gives master image specifications for modern, clean, high-contrast documents created with laser printed type as 8-bit grayscale at 300 or 400 PPI and for documents where color is important for interpretation, at 16 bits with 300 or 400 PPI. The "Guidelines" also provide image specifications for other media types being digitized. The FADGI document "Technical Guidelines for Digitizing Cultural Heritage Materials,"[7] dated September 2016, gives similar specifications. It is well worth your time to review this FADGI document.

Naming Conventions

Digital projects create lots of files and if you create a master file with derivative copies as recommended you create multiple files of the same image. This means it is easy to get confused managing these files. Using a naming convention to consistently name your files is one way to avoid confusion. Whatever naming convention you choose should be used for all your digitization projects, so it should be simple and easily replicated. The publication "BCR's CDP Digital Imaging Best Practices Working Group,"[8] dated 2008, provides the following recommendations for file naming conventions:

- Use lowercase letters of the Latin alphabet and the numerals zero through nine.
- Avoid punctuation marks other than underscores and hyphens.
- Begin each file name with a two- to three-character acronym representing the institutional name followed by a second two- to three-character acronym representing the department or unit name (when applicable).
- Follow the institutional and departmental acronyms with an object ID. The object ID consists of any unique numbering scheme already in use to represent the object or, if no such number exists, a short description representing the item.
- File names should be limited to thirty-one characters, including the three-character file extension.
- When saving files, the file names should be limited to eleven characters, including the three-character file extension, in case a recipient's computer does not support long filenames.
- Use a single period as a separator between the file name and the three-letter extension.
- Include a part designator after the object ID, when applicable.

As an example of a file naming convention, if you are from the Spring Valley Historical Society archives department working on a digital project that creates a 300 DPI master file image, a 64-DPI thumbnail image of that master file, and a 200 DPI use image of the same master file your file names might look like this:

SHSAR12345Mas.TIF
SHSAR12345Thm.JPG
SHSAR12345Use.PDA
SHS represents the Spring Valley Historical Society
AR represents the archives department
12345 represents the unique file number of the image
Mas represents the 300 PDI master copy of the image, which is a lossless TIFF file
Thm represents the 64 DPI thumb nail copy of the image, which is a lossy JPEG file
Use represents the 200 DPI use copy of the image, which is a lossless PDF/A file

When saving these files, I would create a directory entitled *The Spring Valley Historical Society's Archives Department digitized Collection of XXXX* (whatever the collection was) and then name the files on the CD 12345Mas.TIF, 12345Thm.JPG, 12345Use.PDA, so on.

Section II: Project Planning

Now that you understand the basics terms of digitization, we can discuss planning a project. Planning a digital project means making decisions about what you are going to do. The first decision you must make, the first question you must ask is this: What do you want to digitize and why do you want to digitize it? What is the audience you are trying to serve by digitizing this material? What are the implications for you if the project succeeds? What risks do you face if the project fails? The better you answer these questions: the better you define your project. It is much easier to successfully complete a well-defined project than a vague project. If you don't clearly know what you are doing and why you are doing it, how can you know if you have done it well? The kinds of questions you want to answer about your digital project are listed in the "Getting Started in Your Digitization Project,"[9] a questionnaire created by the Collaborative Digitization Program and revised by the Bishoff Group in 2011.

CoSA, the Council of State Archivists, has created an excellent guide on how to start planning your digital project entitled "Digitization Projects."[10] The CoSA guide focuses on the digitization of textual resources (government records), but its project planning advice applies to any digital project. This document is well worth your time if you are considering a digital project.

Planning a digital project can be complicated. Do you select the collection to digitize first or do you create a basic project plan first? In some ways you do them together. To keep things simple, I am going to cover selecting a collection for digitization before project planning, but in practice these activities are often done at the same time.

Selecting the Collection to Be Digitized

Selecting the collection or items to digitize is the first step in your project plan. You want to select a collection that is widely used, that can be digitized without physical harm to the collection, and a collection that you have the legal rights to digitize. Consult with your reference staff and with your users about which of your collections is popular with your users. Check to make sure that you have the copyright to the collection being considered or that you have the right to digitize it. Next consider the historical value of the collection[11] and review its physical condition. Can it be handled and subjected to intense light without harm?[12] Finally, if there are other copies of the collections in existence search the web to see if any other institution has digitized the collection or parts of it.

I have made the selection process sound harder than it is. You know which collections are important to your users; you know which collections make you think, "Wow, this is great stuff" every time you see them. Those are the kinds of collections that make your draft list of what you want to digitize. The copyright and physical condition issues help narrow the list down. Once you have the draft list of collections down to five or less, meet with the staff and management of your institution or survey them in some fashion to make the final selection. You might consider asking some of your researchers their thoughts on the list as well.

There are several good publications on selecting a collection for digitization. National Information Standards Organization's 2007 "A Framework for Guidance for Building Good Digital Collections,"[13] the Council on Library and Information Resources' 1998 "Selecting Research Collections for Digitization,"[14] and the NEDCC reformatting pamphlet "6.6 Preservation and Selection for Digitization"[15] are among the best.

If you are submitting a digitization project as part of a grant submission, the grant guidelines will define the kind of collection they want selected. The first three digitization projects I was involved in were grant submissions, so the selection process was very easy for me.

Project Plan

Now that you have selected the collection to digitize you need to make some decisions about what you are going to do. You can talk to prospective users about these questions or you can make assumptions about them, but you have to make some decisions based on the questions below before moving forward. The decisions you have to make include:

- Who are the users for this digital collection? Who is the audience we are trying to reach?
- How will we make the digital collection available to the audience? In the vast majority of cases you will want to make the digital collection available via the internet. Publishing digital collections to CDs has been used, but it is too difficult to distribute the CDs widely.
- What kind of derivative images will you create for your audience? Will you create 64-DPI thumbnail images for search results that link to higher resolution images for the users to view? What will the high resolution images be—200 DPI, 300 DPI, or something else? Will they be grayscale or color?
- Will you watermark or somehow designate that the images from this digital collection downloaded by users is copyrighted by your institution? Will you ask that those using the images of the collection in publications cite them in a particular way?
- How will the users search for items in this digital collection? What kind of descriptive metadata will they need? Digital collections that have full text search still use descriptive metadata to narrow search parameters. You will need descriptive metadata; the question is how much?
- Will images be enough for our audience or will they want full text search capabilities? Do we need to do OCR or not?

These last two questions about descriptive metadata are covered in detail a bit later in this section.

Project Goal Statement

Now that you have the broad parameters of the project plan figured out, you can write the project goal statement. Writing a good goal statement is not easy. I was taught the SMART goal system, which says that goals should be

- Specific—the goal must be clear and concise.
- Measurable—you must be able to measure progress toward reaching your goal.
- Achievable—reaching the goal must be possible.
- Results focused—goals should measure outcomes, not activities.
- Time bound—you must create deadlines for reaching the goal.[16]

For your first project, your goals should be simple and be easy to reach. At the same time, you should need to work diligently to meet your goals. The measureable aspect of goals is the most difficult for me. What do you measure? Do you measure simple facts or do you measure something more meaningful that tells you what the project has accomplished? In the case of a digital project, do you measure the number of pages scanned or do you measure the use rate of the pages scanned? "Both" is a good answer. The number of pages scanned tells you how much work was accomplished while the use rate of those images gives you some idea of outcome, the impact of the project.

An example of a good digital project goal is: "The Spring Valley Historical Society is going to digitize 500 pages of the John Grey papers and make them available to the public via the Society's website by March 2018. The John Grey images will be accessed at least 10,000 times in the first six months."

Descriptive Metadata

The purpose of descriptive metadata is to enable users to find the information they seek. So you need to figure out how users will search for and find information in this collection. Will images meet their needs or will they want OCR and full-text search?

As you may recall from the chapter on digital records, there are two kinds of metadata, defined or free text. In my opinion the best descriptive metadata is made up of both, but defined metadata may be of more importance. Defined metadata is used by search engines to identify collections for users. Meaning if you are searching the internet for a primary source on the use of balloons in the American Civil War, Google and similar search engines will use defined metadata to identify collections that meet that search criteria.

Dublin Core is the premier descriptive metadata set in use in the English speaking world. It is "a vocabulary of fifteen properties for use in resource description."[17] The fifteen metadata elements are

Contributor—an entity responsible for making contributions to the resource
Coverage—may be a named place or location, date, or date range
Creator—entity primarily responsible for making the resource
Date—a point of time associated with an event in the lifecycle of the resource
Description—includes but not limited to: abstract, a table of contents, or a free-text account
Format—file format, physical medium, or dimensions of the resource
Identifier—unambiguous reference to the resource
Language—language of the resource
Publisher—entity responsible for making the resource available

Relation—a related source
Rights—information about rights held in and over the resource
Source—related resource from which the described resource is derived
Subject—topic of the resource
Title—name given to the resource
Type—nature or genre of the resource

You do not have to use all fifteen elements to create a valid Dublin core record. For most digitization projects, I would recommend the following elements:

ID
Title
Creator
Publisher
Date
Description
Subject

The Dublin Core elements are strictly defined. The elements are explained in depth on the Dublin Core site cited above. The description and subject elements are open to interpretation. While the descriptive element can be anything you want, in my opinion, the subject element should use some sort of controlled thesaurus, a defined set of subject headings. I always favored the Library of Congress Subject Headings.[18] They are free, easy to use, and widely adopted.

You now face a choice about how much metadata you use: Do you create Dublin Core metadata at the collection level or at the item level? The answer lies with the collection, its importance, and how you think users will search for specific items within the collection. You could OCR the collection, thus enabling full text search. The combination of Dublin Core metadata at the collection level and full text search at the item level should be sufficient for most collections.

If you do not want to OCR the collection, you can create Dublin Core elements for each item or you can create your own metadata fields to enhance search. Remember that creating metadata is time consuming, so be sure you think about this step before you take it.

You can create your own subject headings based on the contents of the collection and categorize the items in the collection based on those subject headings. Let's say that the collection you have selected for digitization lends itself to categorization because it covers a limited number of topics that are easily understood. As an example, if you are digitizing the papers of Senator X, the categories in this collection might include the following: legislation, correspondence, subject files, and public relations. You could create a free text field and tag every item in the collection with one of these categories to enhance search. You could go even further if the collection warrants it and create subcategories for the main headings. Legislation could be broken down into pending and successful legislation, or it could be referenced by topic and bill number. Correspondence could be broken down into legislative, voter concerns, and personal correspondence or it could be referenced by date, author, and topic. The free text metadata you create is limited only by your imagination and the needs of the collection.

Just remember that it takes time and effort to create metadata and that the headings for the categories you create have to be logical and make sense. The goal of metadata is to help users find the information they seek, so think about metadata from the user's point of view. How would a user find information in this collection? What would they look for? If you take the needs of the collection and the needs of those using the collection into account, the metadata you create will work. If not, feedback from users will tell you what kind of metadata you should have created.

Outsourcing Project Scanning

Now you have another decision to make: Do you digitize the collection yourself or do you outsource the scanning to a vendor? The answers to the questions above could become the basis of an RFP or RFQ (request for a proposal or quote), a written description of the work you want done should you decide to outsource the scanning part of your digitization project. You send the RFP to vendors in your area and pick the one you like the best based on their responses to the questions. A diligent vendor will want to inspect the collection selected for scanning so that they can give you an accurate quote.

Using a vendor has its upside, they have the equipment and expertise to scan your items at what can be a reasonable price.[19] The downsides to using a vendor are the costs and the time spent supervising the vendor to ensure that you get what you want. You are entering into a partnership with your vendor. That partnership needs good communications and a willingness to compromise if it is to be successful.

There are two kinds of digitization vendors. There are those with experience scanning archival collections, and there are those that scan business documents. If the focus of the vendor you use is scanning business documents, they may not understand the value of archival collections and the need to preserve them. This means you might need to be very specific about the care the vendor needs to take when handling an archival collection. Some digitization vendors will want to use automatic feed scanners to scan your collection. I strongly advise against using autofeed scanners on an archival collection. Autofeed scanners jam on a fairly frequent basis, and when they do there is a strong possibility that the page causing the jam will be torn or destroyed. In my opinion, this is an unacceptable risk for an archival collection.[20]

Pilot Projects

If you choose to scan the collection yourself, you can now start to obtain the hardware and software needed for the project. When you have the hardware and software in place and you have created your plan of work (all of which will be covered in the next section), I strongly recommend that you run a pilot project. Run a few items through the entire plan of work (twenty-five should be more than enough) and ask some users to use the digital collection. See if it meets their needs and find out what they like and don't like about your digital collection. Is the metadata you created for search good enough? Do you need to augment that metadata or change it? Adjust your plan of work and project results accordingly. You created your project plan based on assumptions and/or limited input from your users. A pilot project enables you to confirm your decisions and make adjustments in your project before you have a lot of time and money invested in it. Pilot projects are always a good idea regardless of the size of your project.

Section III: Hardware and Software

If you decide to do your digitization project yourself, what hardware and software do you need to get the project accomplished? To a large extent those answers depend on the items being digitized. Because of that and the rapid change of technology, I am going to give you general principals to guide you in selecting hardware and software rather than specific recommendations.

Hardware

Scanning projects create lots of large files, so one of the primary considerations when purchasing hardware is how fast can you load, use, and transfer large files? You want to have computer[s] dedicated to your scanning project. These computers should have large monitors with high resolution. The quality of the monitor is of particular importance if you are scanning color photographs. Someone is going to spend a lot of time looking at these monitors, so get the biggest and best you can afford.

Computers dedicated to scanning projects should have as much RAM (random access memory) as possible. RAM enables you to view and move from image to image quickly. If you are scanning, reviewing, and doing quality control on 1,000 images, you do not want to waste time waiting for an image to load. These computers should also have processors optimized for the manipulation of images along with the necessary graphics cards.[21]

Computers dedicated to digitization should have lots of hard drive space to hold images and large network connections to enable large-scale data input and transfer. Portable hard drives are a great capability to add to any project using large numbers of large files. They are cheap and easy-to-use devices for backing up and transferring large amounts of data. The speed with which all the computers and other technical devices operate depends on your network connections, so get the best and biggest network connections you can.

Don't be afraid of asking for advice from the experts on what computer capabilities you need. Archivists who have run their own digital projects are a great place to start. Your local computer store is filled with folks that would enjoy providing you with recommendations on the latest and greatest computers for digitization projects. Tell them about your digitization project, and give them as much detail about the size and number of files as you can. This will enable them to give you specific recommendations based on the needs of your project. Remember, buyer beware: the computer store staff may want to sell you capabilities you don't need!

Scanners

There are several different types of scanners, flatbed scanners, book scanners, automatic feed drum scanners, microfilm/microfiche scanners, and large-format scanners (sometimes called planetary scanners).[22] Given that you are creating images, you can also use a 35 mm digital single lens reflex camera, provided you have the right accessories. These accessories include a tether, USB, or Firewire connection to your computer, and a camera stand with lights. For those starting their first digitization project, I strongly advocate a good flatbed scanner. They are simple to use, relatively cheap, and versatile. When looking for a flatbed scanner, make sure it will give you an option for high resolution images and that the plate (the scanning surface) is big enough to handle the collection you want to scan. One of the things that differentiates scanners is the software they come bundled with, which leads us to software.

Software

Depending on the needs of your project, you are going to need three or four different software capabilities. Most scanners come with basic digitization software that will have at least some of the capabilities you need. The areas where you may need more advanced software capabilities are image manipulation, OCR, and digital asset management.

Image manipulation software gives you the ability to modify and/or enhance the images you create. The question you need to ask yourself before purchasing image manipulation software is this: "Are the image manipulation capabilities in the software that come with my scanner enough for my project?" Only you can answer that question, and it depends both on what the scanning software will do and the needs of your collection. If the software that comes with your scanner can create images that are clear enough to be read at low resolutions and you can create master and derivate copies of images, I would say you are fine with what you have.

There is a philosophical question involving image manipulation that deserves some consideration. How much can you manipulate and/or modify an image without harming the integrity of the original? If you take a black and white image and you colorize it, is it the same image? If you take a page of text where the original document is yellow, faded, and the text is in a small font that is no longer in use, and you turn it into a black and white image with 12-point Times New Roman font, have you lost the experience of using the original document? Or is the information in the document the only thing of value? I hate to go back to the same old answer but, it depends. How much you can manipulate images before they lose integrity can be decided on a case-by-case basis or it can be decided at the collection level? The best option means a lot of work—giving the users the ability to see both the image of the original document along with a transcription, an OCR'd version of black and white text. This option is not appropriate for every collection, but it is for some.

OCR

If your project calls for you to OCR images, you may need more OCR capability than comes bundled with the software you get with your scanner. Better OCR gives you lower error rates. An OCR error rate is the number of letters that are assigned wrong characters out of 100 characters. OCR error rates can be deceptive. As an example, if your OCR application gets 30 letters wrong out of 3,000 the error rate is 0.01 percent, which sounds great. But if the 3,000 characters represent 600 words on a page and the search engine skips 30 words because of OCR errors, the search results are off by 0.05 percent, 5 times the error rate.

You need more OCR capability when the error rate you get using an automated OCR process is higher than 3 percent. A 3 percent error rate can mean that 15 percent of the words are unrecognizable. Whether or not this error rate is too high depends on what you're scanning. If you are scanning an index of names with death certificate numbers to enable genealogists to request death certificates, a 3 percent error rate is too high. If you're scanning the 1920 documents of a member of the Ohio House of Representatives, a 3 percent error rate might be fine. Most people do not have the time and/or patience to verify OCR, meaning reviewing and correcting OCR'd text. If your project needs OCR, get the best OCR software you can find. It doesn't cost all that much.

Digital Asset Management

Digital asset management (DAM) software enables users to store, organize, search for, retrieve, and share digital files. Wikipedia defines digital asset management as the "management tasks and decisions surrounding the ingestion, annotation, cataloguing, storage, retrieval, and distribution of digital assets."[23] DAM software suites have lots of different capabilities including but not limited to metadata and taxonomy (classification systems) management, search and guided navigation features, life cycle and rights management capabilities, access and identity management, asset editing, manipulation, and transcoding (moving from one file format to another), task management, workflows, approving, and reporting. To me, one of the most important capabilities of DAM software is its ability to publish digital assets to the internet. DAM software can do a lot of different things, and it can be expensive if you get a suite that will do all the things mentioned above. Some DAM software suites are simple and relatively inexpensive, and you can get DAM as open source software, so look around before you make a decision.

Do you need DAM software? If you are managing small digitization projects that are easily separated and you have a way of publishing images to the internet, you do not. But if you see your institution going from one digitization project to another, and some of those projects will create a large number of files with search and retrieval issues, it will be worth your time to look at DAM software suites.

Section IV: Digitization Procedures and Workflow

Now that you have your collection selected for digitization, a project plan together, and the hardware, software, and network infrastructure ready to go to support the project what do you do next? You create procedures that define how you are going to do things and create a plan of work that defines what you are going to do. Then you get started and modify your procedures and plan of work based on your experiences.

Project Leadership

If you have not already done so now is the time to choose the leader of the project. This person has to have the authority to implement the project plan as they see fit. There are too many small decisions that need to get made every day for the project leader to seek guidance from their superiors. Most of these decisions will be technical, so individuals outside the project will not have the context with which to provide good advice anyway. These small decisions define the project and the project leader should consult with the project staff when making them. The project leader should not be a tyrant. He or she needs to be smart enough to respect the expertise and thoughts of the project staff when making decisions. But make no mistake, the leader makes the decisions and the staff must respect those decisions. With that decision making authority goes the ultimate responsibility for the success or failure of the project. Some people will not want to be a project leader because of the constant decision making and stress.

There are two actions you can take early in small projects that will help you gage their success or failure. First is taking actions to measure the use of the project results, and second is keeping track of any lessons learned. Measuring the use of the project can be as simple as collecting statistics on how many individuals hit the project web pages to complex surveys of user satisfaction. No matter how you do it you need to get user feedback from those using your project to determine its success or failure.

Going over project lessons learned helps project staff grow their expertise and helps the institution make better decisions about digitization projects going forward. I always found it helpful to keep a project journal, detailing the issues and decisions along with a brief explanation of why I made the decision I did. Identifying the major decisions in the project and talking about their effects is the best way to define lessons learned.

Procedures

Procedures are specific actions you take to reach a defined result, a set of directions that may be given in sequential steps. You need procedures to get consistent results. There are two primary sets of procedures for digitization projects: procedures about metadata creation and procedures defining how you are going to create, manage, and store images. Procedures should result in a checklist or some other easy-to-understand set of directions that can be followed by anyone working on the project.

Metadata procedures are easy to create and difficult to implement. The project plan defines what metadata you are going to use, and the procedure tells you how to create that metadata. General metadata is not a problem: the title is this, the publisher is that, the date is this, and so forth. Descriptive metadata is the issue. If you do not have procedures defining how descriptive metadata is created, you will have different people describing the same thing differently. As an example, are you scanning the John Grey papers, the Papers of John Grey or the Grey, John papers? Perhaps you are scanning the John Grey correspondence? You want consistent metadata. Without procedures you will get inconsistent metadata.

To get consistent metadata you need to have instructions for every metadata field. If you have a free text field of 256 characters for an abstract, you need directions for how that abstract is written and what is included in it. If you use subject and/or classification headings, you need to define the list of options with directions for how to choose the options. Choosing the options consistently when several different people are making those decisions is where implementation gets difficult. Procedures help; you also need a common understanding of how metadata is applied to the items in the collection over time.

Imaging procedures define what steps you are going to take to optimize images, how to implement naming conventions, create derivative images, and where you store images. These procedures should include the standard to which you are going to optimize images. They may also include calibration procedures, which are covered in more detail a bit later. Imaging procedures are technical; you are going to use X control or tool Y to create an image of Z resolution. Depending on the capabilities of your software, your procedure may be to use the automated function of the application to optimize the images it creates. The specifications of the images your project creates should have been defined in the project plan, if not you need to define them as part of this step. File naming convention procedures are easy; you rename the files with the names, as appropriate. Storage procedures are also pretty simple: put X files in Z storage area.

You may not need all of these procedures, but creating and following procedures enables you to create a consistent product. They also make it easier to bring new staff into the project. Procedures are particularly important if you are going to run different scanning shifts or if you going to have different people operate the scanner at different times. If you do not have procedures, you will find yourself with wildly different metadata and images at the end of the project.

Digitization Work Plan

There are several good sources for digitization work plans.[24] I would urge you to review them before creating your own work plan. In my opinion there are seven essential steps in a digitization work plan:

1. Review of the physical condition of the items being scanned
2. Scanning prep

3. Scanning
4. Postscanning
5. Quality control
6. Publishing the images
7. Review, revision, and maintenance

Reviewing the Items to Be Scanned

The first step in your plan of work should be to review the physical condition of the items that are going to be digitized. You did this in a general way as part of the selection process, but now it is time to look at each item individually before it is scanned. Can this item be handled and scanned without harming it? Remember the underlying philosophical theme of archival work: *as archivists we need to preserve the collections in our care while providing access to them.* You cannot provide access to an item in a collection if such access threatens the preservation of that item.

If you think you will harm an item by scanning it, do not scan it. See if you can repair it, then scan it later and insert the image into the collection at the appropriate place. If you cannot make repairs to the item so that you can safely scan it, perhaps you can find some way of replacing it. If the item was a page from a document, I would consider retyping it from the original and insert that page of text into the images of the original document. Then footnote the recreated page with the reasons why it was recreated. If you cannot create a copy of the original to scan, skip the item altogether. Describe it in a note and say that its condition prevented it from being scanned. Always be upfront with your users. You have nothing to hide. Reviewing the physical condition of the items to be scanned can certainly take place during the scanning prep step, but I feel it is important enough to be mentioned as a separate step.

Scanning Prep

The point of scanning preparation is to make sure that everything that can be done before you start scanning gets done. Preparing the items to be scanned involves mental and technical preparation. As part of the mental preparation you want to review the naming conventions you are going to use along with how you are going to create descriptive metadata including classification schemes if you are using one.

The technical preparation for scanning involves moving the items to be scanned to the scanner work area, calibrating the scanner, and checking the computer and its network connection to make sure they are working properly. When you move the items to be scanned into the scanner work area, you want to create two holding areas, one for items to be scanned, and the second for items that have been scanned. Think about how you are going to handle the items being scanned: How brittle are they? Do you need to wear gloves? Are you going to put the items in the "scanned" holding area face down?

Calibration is an important step that should be taken at the start of every work session. Calibrating the scanner is testing how the equipment works against a defined standard. In most cases calibrating a scanner means scanning a target usually provided as part of the scanner and adjusting the output of the scanner to optimize the image created of that target. Making sure your computer works properly and that your network connection works is something that all of us do every day.

Some projects will create a scanning prep checklist that is used and signed off on by every scanner operator before they begin work. You may not need to go to that extreme.

Scanning

Once the scanning prep step is done you can start scanning. Scanning itself is pretty easy. Assuming you are using a flatbed scanner, you take the item to be scanned from the "to-be scanned" holding area, open the lid of the scanner, place the item on the scanner plate, close the lid, and hit the scan button. Depending on the software you are using, you might see a preview of the image that is going to be created or you might select the area to be scanned. After taking whatever measures are needed, wait for the light bar to scan the item, open the lid, and take the item off the plate and place it in the "scanned" holding area. You might name the file at this point or you might reply on the file name created by the scanner software.

Post scanning

Most of the work gets done in the post scanning phase. In this phase, might you manipulate the image and create descriptive metadata at the item level. You might rename the file according to your naming convention, and move it to a storage location that the quality control staff have access to. You may also create, rename, and store derivative images. You might run OCR software to create searchable text and rename and store those files as well. What you do in this phase is defined by the project plan and the people and technical assets available to the project. The work done in this phase should be defined by procedures.

Quality Control

Someone other than the person operating the scanner should review 100 percent the images to make sure there are no mistakes in image creation, clarity, metadata creation, and naming convention. This quality control (QC) individual should have access to image manipulation software so they can repair images as needed and they should have the ability to order re-scans. If you are creating derivative images, OCR, and/or descriptive metadata, QC needs to review them as well. QC uses the procedures you created to judge whether or not the scanning product and its associated metadata meet the specifications defined in the procedures. You still need to do QC if you do not have procedures. Procedures just make QC easier and less subjective. You may think you do not need a quality control step for your project. In my opinion, this is an error in judgment. Without a quality control review of the products, you will end up creating a lot of bad images and metadata.

Publishing the Images

The last step in your work plan is publishing the images. You might have one last review of the images and metadata before you publish them or not. It depends on the circumstances and your level of paranoia. Basically, you move the derivative images and their associated metadata into the application you use to make the images available to your users. Check to make sure the publishing application works and that the images and associated metadata show up as they should. Then take a breath and congratulate yourself on a job well done.

Review, Revision, and Maintenance

Larger projects may have a more formal debrief where they review the project, the decisions made, lessons learned, and feedback from their users. In many ways user feedback ultimately determines the success or failure of the project. I am not sure this needs to be a formal meeting but the results of the project, its use rate, user satisfaction, and lessons learned need to be shared within the project staff and institution in some manner.

Taking user feedback into account and making revisions is an important part of your project. In the vast majority of cases the fixes you make due to user feedback will be minor. Things like "this image is out of focus" or "this metadata element is wrong." You may need to create another procedure documenting how modifications are made so the changes get done consistently.

In some cases user feedback will encourage you to modify your descriptive metadata to enhance search. Feedback may even force you to create another search method, like adding OCR or new search terms. Let us hope that is not the case, but if it is, fix whatever the problem is and move on. The whole point of creating digital projects is to give your users an information resource, a product they can be happy with. If they are not happy, you need to make them happy. You need to court your users. They can be your biggest supporters or your biggest problems. Take the steps necessary to make them your friends.

There are three on-going tasks that need to be done at the close of the project: creating backup copies of the project, maintaining the project, and preserving the project.

Creating backup copies of the project is not a big chore. I would advocate that you have two or three backup copies of the project kept in different physical locations. One backup should be kept at a distant location in case a major catastrophe, like a fire or flood, hits your primary location. Project maintenance is an on-going task, and as you modify the project products because of this maintenance, you will need to remember to update your backup copies as well.

There are three different parts of project maintenance. First is making changes to the project due to user feedback, which we have already covered. The second is server maintenance, making sure the publishing application works consistently and that your server has enough computer power and bandwidth to support the increased use of your site. Third, you need to think about migrating the project from one publishing platform to another. Changes due to user feedback will taper off sometime after the initial launch of the project. Server maintenance and getting ready to move the project from one publishing platform or application to another will be reoccurring events.

You have taken nondigital records, probably paper records, and turned them into digital records to increase their use. That is great for access purposes, but now you have created a digital preservation task for you to deal with. Chapter 12 deals with digital preservation issues in detail, so I will not go into them here. I will say that you need to protect and monitor the digital health of the digital objects you have created. You have worked too hard on this project to see its products go bad or vanish in a few years. Take heed: you owe it to the project staff, the institution, and your users to take the digital preservations steps necessary to make your project last over time.

Section V: Summary

Do not be afraid of digitization. Provided you do not harm the original items being scanned, you can redo every step in digitization without problems. If you make a mistake, you can fix it. I was thrown into my first digitization project with no warning and no experience. It was a successful project because of the quality of the people who worked with me and because we learned from our mistakes. I have tried to warn you of those mistakes in this chapter so that you do not repeat them.

My recommendation to you is just do it. Your first digitization project should be small and simple. Think of it as a pilot project for all the digital projects to come, a learning experience rather than creating a product for public consumption. Start with modern text documents, use a metadata scheme to enable search, and make them available to an internal audience for review. If the metadata scheme doesn't work well enough for search, your audience will tell you so. Perhaps give OCR a try. The point of this project is for you to learn what you are doing without pressure.

Digitization is not hard, but it can be very detailed and repetitive work. The digital projects your institution creates will enhance its reputation and add to the mass of research resources available online. They will also create a loyal group of supporters provided you meet their needs. Digitization is well worth the time, money, and effort, and done well it creates a digital research resource than can be used world-wide.

Partial List of Digitization Resources

Council of State Archivists (CoSA)

"Digitization Projects" created by the State Electronic Records Initiative (SERI) is a three-part module on the best practices for managing digitization projects: https://www .statearchivists.org/files/6015/0272/2035/COSA_DigitizationProjects_final.pdf

Council on Library and Information Resources

Selecting Research Collections for Digitization "proposes a model of the decision-making process required of research libraries when they embark on digital conversion projects": https://www.clir.org/pubs/reports/hazen/pub74/

Dublin Core

Defines the Dublin Core Metadata Element Set, Version 1.1 used by many institutions to describe resources: http://dublincore.org/documents/dces/

Federal Agency Digitization Guidelines Initiative (FADGI)

- List of 13 published guidelines on various aspects of digitization: http://www .digitizationguidelines.gov/guidelines/
- List of resources used: http://www.digitizationguidelines.gov/resources/
- "Raster Still Images for Digitization: A Comparison of File Formats": http:// www.digitizationguidelines.gov/guidelines/FADGI_RasterFormatCompare_ p1_20140902_r.pdf
- "Technical Guidelines for Digitizing Cultural Heritage Materials": http://www .digitizationguidelines.gov/guidelines/FADGI%20Federal%20%20Agencies%20 Digital%20Guidelines%20Initiative-2016%20Final_rev1.pdf

Library of Congress

- Preservation Guidelines for Digitizing Library Materials lists some of the things you should consider when choosing items to digitize: https://www.loc.gov/pres ervation/care/scan.html
- Subject Headings are used in conjunction with the Dublin Core to describe resources: https://www.loc.gov/aba/publications/FreeLCSH/freelcsh.html
- Illustrated Book Study: Digital Conversion Requirements Printed Illustrations is the results of the Cornell University Library Department of Preservation, Conservation, and Picture Elements, incorporated joint study to determine the best means for digitizing the vast array of illustrations used in 19th and early 20th century commercial publications: https://www.loc.gov/preservation/resources/rt/ illbk/index.html

LYRASIS

Is a library, archives, and museum membership organization that makes available a number of digital resources in its:

- Digital Toolbox: https://www.lyrasis.org/services/Pages/Digital-Toolbox.aspx
- Western States Digital Imaging Best Practices V. 1.0 provides "minimum digital imaging recommendations to institutions that are planning for or are involved in digitization projects": https://www.lyrasis.org/services/Documents/Digital%20 Toolbox/Western%20States%20Digital%20Imaging%20Best%20Practices%20Ver sion%201.0.pdf
- BCR's CDP Digital Imaging Best Practices Working Group, "a guide for practitioners in cultural heritage institutions that seek to create images from physical objects": https://www.lyrasis.org/services/Documents/Digital%20Toolbox/BCR's%20 CDP%20Digital%20Imaging%20Best%20Practices%20Version%202.0.pdf

National Archives and Records Administration (NARA)

Technical Guidelines for Digitizing Archival Materials for Electronic Access: Creation of Production Master Files–Raster Images "defines approaches for creating digital surrogates for facilitating access and reproduction": https://www.archives.gov/files/pres ervation/technical/guidelines.pdf

National Information Standards Organization

A Framework for Guidance for Building Good Digital Collections "provides an overview of some of the major components and activities involved in the creation of good digital collections": https://www.niso.org/publications/framework-guidance-building -good-digital-collections

North East Document Conservation Center (NEDCC)

NEDCC has seven documents on reformatting resources, of particular interest are:

- 6.6 Preservation and Selection for Digitization discusses the selection and preservation of resources for digitization: https://www.nedcc.org/free-resources/preser vation-leaflets/6.-reformatting/6.6-preservation-and-selection-for-digitization
- 6.7 Outsourcing and Vendor Relations which discusses choosing a vendor for a digitization project: https://www.nedcc.org/free-resources/preservation-leaflets/6 .-reformatting/6.7-outsourcing-and-vendor-relations

University of Exeter

Digitization Workflow and Guidelines "outlines the workflow and best practice required to implement the digitization of physical objects": https://projects.exeter.ac.uk/ charter/documents/DigitisationWorkflowGuidev5.pdf)

Yale University Library

Digital Workflow Tool "is an application to track physical material and their digital surrogates as these items travel to and from the originating department to the digitization vendor": http://web.library.yale.edu/lit/projects/digitization_tool

Digitization Quiz

See the answers on page 325.

1. Is digitization an access tool with preservation implications or is it a preservation tool with access implications?

2. True or false—When you scan an analog item, you create a digital image of that item
3. True or false—Full-text search works on images.
4. OCR stands for what?
5. DPI stands for what?
6. True or false—Bit depth or tonal resolution defines the number of black and white shades in an image or the number of colors used in a color image.
7. True or false—Archivists prefer lossy compression file formats.
8. Is it more important to provide access to archival materials or is it more important to preserve archival materials?
9. What are derivative copies?
10. True or false—Dublin Core is a list of free text metadata.

Notes

1. One of the best explanations of digitization as an access tool is found in—Arms, Caroline R. 1999. "Getting the Picture: Observations from the Library of Congress on Providing Online Access to Pictorial Images." *Library Trends*, Vol. 48, No. 2, Fall 1999, pp. 379–409.

2. Society of American Archivists, "Glossary." https://www2.archivists.org/glossary/terms/d/digitization

3. For more in-depth information about images see National Archives and Records Administration. "Technical Guidelines for Digitizing Archival Materials for Electronic Access: Creation of Production Master Files—Raster Images." https://www.archives.gov/files/preservation/technical/guidelines.pdf

4. https://en.wikipedia.org/wiki/Lossless_compression

5. Federal Agencies Digital Guidelines Initiative. "Raster Still Images for Digitization: A Comparison of File Formats." http://www.digitizationguidelines.gov/guidelines/FADGI_RasterFormatCompare_p1_20140902_r.pdf

6. National Archives and Records Administration. "Technical Guidelines for Digitizing Archival Materials for Electronic Access: Creation of Production Master Files—Raster Images." https://www.archives.gov/files/preservation/technical/guidelines.pdf

7. Federal Agencies Digital Guidelines Initiative (FADGI). "September 2016 Technical Guidelines for Digitizing Cultural Heritage Materials Creation of Raster Image Files." http://www.digitizationguidelines.gov/guidelines/FADGI%20Federal%20%20Agencies%20Digital%20Guidelines%20Initiative-2016%20Final_rev1.pdf

8. FADGI 2016 "Technical Guidelines for Digitizing Cultural Heritage Material." http://www.digitizationguidelines.gov/guidelines/digitize-technical.html

9. Collaborative Digitization Program. 2011. "Getting Started in Your Digitization Project," located at the LYRASIS Digital Toolbox site at http://www.lyrasis.org/LYRASIS%20Digital/Pages/Preservation%20Services/Resources%20and%20Publications/Digital-Toolbox.aspx

10. https://www.statearchivists.org/files/6015/0272/2035/COSA_DigitizationProjects_final.pdf

11. As you may recall from chapter 12, "Digital Records," historic value is defined by four factors. First, does the collection or item have credibility; is it a reliable source? Second, what is the time frame covered by the collection? Longer timeframes are usually better but a significant point in history can be just as important. Third, does the collection or item support the accepted view of history or does it tell us something we did not know? Fourth, does the collection increase our understanding of history?

12. See Library of Congress, "Preservation Guidelines for Digitizing Library Materials." https://www.loc.gov/preservation/care/scan.html

13. http://www.niso.org/apps/group_public/download.php/2/framework3.pdf

14. https://www.clir.org/pubs/reports/reports/hazen/pub74.html

15. https://www.nedcc.org/free-resources/preservation-leaflets/6.-reformatting/6.6-preservation-and-selection-for-digitization

16. For more information on SMART goals, see the University of Virginia "Writing S.M.A.R.T. Goals." http://www.hr.virginia.edu/uploads/documents/media/Writing_SMART_Goals.pdf

17. http://dublincore.org/documents/dces/

18. https://www.loc.gov/aba/publications/FreeLCSH/freelcsh.html

19. For more information about the pros and cons of outsourcing digitization projects see the Western States Digital Standards Group, Digital Imaging Working Group. 2003. "Western States Digital Imaging Best Practices V. 1.0," pgs. 8, 9, and 15, located at the LYASIS Digital Toolbox site at http://www.lyrasis.org/LYRASIS%20Digital/Pages/Preservation%20Services/Resources%20and%20Publications/Digital%20Toolbox/Digitization.aspx

20. For more information on the dangers of digitizing items, see Library of Congress. "Preservation Guidelines for Digitizing Library Materials." http://www.loc.gov/preservation/care/scan.html

21. For more information about what is needed for digitization computers, see CPR's CDP (Colorado Digitization Program) Digital Imaging Best Practices Working Group. June 2008. "Digital Imaging Best Practices V. 2.0," pgs. 14 and 15, located at the LYASIS Digital Toolbox site at http://www.lyrasis.org/LYRASIS%20Digital/Pages/Preservation%20Services/Resources%20and%20Publications/Digital%20Toolbox/Digitization.aspx

22. For more information on scanners, see the FADGI 2016, "Technical Guidelines for Digitizing Cultural Heritage Material." http://www.digitizationguidelines.gov/guidelines/digitize-technical.html

23. https://en.wikipedia.org/wiki/Digital_asset_management

24. See the FADGI 2016 "Technical Guidelines for Digitizing Cultural Heritage Material." http://www.digitizationguidelines.gov/guidelines/digitize-technical.html

Yale University Library's Digital Workflow Tool, http://web.library.yale.edu/lit/projects/digitization_tool

University of Exeter, "Digitization Workflow and Guidelines." https://projects.exeter.ac.uk/charter/documents/DigitisationWorkflowGuidev5.pdf

Conclusion

This book, and the course that inspired it, were created as an exercise in practical education. At the institutional level, I hope that the policy templates, checklists, and various other documents provided bring some structure and process to your archival work. Every archival institution needs a collections and reference policy, legal instruments that document the ownership of the collections it acquirers, accession records, finding aids, and a disaster plan. These documents are the foundation on which you build your historic records program. If you already had these documents I hope you used this book as an opportunity to review and revise them as needed.

On a personal level there are two themes running through this book that I want you remember. First is the underlying philosophical theme of archival work: *archivists need to preserve the collections in our care while providing access to them*. Preservation and access are what archivists do. You should be very reluctant to take a collection you cannot preserve or provide access to. Second, circumstances dictate the correct course of action in the archival world. Context, the collection, your resources, and the needs of your researchers are all inputs in making archival decisions. Preservation, access, and context are the watchwords of an archivist.

Reading this book does not make you an archivist, but it does put you well on your way to becoming a well-informed archival assistant or volunteer. To continue on this journey toward archival competency, I urge you to do the following:

- Use the additional resources listed in the book to go into specific archival topics in more depth. Review the educational offerings by AASLH, SAA, CoSA, and ARMA, and take those that are appropriate for you. Working in archives requires lifelong learning; things change, and you need to keep on top of developments in the field.

- In the first chapter, I mentioned the "Archival Fundamental Series II," published by SAA. Every archivist, regardless of their experience and training, should have access to these books for reference purposes. If your archival institution does not have a copy of this series, encourage them to get them. They are available via the SAA bookstore at https://saa.archivists.org. There are six titles in this series:
  - *Arranging and Describing Archives and Manuscripts*
  - *Managing Archival and Manuscript Repositories*
  - *Preserving Archives and Manuscripts*
  - *Providing Reference Services for Archives and Manuscripts*
  - *Selecting and Appraising Archives and Manuscripts*
  - *Understanding Archives and Manuscripts*

Together, these books define the standards and best practices of the archival profession. Don't be overly concerned if your institution does not meet these professional standards and best practices. Meeting them may be beyond your resources. Work toward meeting those standards and best practices that fit your needs, circumstances, and abilities. Perfection is unobtainable. Do the best you can with what you have.

- Join your state or regional archival organization. SAA maintains a *Directory of Archival Organizations in the United State and Canada* at https://www2.archivists.org/assoc-orgs/directory. Find an organization near you and attend their conferences. Start creating a professional network of people that you can ask for advice. You will enjoy meeting people who face the same archival challenges and issues that you do.
- Do the work. If you are not working or volunteering in an archives find one and get started. Every archives needs help because there is always more work than there is staff to do it. Experience is the best teacher.

Thanks again for your efforts and your commitment to saving the history of your community, state, and our nation. Good luck in life and in your archival endeavors.

Charlie Arp

Appendix A

Assess Your Resources Worksheet

The questions within this assessment are general. Make sure you include the particular circumstances of your institution in the discussion of resources.

1. What are your program's financial resources? What money is available for staff salaries, supplies, and other items? Given your financial resources, should your collecting program be small, medium, or large in size and scope?

2. How much space is available? Is your storage area full or empty, or somewhere in between? How much more can you collect before your storage area is filled?

3. What formats of material can you support? Are you able to preserve and provide access to the type of records that are in your care?

4. Can your program support materials that are in poor physical condition? Can you afford to reformat? Can you afford to hire a conservation specialist?

5. Does your program have sufficient staff who are trained appropriately to manage and make available the records?

6. Who uses your collections? What kind of historical records interest them?

7. Is there a collecting theme or focus that your historical records program wants to, or is mandated to, pursue? Should you focus on a specific geographic area, a particular time period, a particular group of people, a specific event?

Appendix B

The Mills Archive Collection Development Policy

Introduction to the Mills Archive

The Mills Archive is a permanent repository for the documentary and photographic records of traditional and contemporary mills and milling, as well as similar structures dependent on traditional power sources. It was set up in 2002 in response to an expressed need to preserve and, where possible, integrate the various threatened sources of information on the windmills and watermills of the UK and the rest of the world. It is a wholly independent organization operated by the Mills Archive Trust.

The mission of the Mills Archive is to preserve and protect the records of the UK's milling heritage; to make them freely available to the public. The Mills Archive holds over 200 archival collections with more than 3 million documents. Go to: https://millsarchive.org for more information on the Mills archive.

Collections Development Policy

1. Introduction
    1.1. In order to fulfil its mission statement "to preserve and protect records of our milling heritage and to make them freely available to the public," the Mills Archive will seek and acquire historical and contemporary records of traditional mills and milling. This policy defines the scope of the material collected and describes the collection process.
2. Scope of material collected
    Subject: The archive collects historical and contemporary material on mills and milling, including millwrighting and the place of the mill in social as well as technological and architectural history. There is a strong emphasis on mills and similar structures that are or were powered by wind, water, muscle or steam. We will retain items not directly related to our subject area when these are donated as part of a larger collection and their disposal would damage the archival integrity of the collection.
    2.1. Geographical area: Worldwide, although the focus will be on the United Kingdom
    2.2. Chronological period: All periods, but the main focus will be the modern period from the 18th to the 21st centuries inclusive.
    2.3. Genre or media of records held: The archive will collect the following:
        - photographs (prints, slides, negatives etc.)
        - documents (field notes, architectural plans, deeds, business records etc.)
        - published material (books and reports)
        - digital files which can be converted into the preservation formats specified in the digital preservation policy
        - small artefacts of milling relevance
    Records in other formats (e.g. film, other forms of digital material) will not be actively sought. Where such material is offered to the archive we will attempt to find a home for it with other organisations (e.g. the regional film archives), but we may choose to act as the repository of last resort if it would otherwise be discarded.
    2.5. The archive will identify gaps in its holdings and seek to acquire collections accordingly. This will be the subject of the Collections Development Plan which will be produced by the archivist in consultation with the trustees and reviewed annually.

3. Cooperation and demarcation with other repositories whose collection policy overlaps
   3.1. The Mills Archive Trust does not seek to compete for material with other archives. In acquiring records every effort will be made to avoid conflict and duplication with the collecting policies of other repositories. In all cases we shall work with other archives and donors to ensure material is placed in its most appropriate home.
   3.2. No attempt will be made to secure the acquisition or removal of any records held in another record repository, except with the consent of the owner of the records and in consultation with the archivist in charge and governing body of that repository.
   3.3. The archive will make every effort to avoid splitting collections. Where the majority of the collection falls within the scope of the archive (see section 2), we will retain the whole collection, including the material on related subjects which are not directly in our scope. Where we are offered part of a collection of which part is held already at another repository, we will recommend that the collection donor first offer the material to that repository.
   3.4. Collections where the majority of the material falls outside of the scope of the archive will not be accepted.
   3.5. Where the collection falls within our scope, but relates entirely to a specific location we will notify the relevant local authority archive service and discuss the most appropriate deposit arrangements. Factors which may be taken into account include the location of related records, the significance of the specific site to the subject area and the wishes of the depositor.
4. The collection process
   4.1. Collections will be acquired by donation and purchase; deposits on loan will only be considered in exceptional circumstances.
   4.2. Responsibility for deciding whether to accept material lies with the archivist in consultation with the chairman of trustees.
   4.3. Conditions associated with accessions:
      4.3.1. It is a condition of acceptance that documents shall be available for public access either immediately or at the expiry of a specified period.
      4.3.2. Acquisition of records will depend on the appropriateness of the Mills Archive as a suitable place for their custody and consultation and will respect the principles of archival integrity.
      4.3.3. No records will be acquired or disposed of in contravention of the terms of any current legislation and in particular the Public Records Acts, the Manorial and Tithe Documents Rules and the Parochial Registers and Records Measure.
      4.3.4. Before accepting records, the Mills Archive Trust must be satisfied that the donor has proper authority or title to transfer them and in the event of acquisition by gift the Governing Body and the donor or owner of the records shall fully acquaint each other in writing of any terms or conditions attaching to the transfer.
      4.3.5. We will also seek to acquire intellectual property rights to the material from the owner of these rights, if known, or agree on a licence permitting us to reproduce the material.

4.4. When the archive has agreed to accept a collection of material, the donor will be given an acquisition form to complete, transferring ownership, detailing the agreement we have reached regarding intellectual property rights and specifying any further conditions or restrictions. This and any related correspondence will be stored in the accessions files. The material will be accessioned in line with the specifications of the accessions procedure.

5. Selection and deaccessioning policy

5.1. The Mills Archive Trust believes that there should be a presumption against disposal by sale of documents in its ownership except when they are duplicates of published material. In accordance with the wishes of depositors, as expressed at the time of transfer, we shall evaluate and remove from the archive those documents deemed not to be worthy of permanent preservation.

5.2. In all other cases there is a presumption against the disposal, by any means, of records accepted into the record repository unless:
   - it is found that they belong more properly with records in another repository, in which case they may be transferred there with the consent of both governing bodies.
   - the Mills Archive becomes unable, either temporarily or permanently, to provide proper care for them, in which case they will be transferred to another appropriate repository with similar overall objectives on such terms as may then be agreed in writing with both governing bodies.
   - the donor requests their return.

6. Contact with donors

6.1. The archive will maintain contact with donors of material by adding them to the mailing list for our newsletter and inviting them to any events held at the archive.

7. Responsibility and review

7.1. This policy statement is based on that originally approved by the Trustees in January 2002. Responsibility for ensuring the policy is adhered to lies with the Archivist. The policy will be reviewed every three years.

Appendix C

Collections Policy of the Hamilton Public Library, Local History and Archives

55 York Blvd. Hamilton, Ontario, Canada L8N 4E4

The Local History and Archives collection exists to

- Collect and preserve materials which illustrate the growth and development of Hamilton-Wentworth, both before and after incorporation, or which pertain in whole or in part to activities within the geographic boundaries of Hamilton-Wentworth;
- Arrange and describe these materials according to archival principles and make them accessible to the general public on a regular basis, unless access is restricted by legal requirements or written agreement with the donor;
- Provide adequate and appropriate conditions for the storage, protection, and preservation of archival material;
- Provide regular reference services to individuals, organizations, the municipal government, or other groups interested in the activities and holdings of the Archives;
- Provide educational and outreach programming whenever possible to increase public awareness of Hamilton-Wentworth's history and development.

Material acquired by Local History and Archives shall become the permanent property of the Archives and, therefore, the Hamilton Public Library, until such time as the archivist deems it no longer relevant to the Archives, in which case the material may be deaccessioned.

Deaccessioning will not take place without the written approval of the department head responsible for the Archives. All information pertaining to the deaccessioning and disposition of material will be retained in the Archives' records.

The Archives retains the right to reproduce materials by mechanical, electronic, or photographic means for security, conservation, or research purposes.

The Archives will accept historical material of any medium, including textual records; photographs and other visual records; maps, plans, and architectural records; and sound recordings and oral history tapes. The Archives will only accept books, printed materials, artifacts, and electronically stored data at the discretion of the department head or archivist.

The Archives retains the right to charge for any reproduction or other research service. A schedule of fees will be made available to the general public on a regular basis.

The Archives will only accept material on a permanent basis, except when borrowing material for short-term loans to reproduce or to include in displays or exhibits.

Materials from the Archives may be loaned to other institutions or organizations only under the following circumstances:

- Written authorization is obtained from the manager, Local History and Archives (or designate)
- The borrower ensures adequate care and handling of the material on loan. If at any time the Archives determines that the material on loan is not being cared for adequately, the manager or archivist may cancel the loan and request the immediate return of the material.

No person shall be prevented from using archival materials unless is it determined that the materials will be physically abused or used in a libelous or illegal manner.

Appendix D

Collection Policy References

These are just a few references to collections policies that can be found on the internet, many more are available via search. All these citations were accessed in March 2018. The citations are in alphabetical order.

American Jewish Archives
http://americanjewisharchives.org/publications/starting2.php

Amherst College
https://www.amherst.edu/library/archives/collectiondevelopment

Chevy Chase Historical Society
http://www.chevychasehistory.org/chevychase/cchs-archival-collection

Council of Nova Scotia Archives, Members Acquisitions Policy
https://www.councilofnsarchives.ca/cooperative-acquisition-strategy/members-acquisition-policies/

Frick Art Reference Library
https://www.frick.org/research/library/collection_development_policy

Harvard University Archives
https://library.harvard.edu/university-archives/donating-materials/policies

Historical Society of Central Florida
http://download.aaslh.org/StEPs+Resources/Collections+Management+Policy+Historical+Society+of+Central+Florida%2C+Inc.pdf

Historical Society of Pennsylvania
http://hsp.org/sites/default/files/hsp_collections_management_policy_rev__11-23-15.pdf

Houston Public Library
http://www2.houstonlibrary.org/hmrc/docs/ArchCollManWeb.pdf

Lima Historical Society
https://limahistorical.org/wp/index.php/collection-policy/

Metropolitan Museum of Art—Cloisters Library and Archives
https://www.metmuseum.org/art/libraries-and-research-centers/the-cloisters-library-and-archive

Appendix E

Collections Policy Worksheet

Use this form to identify the components of your organization's collection policy. Then, place your answers in the policy template. Remember that this policy should provide structure to decision making, but it also should be flexible and amendable as needed.

Element 1

Name of program:

Name of parent organization (if applicable):

Under what authority does your program operate or is governed? A board? Government agency? Director? Company president? Archivist?

Element 2

What is the purpose (or mission) of the program?

Element 3

What is the focus of the collection? Describe the topics and areas of emphasis your program specializes in. List the subjects, people, timeframes, and geographic areas that your program focuses on. Also, describe the specific kinds of materials your program collects.

Element 4

What formats can the repository responsibly manage? (Example: Oral history interviews on cassette tape will be accepted, but we prefer that a typewritten transcript accompany them; these will have a higher collecting priority.)

Element 5

How will materials be accepted into the collections? Will records be actively sought? Who will approve acceptance of materials? Through what means will legal custody be obtained?

Element 6

Under what authority and circumstances will unwanted materials be removed from the collections? What procedures will be used to document this activity?

Element 7

Will loans of materials be made to other organization and will they be accepted by your organization? Under what circumstances? What are the general conditions of the loan and conditions for termination of the loan?

Collection Policy Template

NAME OF THE PROGRAM

PURPOSE

AUDIENCE

COLLECTING FOCUS and LIMITATIONS

ACQUISITION OF MATERIALS

LOAN OF MATERIALS

DISPOSAL OF MATERIALS

Appendix F

Appraisal Scorecard

Collection name:

Donor:

Date of appraisal:

Individual doing the appraisal:

Score a yes as 5, score a no as 1

Section 1—When Were the Records Created?		
	Score	Notes
1a. Are the records old?		
1b. Are the records scarce?		
1c. Are the records from an important time period?		
1d. Do the records cover a long or short period of time?		
Section 2—Why Were the Records Created?		
2. Do they document the principal activities or functions of the creator?		
Section 3—What Is in the Records?		
3a. Do they document important activities?		
3b. Are they the only source of information?		
3c. Are they the best source of information?		
3d. Do they dispute other records?		
3e. Do they provide unique information?		
Section 4—Who Created the Records?		
4a. Do the records reflect a routine or unique point of view?		
4b. What was the position of the creator?		
4c. Was the creator personally involved in the activities recorded?		
4d. Did the creator possess the necessary expertise to understand the events recorded?		
4e. Does the creator display a bias?		

Section 5—How Do These Records Fit with Your Program?		
5a. Do the records meet the requirements of our collection policy?		
5b. Where is the geographical focus?		
5c. Do they duplicate or support current holdings?		
5d. What is their research potential?		
5e. Do they meet researchers' needs?		
5f. What is the condition and size of the group of records?		
5g. Can we support the storage and staff costs, necessary preservation and conservation of the records?		
5h. Are there political considerations in accepting or rejecting these records? Any positive or negative repercussions from donor? Any precedent set if accepted?		
Section 6—Accept or Reject Records?	Y/N	
6. Are the records valuable and appropriate for our program?	Total Score	

Appendix G

Sample Deposit Agreement

SAMPLE DEPOSIT AGREEMENT BETWEEN HISTORICAL SOCIETY AND MUSEUM OF RIVEROAKS and

NAME CHARLOTTE TOMLINSON
INSTITUTION NONE
ADDRESS 300 N. STATE STREET
CITY RIVEROAKS   STATE NA   ZIP CODE 00001
TELEPHONE (001) 001-1001

DESCRIPTION OF ITEMS ON DEPOSIT:

This agreement covers the deposit of the "CHARLOTTE TOMLINSON PAPERS," hereafter referred to as "Papers."

The Papers consist of the private collection of materials bought, collected, and produced by Charlotte Tomlinson from 1940 to the present. This includes personal letters, oral history tapes and transcriptions, newspaper clippings, photographs, scrapbooks, slides, a card catalog of historical fact cards, manuscripts (published and unpublished), and a library of history books.

APPROXIMATE VALUE OF ITEMS:

A third party appraisal valued the items at $50,000.00

INSURANCE WILL BE CARRIED BY:

Society's insurance policy _____

I own the materials described above and voluntarily agree to deposit them with the HISTORICAL SOCIETY AND MUSEUM OF RIVEROAKS, with the intention of transferring title to said organization upon my death. At that time all rights, title and interest I possess in these materials will transfer and be assigned to said organization.

No arrangement or preservation work may be performed on these materials without my written permission. The repository is responsible for all damages, accidental or otherwise, that occurs to the material while in its custody. A description of these materials may be added to the access records of the organization.

Access to these records is permitted and unrestricted. The records may be reproduced with the supervision of the *receiving* repository.

I agree to the above conditions of deposit and I am authorized to agree thereto:

For the _____   For the _____

Signature _____   Signature _____

Title _____   Title _____

Date _____   Date _____

Appendix H

DEPOSIT AGREEMENT

Type your program name here.

AND

NAME _____

INSTITUTION _____

ADDRESS _____

CITY _____ STATE _____ ZIP CODE _____

TELEPHONE NUMBER

DESCRIPTION OF ITEMS ON DEPOSIT:

APPROXIMATE MONETARY VALUE OF ITEMS:

INSURANCE WILL BE CARRIED BY:

I own the materials described above and voluntarily agree to deposit them with the **TYPE YOUR PROGRAM NAME HERE**, with the intention of transferring title to said organization upon my death. At that time all rights, title, and interest I possess in these materials will transfer and be assigned to said organization.

No arrangement or preservation work may be performed on these materials without my written permission. The repository is responsible for all damages, accidental or otherwise, that occurs to the material while in its custody. A description of these materials may be added to the access records of the organization.

Access to these records is permitted and unrestricted. The records may be reproduced with the supervision of the *receiving* repository.

I agree to the above conditions of deposit and I am authorized to agree thereto:

For the _____   For the _____

Signature _____   Signature _____

Title _____   Title _____

Date _____   Date _____

Appendix I

Example Deed of Gift

In consideration of mutual benefits, ELBERT MARVEL, later called PERSON, and the QUILL COLLEGE ARCHIVES, later called COLLEGE, enter into this agreement for access, use, disposition, and ownership of the PERSON'S PAPERS, later called PAPERS.

I. COLLEGE shall: have ownership of PAPERS upon receipt, store PAPERS according to accepted archival standards, catalog them, and prepare finding aids to assure ease of access to PAPERS.

II. At the time of their presentation to the COLLEGE, PERSON will designate all boxes or folders of PAPERS as either Unrestricted or Restricted.

   A. UNRESTRICTED PAPERS:
      1. All PAPERS not specifically designated Restricted, shall be Unrestricted. It is specifically understood that news releases, speeches, newspaper clippings, photographs, commonly available publications, and like materials of a public nature in the donated property are Unrestricted, even if found in boxes designated by PERSON as Restricted.
      2. At time of receipt PERSON transfers both property rights and all copyrights he/she may own in Unrestricted PAPERS to COLLEGE. COLLEGE will permit free public access to, quotation from, and publication of these unrestricted PAPERS.

   B. RESTRICTED PAPERS:
      1. PERSON hereby reserves any copyrights he/she possesses in and the right to control access to Restricted PAPERS which have been turned over to COLLEGE by PERSON and which by their year date are less than 50 years old provided, however, that COLLEGE shall have access to PAPERS at all times solely for the purposes of listing, cataloging, storing, and preserving them. THE RESTRICTED PAPERS SHALL CONSIST OF ALL ARCHITECTURAL DRAWINGS OF BUILDINGS NOT OWNED BY THE COLLEGE.
      2. PERSON reserves to him/herself the right of access to and use of Restricted PAPERS. Except as noted in paragraph II.B.1., COLLEGE shall only allow access to and use of Restricted PAPERS by other persons approved in writing by PERSON. Persons granted such access by PERSON may quote or publish from the PAPERS under the fair use provision of the copyright law, provided that they shall signify understanding of and due regard for legal and ethical considerations including matters of copyright, invasion of privacy, libel, slander, and accurate attribution of sources. For quotation or publication beyond the fair use provision of the copyright law, written approval of PERSON or his/her designee must be secured by said persons prior to such quotation or publication.
      3. PERSON may, during his/her lifetime, name one or more persons who shall have the unrestricted right of access to and use of Restricted PAPERS, and shall keep COLLEGE advised at all times of the name(s) of said person(s).
      4. Restrictions as specified in Sections II. B. concerning use of said PAPERS shall cease for all PAPERS which by their year dates are more than NUMBER (—) years old—or, regardless of the age of the PAPERS, upon the death of PERSON—and COLLEGE shall acquire all rights (including all copyrights owned by PERSON, and the right to control access) in and to the same. Moreover, PERSON may at any time authorize earlier free public access to any or all of restricted PAPERS as PERSON shall in his/her judgment deem appropriate. Once restrictions lapse, PERSON, his/her heirs and assigns, shall have no further legal interest therein nor right to control their disposition or use.

5. PERSON shall save COLLEGE and hold it harmless from liability from any use of the Restricted PAPERS, or any quotation or publication based on them, without written permission of PERSON, if COLLEGE has followed procedures established according to this agreement.

III.

(Check one based on previous conversation with donor:)

COLLEGE may dispose of any PAPERS not selected for permanent retention.

If COLLEGE chooses not to permanently retain some of the PAPERS which it accepts, then it shall offer to return such PAPERS to PERSON; however, if PERSON does not accept such PAPERS within 90 days of their being tendered to it, COLLEGE may dispose of them.

IV.

This agreement shall be binding upon and ensure to the benefit of the heirs, assigns, and legatees the parties hereto.

_____

Staff Member, Title   Date

_____

PERSON   Date

Appendix J

Deed of Gift

Name of institution	Address	Telephone/email
Date	Accession number(s)	
Donor	Street	City/state/ZIP
Contact person	Telephone/email	

The donation has been received by the Archives as a gift, and the owner or his agent with full authority, desiring to absolutely transfer full title by signing below, hereby gives, assigns, and conveys finally and completely, and without any limitation or reservation, the property described below to the Archives and its successors and assigns permanently and forever, together with (when applicable) any copyrights therein and the right to copyright the same.

Description of donation

Credit line

Signatures

Donor _____   Date _____

Printed name _____

Director _____   Date _____

Conditions Governing Gifts

1. It is understood that all gifts are outright and unconditional unless otherwise noted upon this gift agreement. The collection covered by this gift will be used for research, exhibit, and any related educational purposes defined by the Archives.
2. Gifts to the Archives may be deductible in accordance with provisions of federal income tax laws.
3. The donor name on this form has not received any goods or services from the Archives in return for this gift.
4. The staff of the Archives is not permitted to furnish appraisals.
5. The Archives gratefully acknowledges your gift.
6. Please indicate on the form beside "CREDIT LINE" how you would like to be acknowledged in any news releases, exhibit labels, or other publicity regarding this donation.

(This form may be a multipart form.)

Appendix K

Sample Accession Form

Date Received	Accession No.	
Title		
Creator		
Donor Name/Address		
Restrictions	Location	Total Size
General Description and Condition of Material		

Specific Description of Material:

Type	Amount	Type	Amount
☐ Audio Recordings	_____	☐ Photographs	_____
☐ Bound Volumes	_____	☐ Microfilm	_____
☐ Storage Boxes	_____	☐ Movie Film	_____
☐ Newspapers	_____	☐ Scrapbooks	_____
☐ Maps	_____		

☐ Other _____

Arrangement of Material:

☐ Alphabetic   ☐ Chronologic   ☐ Numeric

☐ Topical (Subject)   ☐ Not Arranged   ☐ Other _____

Approximate Inclusive Dates	Accessioned By	Date

Additional Comments

Appendix L

Preprocessing Checklist

1. Who was the creator or accumulator of the records? What do you know about the people (individual or organization) who created and used the records?

2. What was the purpose of the records? Why were they created? How were they used?

3. What do you know about the time, place, and subjects of the records?

Sources consulted:

Appendix M

[THIS FINDING AID HAS BEEN REVISED FROM ITS ORIGINAL FORM
AND IS INTENDED FOR EDUCATIONAL PURPOSES ONLY]

OHIO HISTORICAL SOCIETY
Manuscript Collections

MSS 60 [unique collection number]
Pearl R. Nye Collection [collection title]
1851–1962 [collection dates]

OVERVIEW OF THE COLLECTION

Number:	MSS 60, MSS 60 AV	[unique collection number]
Title:	Pearl R. Nye Collection	[collection title]
Creator:	Pearl R. Nye	[record creator]
Dates:	1851–1962; 1870–1913 (bulk)	[dates]
Media:	Papers, photographs	
Quantity:	1.67 c.f.	

BIOGRAPHY OF Pearl R. Nye
[Biographical Sketch or Organizational History]

Pearl R. Nye was born February 5, 1872, on a canal boat, the *Reform*. At that time, the *Reform* was docked at Chillicothe, Ohio, on the Ohio-Erie Canal. Nye was the fifteenth of eighteen children of Captain and Mrs. William Nye. Nye was raised and educated by his parents on the canal boats, eventually becoming a canal boat captain. During Nye's career, the Ohio canal system was in a continual state of decline. The railroads were the primary reason for this decline, replacing the canals as the preferred method of transporting passengers and freight. The final blow to the canal system came in the spring of 1913, when disastrous flooding across the state of Ohio damaged the canals so severely that the state decided to close them.

After the closing of the canals, Nye built a permanent home on the remains of an abandoned canal lock near Roscoe (Coshocton), Ohio. His home was built to resemble a canal boat and was named Camp Charming. Nye's goal in his later years was to preserve the history and culture of the "canallers." Nye learned a large repertoire of ballads, gospel hymns, minstrel tunes, and popular songs from the late-nineteenth and early twentieth century. He drew on his memories of his parents and his years spent as a canal boat captain for inspiration. He adapted the lyrics of well-known songs such as "Tipperary" and "Rock-a-Bye Baby" to become new songs describing canal life. He also wrote original lyrics and music.

Nye developed a reputation as a folk singer. He was recorded by John and Alan Lomax for the Library of Congress in 1937. In 1945, Nye was recorded by Edith Keller, Music supervisor for elementary and secondary education in Ohio, and Cloea Thomas of the Ohio State University School of Music. Nye performed at the National Folk Festivals in 1938, 1942, and 1946, at Madison Square Garden in New York and Constitution Hall in Philadelphia. Nye passed away in a nursing home in Akron, Ohio, on January 4, 1950.

SCOPE AND CONTENTS OF THE COLLECTION [Description]

The manuscript component of the collection contains the lyrics and music of songs authored or performed by Pearl R. Nye. Nye's repertoire included traditional ballads, gospel hymns, popular songs, and songs describing the conditions of life on the canal. While Nye wrote original lyrics and music, he also adapted the lyrics of well known songs such as "Tipperary" and "Rock-a-bye Baby" to reflect canal related themes. Series I contains song lyrics hand written by Nye. Filed with the hand-written lyrics are typed copies. Series II consists of transcripts and music of songs authored or performed by Nye. The transcripts were compiled by Cloea Thomas of the Ohio State University School of Music from audio recordings.

The audiovisual component of the collection consists of 399 mostly black and white photographs of various sizes depicting the Ohio canal system. The majority of the photographs appear to be reproductions. The most documented canal is the Ohio-Erie Canal. The Ohio-Erie Canal, which stretched 309 miles, was the longest canal in Ohio. The photographs depict cities, small towns and canal structures from the canal's northern terminus in Cleveland on Lake Erie to its southern terminus in Portsmouth on the Ohio River. There are also photographs depicting three feeder canals that connected to the Ohio-Erie Canal: the Hocking Canal, the Muskingum Improvement, and the Walhonding Canal. The Miami-Erie Canal, the state's second longest canal, which connected Toledo and Cincinnati, is represented by fewer images. The bulk of the photographs document the years 1870 through 1913 when the canal system was closed. The deteriorating physical condition of the canal system and the declining amount of freight traffic during this period is illustrated by the images. There are some images that depict canal scenes and towns along the canals as early as the 1850s when canal traffic was at its peak. Some photographs illustrate what remained of the canal beds and canal structures in the 1930s and 1940s.

ORGANIZATION OF THE COLLECTION [Arrangement]

The Pearl R. Nye Collection consists of three series: papers, transcripts, and photographs. Series I, the papers, are arranged alphabetically by song title. Series II, the transcripts, consists of two subseries. Within each subseries, the transcripts are arranged alphabetically by song title. Series III, the photographs, consists of five subseries. Within each subseries the photographs are arranged alphabetically by subject.

Series I: Papers contains the hand written lyrics of 136 songs authored or performed by Pearl R. Nye. For the majority of titles there is also a typed copy of the lyrics. The songs are arranged alphabetically by title and housed in Box 1. Also included in Series I are copies of newspaper clippings about Nye.

Series II: Transcripts contains the typed lyrics and music of 118 songs authored or performed by Pearl R. Nye. There is not music for every song title. Also included in Series II is an index to the location of Pearl R. Nye recordings.

Series III: Photographs contains 394 photographs of canal scenes. Subjects depicted by the photographs include canal boats, locks, dams, aqueducts, water powered mills, towns located on the canal, Pearl R. Nye, and the Nye family.

SEE ALSO

Scenes and Songs of the Ohio-Erie Canal (3 copies) by Pearl R. Nye and Cloea Thomas, call numbers 784.49771 T361s; 784.49771 T361 1971 and PA Box 422, 15.
A Photo Album of Ohio's Canal Era, 1825–1913 by Jack Gieck, call number 386.4809771 G361p 1988.
Songs by Pearl R. Nye, call Number PA Box 281, 13.
SC 20 Aqueducts; SC 964 Canals–Barges/Boats; SC 965 Canals–Locks; SC 966 Canal Scenes; SC 967 Canals–Ohio; SC 4456 Ohio Canal (Chillicothe, Ohio)

ADMINISTRATIVE INFORMATION

Access:	This collection is open under the rules and regulations of the Ohio Historical Society.	[access restrictions]
Preferred Citation:	Researchers are requested to cite the collection name, collection number, and the Ohio Historical Society in all footnote and bibliographic references.	
Property Rights:	The Historical Society owns the property rights to this collection.	[copyright]
Copyrights:	Pearl R. Nye has not dedicated such copyrights, as he possesses in this collection to the public. Richard H. Swain has dedicated such copyrights, as he possesses in this collection to the public. Consideration of all other copyrights is the responsibility of the author and publisher.	[copyright]

DETAILED DESCRIPTION OF THE COLLECTION

Note to researchers: To request materials, please note both the location and box numbers shown below.

[Inventory]

Series I: Papers contains the hand written lyrics of 136 songs authored or performed by Pearl R. Nye. The songs are arranged alphabetically by title.

Box	Folder	File Title	Dates
1	1	Song titles A–C	
	2	Song titles D–I	
	3	Song titles J–M	
	4	Song titles N–P	
	5	Song titles R–Z	
	6	Newspaper clippings about Pearl R. Nye	1936; 1940

Series II: Transcripts contains the typed lyrics and music of 118 songs authored or performed by Pearl R. Nye. The transcripts have been divided into two subseries.

Box	Folder	File Title	Dates
2	1	Song titles B–L	
	2	Song titles M–W	
	3	Song titles B–J	
	4	Song titles K–W	
	5	Index to location of Nye Recordings	

Series III: Photographs contains 394 photographs of canal scenes.

Box	Folder	File Title	Dates
3	1	Ohio-Erie Canal: Adams Mills	
	2	Ohio-Erie Canal: Akron, Lock 1	1907–1962
	3	Ohio-Erie Canal: Akron, Lock 2	c. 1890–1930
	4	Ohio-Erie Canal: Akron, Locks 3, 6, 7	
	5	Ohio-Erie Canal: Akron Locks 11–15 and 18–21	
	6	Ohio-Erie Canal: Akron Scenes	c. 1855–1905
	7	Ohio-Erie Canal: Akron Scenes	Not Dated
	8	Ohio-Erie Canal: Akron, Upper Basin	c. 1913–1935
	9	Ohio-Erie Canal: Barberton	c. 1880–1910
	10	Ohio-Erie Canal: Bolivar	
	11	Ohio-Erie Canal: Boston	c. 1890
	12	Ohio-Erie Canal: Canal Fulton Lock	
	13	Ohio-Erie Canal: Canal Winchester	
	14	Ohio-Erie Canal: Chillicothe Area	
	15	Ohio-Erie Canal: Circleville Area	
	16	Ohio-Erie Canal: Cleveland Area Locks	c. 1900–1910
	17	Ohio-Erie Canal: Cleveland Scenes	c. 1860–1910
	18	Ohio-Erie Canal: Clinton Lock	
	19	Ohio-Erie Canal: Columbus	
	20	Ohio-Erie Canal: Dover	
	21	Ohio-Erie Canal: Dresden Aqueduct	
	22	Ohio-Erie Canal: Garfield Heights, Lock 8	
	23	Ohio-Erie Canal: Hanover Area	1851
	24	Ohio-Erie Canal: Independence Area Locks	
	25	Ohio-Erie Canal: Jasper Basin	
	26	Ohio-Erie Canal: Lockbourne	
	27	Ohio-Erie Canal: Massillon Area	
	28	Ohio-Erie Canal: Miscellaneous	1890–1898
	29	Ohio-Erie Canal: Navarre	c. 1880–1900
	30	Ohio-Erie Canal: New Philadelphia	c. 1890–1910
	31	Ohio-Erie Canal: Newark Area	
	32	Ohio-Erie Canal: Newcomerstown	
	33	Ohio-Erie Canal: Orange	1884
	34	Ohio-Erie Canal: Peninsula	c. 189–1913
	35	Ohio-Erie Canal: Port Washington	

Box	Folder	File Title	Dates
	36	Ohio-Erie Canal: Portsmouth Area	
	37	Ohio-Erie Canal: Trenton (Tuscarawas)	
	38	Ohio-Erie Canal: Trenton (Tuscarawas), Lower Lock	
	39	Ohio-Erie Canal: Trenton (Tuscarawas), Upper Lock	
	40	Ohio-Erie Canal: Valley View, Lock 14	

Box	Folder	File Title	Dates
4	1	Ohio-Erie Canal: Waverly Area	
	2	Ohio-Erie Canal: Yellowbud	c. 1890
	3	Ohio-Erie Canal: Zoar Area	c. 1880–1900
	4	Ohio-Erie Canal: Zoarville	1888

Box	Folder	File Title	Dates
4	5	Hocking Canal: Carroll	c. 1880
	6	Hocking Canal: Lancaster Area	
	7	Hocking Canal: Lockville Area	
	8	Hocking Canal: Nelsonville	
	9	Hocking Canal: Sugar Grove	
	10	Muskingum Improvement: Lowell	1879
	11	Muskingum Improvement: Malta	1870
	12	Muskingum Improvement: Zanesville, Y-Bridge	
	13	Walhonding Canal: Roscoe (Coshocton) Area	
	14	Walhonding Canal: Walhonding Lock	
	15	Walhonding Canal: Warsaw Mill	

Box	Folder	File Title	Dates
4	16	Miami-Erie Canal	c. 1880–1940
	17	Miami-Erie Canal: Lockington	

Box	Folder	File Title	Dates
4	18	Nye Family: Boats	
	19	Nye Family: Camp Charming	
	20	Nye Family: Mother Nye	
	21	Nye Family: Nye Nephews	
	22	Nye Family: Pearl R. Nye	1903–1946

Box	Folder	File Title	Dates
4	23	Miscellaneous	
	24	Miscellaneous: Boats	
	25	Miscellaneous: Bridges and Basins	
	26	Miscellaneous: Canallers (canal workers)	
	27	Miscellaneous: Locks	
	28	Miscellaneous: Mills	

Appendix N

Finding Aid Worksheet

Unique collection number

Collection title

Collection dates

Biographical sketch or organizational history

Description

Access restrictions

Inventory: list of boxes and folders

Appendix O

Local Sailing Association Records

ABC Department of Archives and Special Collections

Local Sailing Association Minutes, 1899–1960
Series 169
2 cubic feet

Organizational History

The Local Sailing Association was incorporated in 1899. The Sailing Association was a voluntary organization that was prominent in the local community. At its start, the membership consisted mostly of wealthy individuals. During the Depression years, fewer people could afford to maintain sailboats and consequently the nature of the association changed. After World War II, the Sailing Association was an organization of individuals from many socioeconomic groups who shared an interest in sailing. The focus of the association became families and recreation. The association disbanded in 1960 when much of the membership moved west to take jobs in the expanding defense industry.

Description

The collection is comprised of the complete minutes from the Local Sailing Association. The collection is arranged chronologically. The minutes from the early part of the twentieth century are especially rich in social commentary and include detail on the policy debates that took place at the meetings.

Related collections include

Series 170 Local Sailing Association Membership Rosters
Series 171 Local Sailing Association Correspondence
Series 172 Local Sailing Association Photographs of Events

Access Restrictions

The records are open for research without restrictions. The suggested citation to the collection is, "Local Sailing Association Minutes, ABC Department of Archives and Special Collections."

Container Listing

Box 1	Folder 1	Minutes, 1899–1905
	Folder 2	Minutes, 1906–1910
	Folder 3	Minutes, 1911–1915
	Folder 4	Minutes, 1916–1920
	Folder 5	Minutes, 1921–1925
	Folder 6	Minutes, 1926–1930
Box 2	Folder 1	Minutes, 1931–1935
	Folder 2	Minutes, 1936–1940
	Folder 3	Minutes, 1941–1945
	Folder 4	Minutes, 1946–1950
	Folder 5	Minutes, 1951–1955
	Folder 6	Minutes, 1956–1960

Appendix P

Riveroaks Historical Society

Lisa Smith Papers, 1965–2001
MSS 152

Biographical Sketch

Lisa Smith was born in Riveroaks on May 5, 1950. Never trained formally as an artist, she began painting in 1965 when she was fifteen; her first single-artist exhibit was held at the Riveroaks Gallery in 1972. She is well-known nationally and internationally for her portrayal of rural American landscapes and portraits, many of which are based on locations and people from the Riveroaks area. Many of her paintings are held by the Riveroaks Historical Museum, as well as by many major art museums throughout the country. Lisa Smith's art has been highly praised and widely sold and exhibited. In 2001, Lisa Smith decided that she would no longer pursue her art as a career.

Collection Description

This collection consists of five cubic feet of records relating to the art of Lisa Smith. Each file contains information about an exhibit venue and each piece displayed at that venue, including the artist's handwritten descriptions and background of each painting that was later edited and incorporated into exhibit catalogs, brochures, and exhibit publications. Most files contain photographs of each piece of artwork included in the exhibits and photographs of the exhibit venue. Also included are newspaper clippings, exhibit catalogs, and brochures and correspondence between the artist and exhibit organizers.

Exhibit locations include the Riveroaks Museum; the West Side Gallery in New York, New York; the Cleveland Museum of Art; the Museum of Modern Art; and the Gallerie de Francaise in Paris, France.

Although the collection was created as a record of exhibits by the artist, it's greatest strength is the artist's own descriptions of each piece in which she details how the piece was created, the settings, the intent of each piece, and the meanings each piece had for her. These descriptions provide insight into the mind of the artist, how she was affected by the political and social events that occurred, including the Vietnam War, the social upheaval of the 1960s, the environmental movement, and local issues such as plant closings in Riveroaks in the 1970s, economic development in the region, and so forth.

The collection is arranged chronologically by beginning date of the exhibit. When identical dates exist, files are arranged by date, then alphabetically by name of venue.

Access Restrictions

There are no access restrictions to this collection.

Inventory

Box number	Folder number	Folder description
1	1	March 1, 1965; River Valley Public Library
	2	September 23, 1966; City of Riveroaks
	3	January, 13 1967–January 15, 1967; ABC Art Gallery
	4	June 1967; Jack's Art House
2	1	
	2	
	3	
	4	
3	1	
	2	
	3	
	4	

Continue inventory in same pattern as above

Folder description is written exactly
as it is written on the actual folder

Appendix Q

Your Building's Bio

Your Building's Bio

1. What kinds of space do you have?

☐ A separate storage area

☐ A separate research area

☐ A separate area for processing records

☐ Everything in one space

2. What's the space like?

☐ Heated

☐ Air conditioned

☐ Shelves

☐ Windows in areas where records are stored

☐ Overhead pipes

☐ Attic/top floor where records are stored

☐ Basement where records are stored

3. What collections protection systems do you have?

☐ Fire alarm

☐ Smoke detector

☐ Locks of doors

☐ Locks on windows

4. Identify actions and improvements in each category that you could take to improve your storage facility.

Lightning

Fire Protection

Water Protection

Air Quality

Pest Control

Housekeeping

5. Prioritize Your List of Actions and Improvement

Appendix R

Facility Assessment Questionnaire

Complete one form for each location in which historical or archival records are stored.

RECORDS STORAGE AREA

Location _____ ☐ off-site ☐ on-site

If multi-storied building, include which floor: _____

Nature of storage:

☐ basement ☐ attic ☐ closet ☐ at home ☐ warehouse ☐ garage ☐ vault
☐ safe   ☐ fireproof file cabinet   ☐ other (specify)

1. ENVIRONMENTAL CONTROLS

Is the HVAC system for the storage area part of the system for the entire building?

☐ Yes   ☐ No—*go to (2) below*

Is the HVAC system shut down during evenings, weekends, etc.?

☐ Yes   ☐ No

Are there separate temperature zones within the centralized system for the storage area?

☐ Yes   ☐ No

If yes, can the temperature be adjusted by individual users?

☐ Yes   ☐ No

Are there separate humidity zones within the centralized system for the storage area?

☐ Yes   ☐ No

If yes, can the humidity be adjusted by individual users?   ☐ Yes   ☐ No

Do you use supplemental environmental control equipment in areas covered by the system?

☐ Yes   ☐ No

If yes, what do you use (check all that apply):

☐ fan   ☐ heater   ☐ portable humidifier

☐ portable dehumidifier ☐ window air conditioner ☐ other: _____

Do you open doors and/or windows to control temperature and provide ventilation?   ☐ Yes   ☐ No

2. FOR STORAGE IN A BUILDING WITHOUT CENTRAL HVAC, COMPLETE BELOW:

Are any of the following centralized:

Heat: ☐ Yes ☐ No

Cooling: ☐ Yes ☐ No

Do you use local climate control equipment:?   ☐ Yes ☐ No

If yes, please check all you use:

☐ fan   ☐ window air conditioner   ☐ portable heater
☐ portable humidifier   ☐ portable dehumidifier

Do you open doors and/or windows to control temperature and provide ventilation?

☐ Yes   ☐ No

3. **CLIMATE**—FOR THIS INITIAL SURVEY, YOU ARE PROVIDING A GENERAL SENSE OF THE ENVIRONMENT. IDEALLY, YOU SHOULD DO FREQUENT MONITORING OF THE TEMPERATURE AND HUMIDITY OF YOUR STORAGE AREA NOW TO HELP PLAN FOR REMEDIES.

What is the average temperature?

Spring/Fall   ☐ Hot   ☐ Cold   ☐ Comfortable   Temperature: _____°

Summer   ☐ Hot   ☐ Cold   ☐ Comfortable   Temperature: _____°

Winter   ☐ Hot   ☐ Cold   ☐ Comfortable   Temperature: _____°

     Does it fluctuate?   ☐ Daily   ☐ Weekly   ☐ Monthly   ☐ Seasonally

What is the average humidity?

Spring/Fall   ☐ Damp/Humid   ☐ Dry   ☐ Comfortable   Level: _____%

Summer   ☐ Damp/Humid   ☐ Dry   ☐ Comfortable   Level: _____%

Winter   ☐ Damp/Humid   ☐ Dry   ☐ Comfortable   Level: _____%

     Does it fluctuate?   ☐ Daily   ☐ Weekly   ☐ Monthly   ☐ Seasonally

4. **LIGHT EXPOSURE**

Windows?   ☐ Yes   ☐ No;   If yes,   ☐ Covered   ☐ Uncovered

Artificial Light: ☐ Florescent   ☐ Incandescent

5. **SECURITY/DISASTER PROTECTION**

Alarms—does your storage area have:

Smoke/heat alarms   ☐ Yes   ☐ No

     If yes, are they connected to local fire department/dispatch?   ☐ Yes   ☐ No

Intrusion alarms   ☐ Yes   ☐ No

     If yes, are they connected to local police/sheriff?   ☐ Yes   ☐ No

Water alarms   ☐ Yes   ☐ No

     If yes, are they connected to local police/sheriff?   ☐ Yes   ☐ No

Fire suppression:

Sprinkler system   ☐ Yes   ☐ No   If yes, are they   ☐ water based   ☐ gas based

                                  If yes, are they   ☐ wet pipe   ☐ dry pipe

Do you have fire extinguishers in the area?   ☐ Yes   ☐ No

Security:

Doors locked?   ☐ Yes   ☐ No   Windows locked?   ☐ Yes   ☐ No

Who has access/keys to the area? (list below)

6. **GENERAL CONDITIONS OF STORAGE AREA**

What are the conditions of your storage area:

Overcrowded?   ☐ Yes   ☐ No   Cluttered?   ☐ Yes   ☐ No

Dusty?   ☐ Yes   ☐ No

Evidence of mold/rodent/insect damage?   ☐ Yes   ☐ No

Is other material stored in the same room as your archival records?   ☐ Yes   ☐ No

If yes, what is the other material?

☐ Paper supplies   ☐ Packing supplies   ☐ Holiday decorations

☐ Cleaning supplies   ☐ Security/backup copies   ☐ Trophies, banners, objects

☐ Other _____

7. **GENERAL CONDITIONS OF THE RECORDS**

Do the records suffer from any of the following?

☐ Faded   ☐ Mold damage   ☐ Surface dirt

☐ Insect/vermin damage

☐ Folded   ☐ Stains   ☐ Water damage

☐ Enclosures/attachments

☐ Brittle   ☐ Loose bindings   ☐ Use of mending tape

☐ Fasteners/rubber bands

How are the records stored? Indicate storage units used:

☐ Steel shelving   ☐ Wooden shelving   ☐ Wooden cabinets

☐ Metal filing cabinets   ☐ Metal flat files   ☐ Metal storage cabinets

☐ Other (please list)

      ☐ No storage units (piled on the floor or stacked on pallets)

      If you have shelving, is it?   ☐ wobbly   ☐ rusty   ☐ bent

Are your basic paper records stored in (mark all that apply):

☐ Records center cartons   ☐ Cardboard boxes   ☐ Alkaline boxes

☐ Hanging Folders   ☐ Original folders   ☐ Alkaline folders

How are your oversized materials (maps and plans) stored:

☐ Flat   ☐ Suspended   ☐ Rolled

How are your bound volumes stored?

☐ Upright   ☐ Leaning   ☐ Flat   ☐ On spine   ☐ Covered

8. **DO YOU HAVE A DISASTER PLAN FOR YOUR RECORDS?**

☐ Yes   ☐ No

Appendix S

Risk List

List the potential hazards within your facility that you have identified.

    1.
    2.
    3.
    4.
    5.
    6.
    7.
    8.
    9.
   10.

List the natural disasters that could potentially affect your historical records program.

    1.
    2.
    3.
    4.
    5.

List the man-made disasters that could potentially affect your facility.

    1.
    2.
    3.
    4.
    5.

List the collections that are the highest priority for rescue.

    1.
    2.
    3.
    4.
    5.
    6.

Appendix T

Disaster Plan Template

Institution: _____

Date of current revision: _____

Table of Contents

Disaster Response Plan

Immediate Emergency Response
In-House Emergency Team
Facilities: Locations of Emergency Systems
Emergency Services
Responsibilities for Collections Disaster Response and Recovery
Collection Salvage Priorities
Collection Salvage Supplies
Staff Emergency Procedures

Emergency Planning and Recovery Documents

Salvage of Water Damaged Materials
Salvage Glossary
Emergency History
Locations Where This Plan Is on File
Acknowledgments

Evacuation Plan and Maps [added by program]
Copy of Insurance Policy [added by program]
Copy of Disaster Recovery Services Contract [added by program]

This publication was adapted from a Library Disaster Plan that was prepared by The California Preservation Network and supported by the U.S. Institute of Museum and Library Services under the provisions of the Library Services and Technology Act, administered by the California State Library.

Immediate Emergency Response

- Assess your own safety and act accordingly.
- Elicit help from a coworker or another person in the area.
- Act to protect lives, then physical property.

Make the following phone calls in the order shown, based on the type of emergency.

First calls: Type of emergency:	Who to call:
Fire	Fire department
People hurt	Police
Water/electrical emergency	

Second calls: Type of emergency:	Who to call:
People hurt	
Building or equipment damage	
Collection damage	
Computer damage	

Third call: All emergencies:	Who to call:
All emergencies *during* working hours:	
All emergencies *after* working hours:	

In-House Emergency Team

	Name	Responsibility	Office Phone	Home/Cell Phone

Administrator(s): _____

_____

Disaster team

Leader: _____

Building

Maintenance:_____

Preservation

Resource: _____

Disaster team:

1. _____

2. _____

3. _____

4. _____

5. _____

Department head: _____

Department head: _____

Department head: _____

Department head: _____

Department head: _____

See *Responsibilities for Collections Disaster Response and Recovery* for additional instructions.

Facilities: Locations of Emergency Systems

Building: _____

List locations and attach floor plan (use letters to indicate locations on floor plan).

A. Main Utilities

1. Main water shut-off valve: _____

2. Sprinkler shut-off valve: _____

3. Main electrical cut-off switch: _____

4. Main gas shut-off: _____

5. Heating/cooling system controls: _____

B. Fire Suppression Systems (by room or area)

1. Fire extinguishers: _____

2. Fire hoses: _____

3. Other: _____

C. Water Detectors _____

D. Keys

Key boxes: _____

Individuals with master and/or special keys (attach list with names, titles, and keys in possession).

E. Fire Extinguishers (label by number according to type)

1. Type A—wood, paper, combustibles

2. Type B—gasoline, flammable liquid

3. Type C—electrical

4. Type ABC—combination

5. Halon

F. Fire Alarm Pull Boxes (use floor plan)

G. Smoke and Heat Detectors (use floor plan)

H. Radios

1. Transistor radios (for news): _____

2. Two-way radio (for communication): _____

I. Cell Phones

J. First Aid Kits

K. Public Address System

Emergency Services

Company/Service and Name of Contact   **Phone #**

Security: _____

Fire department: _____

Police/sheriff: _____

Ambulance: _____

Civil defense: _____

Other: _____

Maintenance/utilities

Janitorial service: _____

Plumber: _____

Electrician: _____

Locksmith: _____

Carpenter: _____

Gas company: _____

Electric company: _____

Water utility: _____

Insurance

Insurance company: _____

Agent/contact: _____

Policy number: _____
(Attach copy of policy)

Self-insured? _____ If yes, list contact: _____

Conservators/Specialists

Paper and books: _____

Photographs: _____

Computer Records: _____

Recovery Assistance

Preservation resource: _____

Preservation resource: _____

Disaster recovery network: _____

Local freezer companies: _____

_____

Disaster recovery service: _____

Account preestablished? _____   Account number: _____
(Attach copy of contract)

Services available: _____ Water recovery   _____ Freezer

                       _____ Vacuum freeze dryer   _____ Fire recovery

                       _____ Mold remediation   _____ Environmental control

Disaster Recovery Service: _____

_____

Account preestablished? _____   Account number: _____
(Attach copy of contract)

Services available: _____ Water recovery   _____ Freezer

                       _____ Vacuum freeze dryer   _____ Fire recovery

                       _____ Mold remediation   _____ Environmental control

Exterminator: _____

Other

Legal advisor: _____

Architect: _____

_____

_____

Responsibilities for Collections Disaster Response and Recovery

Identify and list at least one person and an alternate for each responsibility. Sometimes a group or committee will bear responsibility.

Assessment and Documentation	Name and Contact Information
Assesses and estimates the type and extent of the damage	
Contacts insurance company or risk management and fills out required forms	
Ensures proper documentation of damage (pictures, videos, etc.)	
Reviews collections priorities list and confirms or adjusts it based upon damage assessment	
Estimates number of personnel needed to complete the work and how long recovery up will take	
Evaluates and recommends if salvage can be done in house with staff, or if a consultant and/or disaster recovery service is needed	
Identifies locations for storing materials out of building if a commercial disaster recovery service is not used	
Formulates logistics for packing out and moving materials from the building if a commercial disaster recovery service is not used	
Records all major decisions and a chronology of events	

Communications	
Handles all public relations and the media	
Provides communication with workers	
Interacts with the organization to which the library reports	

Security	Name and Contact Information
Secures and protects the building's contents.	
Financial Issues	
Tracks the monetary impact of all decisions	
Arranges for funds necessary to buy supplies, equipment, food, etc., and to pay vendors	
Salvage Operations	
Deploys work teams	
Supervises work teams in proper packing and personal safety	
Keeps inventory control of items being removed or discarded	
Supplies and Equipment	
Responsible for ordering, delivery, and dispersal of sufficient quantities of the appropriate materials for packing out	

Responsible for ordering, delivery and dispersal of sufficient quantities of food, water, and other comfort items for the workers	
Building Issues	
All issues leading up to the eventual restoration of the building to normal	
Identification of locations for response and salvage activities	
Personnel Issues	
Provides communications with staff	
Responsible for union issues	
Handles health, safety, and comfort (physical and emotional) concerns	
Coordinates and monitors the use of volunteers	

Collection Salvage Priorities

1. Salvage Priorities—Collections

Listed below are those portions of the collection to which salvage priorities have been assigned.

Priority   Call Number   Location   Size of Collection   Special

Notes:

Collection Salvage Supplies

Basic response supplies should be immediately accessible.
Inventory supplies at least annually.

On-Site Location(s) or Off-Site Source   **Source Phone #**

___ Boxes _____

___ Clothes pins _____

___ Freezer or wax paper _____

___ Gloves, rubber or latex _____

___ Interfacing (pellon) _____

___ Masks, dust _____

___ Newsprint, blank _____

___ Note pads and clipboards _____

___ Nylon cord _____

___ Packing tape with dispensers _____

___ Plastic sheeting _____

___ Sponges _____

_____

Other Equipment and Supplies

On-Site Location(s) or Off-Site Source   **Source Phone #**

___ Aprons, smocks _____

___ Booktrucks, metal _____

___ Boots, rubber _____

___ Brooms _____

___ Buckets and trash cans, plastic _____

___ Camera (to document damage) _____

___ Caution tape _____

___ Dehumidifiers _____

Equipment and Supplies (continued)

On-Site Location(s) or Off-Site Source　　　Source Phone

___ Extension cords, grounded _____

___ Fans _____

___ Flashlights _____

___ Forklift _____

___ Generator, portable _____

___ Gloves, heavy duty _____

___ Hard hats _____

___ Lighting, portable _____

___ Mops, pails _____

___ Pallets _____

___ Paper towels _____

___ Plastic sheeting, heavy _____
(stored w/ scissors, tape)

___ Refrigerator trucks _____

___ Safety glasses _____

___ Sponges, industrial _____

___ Sump pump, portable _____

___ Tables, portable _____

___ Trash bags, plastic _____

___ Vacuum, wet _____

___ Water hoses _____

___ Water-proof clothing _____

___ Other: _____

_____

Staff Emergency Procedures

Employee Evacuation Procedure

In advance, each staff person and volunteer should:

1. Understand the evacuation plan.
2. Recognize the sound of the evacuation alarm.
3. Know at least two ways out of the building from your regular workspace.

When you hear the evacuation alarm or are told to evacuate the building:

1. Remain calm.
2. Immediately shut down any hazardous operations.
3. Leave quickly.
4. The highest ranking person who is physically present in each department is responsible for insuring all members of his/her department evacuate the area. In addition, employees should check that all others in the workspace are leaving as instructed.
5. As you exit, quickly check nearby rest rooms, copier rooms, closets, etc.
6. Accompany and help handicapped personnel, visitors, and any co-workers who appear to need direction or assistance.
7. Take with you: your car keys, purse, briefcase, and so forth. Do not attempt to take large or heavy objects.
8. Shut all doors behind you as you go. Closed doors can slow the spread of fire, smoke, and water.
9. Proceed as quickly as possible, but in an orderly manner. Do not push or shove. Hold handrails when you are walking on stairs.
10. Once out of the building, move away from the structure and meet at prearranged location for a head count.

Medical Emergencies: Staff

If a staff member or volunteer is seriously ill or injured:

1. Notify your supervisor immediately.
2. Render the minimum first aid necessary and decide what additional treatment is required (call fire department, paramedics, ambulance, other).
3. Do not attempt to move a person who has fallen and who appears to be in pain.
4. Avoid unnecessary conversation with or about the ill or injured person. You might add to the person's distress or fears, increasing the risk of medical shock. Limit your conversation to quiet reassurances.
5. After the person has been taken care of and the incident is over, remain available to help the supervisor with pertinent information for a medical report or, if applicable, a workers' compensation report.
6. Contact personnel department for any questions concerning workers' compensation.

Medical Emergencies: Visitor

When an employee or volunteer observes a visitor who appears to be ill or injured:

1. Notify your supervisor immediately.
2. Render the minimum first aid necessary and decide what additional treatment is required (call fire department, paramedics, ambulance, other).
3. Do not attempt to move a person who has fallen and who appears to be in pain.
4. Avoid unnecessary conversation with or about the ill or injured person or members of his/her party. You might add to the person's distress or fears, increasing the risk of medical shock. Limit your conversation to quiet reassurances.
5. Do not discuss the possible causes of an accident or any conditions that may have contributed to the cause.
6. Under no circumstances should an employee or volunteer discuss any insurance information with members of the public.
7. After the person has been taken care of and the incident is over, remain available to help the supervisor with pertinent information for a medical report.

Phone Threat, Mail Threat, and Suspicious Object

If you receive a *telephone threat:*

1. Remain calm.
2. Listen carefully. Be polite and show interest. Try to keep the caller talking so you can gather more information.
3. If possible, signal a colleague to inform administration for you or call yourself as soon as the caller hangs up.
4. Call the police.
5. Promptly complete a telephone threat report, writing down as many details as you can remember. This information will be needed by security and police interviewers.
6. Do not discuss the threat with other staff.
7. If evacuation is ordered, go to a designated area (see map).

If you receive a *written threat* or a *suspicious package* or if you find a *suspicious object* anywhere on the premises:

1. Keep anyone from handling it or going near it.
2. Notify your supervisor immediately.
3. Call the police.
4. Promptly write down everything you can remember about receiving the letter or package, or finding the object. This information will be needed by security and police interviewers.
5. Remain calm. Do not discuss the threat with other staff members.
6. If evacuation is ordered, go to a designated area (see map).

Fire

If a fire occurs in your area:

1. Remain calm.
2. Call the fire department.
3. If the fire is small, attempt to put it out with a fire extinguisher. Do not jeopardize your personal safety.
4. Never allow the fire to come between you and an exit.
5. Disconnect electrical equipment that is on fire if it is safe to do so (pull the plug or throw the circuit breaker).
6. Notify your supervisor of the location and extent of the fire.
7. Evacuate your area if you are unable to put out the fire. Close doors and windows behind you to confine the fire. Go to a designated area (see map).
8. Do not break windows. Oxygen feeds a fire.
9. Do not open hot doors. Before opening any door, touch near the top. If the door is hot or if smoke is visible, do not open the door.
10. Do not use elevators.
11. Do not attempt to save possessions at the risk of personal injury.
12. Do not return to the area until cleared by emergency personnel.

All fires, no matter how small, must be reported to a supervisor.

Toxic Events, Chemical Spills and Fires

If a *chemical spill* occurs within the building:

1. If toxic chemicals come in contact with your skin, immediately flush the affected area with clear water. Use chemical shower if available.
2. Notify your supervisor of the extent and location of the spill.
3. If there is any possible danger, evacuate your area.

If a *chemical fire* occurs within the building:

1. Remain calm.
2. Call the fire department.
3. If the fire is small, attempt to put it out with a fire extinguisher. Do not jeopardize your personal safety.
4. Never allow the fire to come between you and an exit.
5. Notify your supervisor of the location and extent of the fire.
6. Evacuate your area if you are unable to put out the fire. Close doors and windows behind you to confine the fire. Go to a designated area (see map).
7. Do not break windows. Oxygen feeds a fire.
8. Do not attempt to save possessions at the risk of personal injury.
9. Do not return to the area until cleared by emergency personnel.

All chemical spills and fires, no matter how small, must be reported to a supervisor.

In the event of a *toxic spill* outside of the building, most likely caused by a train derailment or tanker truck accident:

1. Notify your supervisor immediately.
2. Call police and fire departments, giving location of spill.
3. Evacuate the building only if instructed to do so.

Earthquakes

In the event of an earthquake:

1. Remain calm.
2. Stay in the building. Take shelter within a doorway, in a narrow corridor, or under a heavy table, desk, or bench.
3. Stay away from windows, mirrors, overhead fixtures, filing cabinets, bookcases, and electrical equipment
4. Do not attempt to leave the building, as exit stairwells may have collapsed or be jammed with people.

After the earthquake has stopped:

1. Remain alert for aftershocks.
2. Listen to local radio stations for instructions.
3. Assist those who have been trapped or injured by falling debris, glass, and so forth. Do not move seriously injured persons unless they are in obvious, immediate danger (of fire, building collapse, etc.).
4. Evacuate the building if safe to do so. Do not reenter until the building has been declared structurally sound.
5. Check for broken water pipes or shorting electrical circuits. Do not use a match, candle, or lighter to find your way, since there may be flammable gas in the air. Shut off utilities at main valves or meter boxes. Turn off appliances.
6. Do not use the telephone, except in a real emergency. The lines should be kept free for emergency rescue operations.
7. Ensure that sewage lines are intact before running water or flushing toilets.

Explosion

1. Remain calm.
2. Be prepared for possible further explosions.
3. Crawl under a table or desk.
4. Stay away from windows, mirrors, overhead fixtures, filing cabinets, bookcases, and electrical equipment.
5. Be guided by the administration. If evacuation is ordered, go to a designated area (see map).
6. Do not move seriously injured persons unless they are in obvious, immediate danger (of fire, building collapse, etc.).
7. Open doors carefully. Watch for falling objects.
8. Do not use elevators.
9. Do not use matches or lighters.
10. Avoid using telephones.
11. Do not spread rumors.

Power Outage

If a power outage occurs:

1. Remain calm.
2. Provide assistance to visitors and staff in your immediate area.
3. If you are in an unlighted area, proceed cautiously to an area that has emergency lights.
4. If you are in an elevator, stay calm. Use the intercom or the emergency button to notify building security.
5. If instructed to evacuate, go to a designated area (see map).
6. Secure the building from vandalism, intrusion, and fire.

Flooding and Water Damage

If a water leak or flooding occurs:

1. Remain calm.
2. Notify building maintenance <u>and</u> your supervisor. Give the exact location and severity of the leak. Indicate whether any part of the collections is involved or is in imminent danger.
3. Do not walk in standing water that may have contact with wiring and may be electrified. If there are electrical appliances or electrical outlets near the leak, use extreme caution. If there is any possible danger, evacuate the area.
4. If you know the source of the water and are confident of your ability to stop it (unclog the drain, turn off the water, etc.), do so cautiously.
5. Be prepared to help as directed in protecting collection materials that are in jeopardy. Take only those steps needed to avoid or reduce immediate water damage: cover shelf ranges with plastic sheeting; carefully move materials out of the emergency area. Do not remove already wet books from shelves.

RECOVERY AND SALVAGE OF MATERIALS

Salvage of Water Damaged Collections

Books: Cloth or Paper Covers

Priority

Freeze or dry within forty-eight hours. *Coated paper* must not be allowed to air dry in a clump or it will permanently block together. If slightly damp and the pages are separable, air dry interleaved pages before items have an opportunity to dry. If saturated, coated paper must by frozen as soon as possible for subsequent vacuum freeze-drying.

Handling Precautions

Do not move items until a place has been prepared to receive them. Do not open or close books or separate covers. Oversized books need to be fully supported, it may only be possible to move one at a time.

Preparation for Drying

Closed books that are muddy should be rinsed before freezing. If air drying is not possible, books should be frozen within forty-eight hours. Separate with freezer paper, pack spine down in milk crates, plastic boxes, or cardboard boxes lined with plastic sheeting.

    Coated paper requires that each and every page be interleaved with a nonstick material such as silicone release paper, Holytex, or wax paper. If the leaves cannot be separated without further damage, the book cannot be air dried successfully and must be prepared for vacuum freeze-drying.

Drying Methods

Air drying is suitable for small quantities for books (less than 100 volumes) that are not thoroughly soaked. Requires space in an area away from the disaster to spread the books out. Books are stood upright and gently fanned open to dry. Keep air moving at all times using fans. Direct fans into the air and away from the drying volumes. Use dehumidifiers as needed to maintain humidity at or below 50 percent RH.

    Oversize volumes must lay flat and should be turned when the blotter is changed. Pages should be interleaved with sheets of uninked newsprint or blotting paper that is changed as it becomes saturated.

    Freeze drying (not vacuum thermal drying) is suitable for large quantities of books and books that are very wet. Pack as described above and ship to drying facility.

    Vacuum freeze drying is suitable for large quantities of books. Wet *coated* paper can only be dried by this method. Pack as described above and ship to drying facility. Pack carefully, as volumes packed with distortions will retain that distortion permanently after vacuum freeze-drying.

Books: Leather or Vellum Covers

Priority

Freeze as soon as possible; vellum will distort and disintegrate in water.

Handling Precautions

Do not move items until a place has been prepared to receive them. Do not open or close books or separate covers. Oversized books need to be fully supported; it may only be possible to move one at a time.

Preparation for Drying

Closed books that are muddy should be rinsed before freezing. If air drying is not possible, books should be frozen, preferably blast frozen, as soon as possible. Separate with freezer paper, pack spine down in milk crates, plastic boxes, or cardboard boxes lined with plastic sheeting.

Drying Procedure

Freeze-drying is the preferred method. Books should be separated with freezer paper and packed spine down in milk crates, plastic boxes, or cardboard boxes lined with plastic sheeting.

Air drying may be used for items that are not very wet. This requires space in an area away from the disaster to spread the books out. Books are stood upright and gently fanned open to dry.

Coated paper requires that each and every page be interleaved with a nonstick materials, such as silicone release paper, Holytex, or wax paper.

Oversize volumes must lay flat and should be turned when the blotter is changed. Pages should be interleaved with sheets of uninked newsprint or blotting paper that is changed as it becomes saturated.

Keep the air moving at all times using fans. Direct fans into the air and away from the drying records. Use dehumidifiers as needed to maintain humidity at or below 50 percent RH.

Paper: Uncoated

Priority

Air dry or freeze within forty-eight hours. Records with water-soluble inks should be frozen immediately to arrest the migration of moisture that will feather and blur inks. Records that show signs of previous bacterial growth should also be frozen immediately if they cannot be air dried.

Handling Precautions

Paper is very weak when wet and can easily tear if unsupported while handling.

Preparations for Drying

Pack flat sheets in bread trays, flat boxes, or on plywood sheets covered with polyethylene. Bundle rolled items loosely and place horizontally in boxes lined with a release layer. Remove drawers from flat files; ship and freeze stacked with 1" × 2" strips of wood between each drawer. Framed or matted items must be removed from frames and mats prior to air or freeze-drying. See section *Paper: Framed or Matted, Preparation for Drying*.

　　Air drying—secure a clean, dry environment where the temperature and humidity are as low as possible. Cover tables, floors, or other flat surfaces with sheets for blotter or uninked newsprint.

　　Freezing—Work space and work surfaces and the following equipment: milk crates and/or cardboard boxes, bread trays, sheets of plywood, and rolls/sheets of freezer or waxed paper.

Drying Methods

Air drying—This technique is most suitable for small numbers of records that are damp or water-damaged around the edges. Keep the air moving at all times using fans. Direct fans into the air and away from the drying records. Use dehumidifiers as needed to maintain 50 percent RH.

　　Damp material—Single sheets or small groups of records are to be laid out on paper-covered flat surfaces. If small clumps of records are fanned out to dry, they should be turned at regular intervals to encourage evaporation from both sides. As a last resort to maximize space utilization, clothesline may be strung for the records to be laid across.

　　If an item exhibits water-soluble media, allow it to dry face up. Do not attempt to blot the item since blotting may result in offsetting water-soluble components. Wet blotter or newsprint should be changed and removed from the drying area.

　　Wet material—When separating saturated paper, use extra caution to support large sheets. If sheets are contained in flat files, standing water should be sponged out first. If items are in L-sleeves, the polyester must be removed to allow drying. Cut the two sealed edges of the film in the border between the item and the seal. Roll back the top piece of polyester in a diagonal direction. If there are any apparent problems with the paper support or media, stop and seek the assistance of a conservator. Support can be given to single sheets by placing a piece of polyester film on top of the document. Rub the film gently and then slowly lift the film while at the same time peeling off the top sheet in a diagonal direction. Lay the sheet flat; as it dries, it will separate from the surface of the film.

　　Freezing—This option is best if there are large quantities or if the water damage is extensive. Place manuscript boxes in milk crates or cardboard boxes. If time permits, interleave each manuscript box with freezer or waxed paper. If the boxes have been discarded, interleave every two inches of foldered material with freezer or waxed paper.

　　Do not freeze framed items. Remove frame assemblage before freezing. See section *Paper: Framed or Matted, Preparation for Drying*.

Paper: Coated

(Including linen drawings [drafting cloth] and paper with sensitized coatings such as Thermofax and fax copies)

Priority

Coated paper must not be allowed to air dry in a clump or it will permanently block together. If saturated, freeze within six hours for subsequent vacuum freezing-drying. If damp, separate and air dry before items have an opportunity to dry.

Handling Precautions

Physical manipulation should be kept to a minimum to avoid disruption of the water-soluble coating and media, which may cause obliteration of the information.

Preparation for Drying

Air drying—Secure a clean, dry environment where the temperature and humidity are as low as possible. Equipment needed: flat surfaces for drying; fans and extension cords; dehumidifier; moisture meter; sheets of polyester film, nonstick interleaving material such as freezer, waxed, or silicone release paper; or polyester nonwoven fabric.

Freezing—Equipment needed: milk crates; cardboard boxes for large items; large flat supports, such as bread trays or pieces for plywood; freezer, waxed, or silicone release paper; or polyester nonwoven fabric.

Remove drawers from flat files; ship and freeze stacked with 1" × 2" strips of wood between each drawer. Framed or matted items must be removed from frames and mats prior to drying. See section *Paper: Framed or Matted, Preparation for Drying*.

Drying Methods

Air drying—This technique is most suitable for small numbers of records that are damp or water-damaged around the edges. Coated paper requires that each and every page be interleaved with a nonstick material such as silicone release paper, Holytex, pellon, or wax paper.

Damp material—Lay single sheets or small groups of interleaved records on paper covered flat surfaces. If small clumps of records are fanned out to dry, they should be turned at regular intervals to encourage evaporation from both sides.

If an item exhibits water-soluble media, allow it to dry face up. Do not attempt to blot the item since blotting may result in offsetting water-soluble components. Wet blotter or uninked newsprint should be changed and removed from the drying area.

Wet material—When separating saturated paper, use extra caution to support large sheets. If sheets are contained in flat files, standing water should be sponged out first. If items are in L-sleeves, the polyester must be removed to allow drying. Cut the two sealed edges of the film between the item and the seal. Roll back the top piece of polyester in a diagonal direction. If there are any apparent problems with the paper support or media, *stop* and seek the assistance of a conservator. Support can be given to single sheets by placing a piece of polyester film on top of the document. Rub the film gently and then slowly lift the film while at the same time peeling off the top sheet in a diagonal direction. Lay the sheet flat; as it dries, it will separate from the surface of the film.

Keep the air moving at all times using fans. Direct fans into the air and away from the drying records. Use dehumidifiers as needed to maintain humidity at or below 50 percent RH.

Freezing—Freezing is best if there are large quantities or if the water damage is extensive. Place manuscript boxes in milk crates or cardboard boxes. If time permits, interleave each manuscript box with freezer or waxed paper. If the boxes have been discarded, interleave every two inches of foldered material with freezer or waxed paper.

Specify vacuum *freeze-drying* for coated paper and linen drawings; do not use vacuum thermal drying.

Pack flat sheets in bread trays, flat boxes, or on plywood sheets covered with polyethylene. Bundled rolled items loosely and place horizontally in boxes lined with a release layer.

Do not freeze framed items. Remove frame assemblage before freezing. See section *Paper: Framed or Matted, Preparation for Drying*.

Paper: Framed or Matted, Preparation for Drying

Priority

Wet paper must be frozen or air dried within forty-eight hours. Framed and matted items must be disassembled prior to air drying or freezing.

Handling Precautions

Caution must be exercised so as to not puncture or tear the wet paper artifact in the process of removing the frame, glazing, and mounting materials.

Preparation for Drying

Place frame face down on a smooth, flat surface covered with blotter paper or plastic bubble pack. Carefully remove dust seal and hardware (place these metal pieces in container so that they do not come in contact with the wet paper and inadvertently cause damage). Check if the paper object is adhered to rabbet of frame by gently pushing up on the glazing to see that the assemblage will release without resistance. Place a piece of board (mat board, Masonite, or Plexiglas) over the back of the frame with all contents still in place. Using two hands, invert frame assemblage as that the glass and image are facing up. Lift off the frame then lift off the glass.

When the paper is in direct contact with the glass, carefully remove them together and lay face down on a flat surface. Consult a conservator if the paper is sticking to the glazing.

If the glass is broken, the pieces may be held together with tape applied lightly over the breaks. The frame may then be laid face down and the paper removed from the back. If pieces of glass has dropped behind the remaining glass, hold the frame in a vertical position to remove the mat and/or paper.

To remove the item from its mat, place the image facing up. Lift window mat board carefully and detach paper object from back mat by carefully cutting hinges. If the object is attached firmly and directly to mat or backing board, do not attempt to remove. Proceed to air dry paper object as recommended in sections *Paper: Uncoated* or *Paper: Coated*, as appropriate.

If difficulty is encountered at any point, consult a conservator for assistance.

Microfiche

Priority

Freeze or dry within seventy-two hours.

Handling Precautions

Do not move items until a place has been prepared to receive them and you have been instructed to do so. If the fiche cannot be air dried immediately, keep them wet inside a container lined with garbage bags until they are frozen.

Drying Methods

Freeze if arrangements cannot be made to air dry the fiche quickly. Fiche should be removed from the paper jackets to dry. Jackets should be retained to preserve any information printed on them, but this information should be transferred to new jackets once the fiche is dry and ready to be stored again. The best air drying method is to clip the fiche to clotheslines with rust-proof clips.

Fiche has been successfully vacuum freeze-dried, though freeze-drying of photographic materials is not widely recommended. If dealing with large quantities of fiche, this option should be investigated.

Microfilm and Motion Picture Film

Priority

Rewash and dry within seventy-two hours. Wet film must be kept wet until it can be reprocessed.

Handling Precautions

Wipe outside of film cans or boxes before opening. Cans that are wet on the outside may contain dry film that should be separated from wet material. Do no remove wet microfilm from boxes; hold cartons together with rubber bands. Dry film in damp or wet boxes should be removed and kept together with the box. Do not move items until a place has been prepared to receive them.

Packing Methods

Wet microfilm in plastic trays in the microfilm vault should be filled with water until reprocessed. Pack wet motion picture film in a container lined with plastic garbage bags.

Preparation for Drying

Contact a microfilm lab or film processor to rewash.

Drying Methods

Contact a disaster and service or microfilm lab to rewash and dry film. The manufacturer or other professional processor should be contacted to rewash and dry motion picture film.

Magnetic Media: Computer Diskettes

Priority

Prolonged storage in water causes leaching of chemicals from the support. *If a back-up copy is available, it is better to discard the water-soaked original.*

Handling Precautions

Store diskettes upright without crowding, in cool, distilled water until you are ready to attempt data recovery. Exposure to water should not extend beyond seventy-two hours. If disks cannot be dried and copied within three days, the disks should be placed wet in plastic bags and frozen until drying and data recovery is possible.

Preparation for Drying

3.5-inch disks—Pack wet disks in plastic bags and ship overnight to a computer media recovery service vendor for data recovery. Do not dry disks first; dried impurities can etch magnetic coating.

    5.25-inch disks—Remove the disk by cutting with scissors along the edge of the jacket. Carefully remove the diskette and agitate the exposed disks in multiple baths of cool de-ionized water or distilled water to remove all visible dirt.

Drying Methods

3.5-inch disks—It is safest to send disks to a professional data recovery vendor for data recovery. *Damage to your hardware could result.* Gently blot surface with lint-free cloth or lay on clean cloth to air dry.

    5.25-inch disks—Dry with lint-free toweling or cheese cloth.

Data Recovery

In order to ensure the preservation of data on disks that have been wet, it is prudent to copy it to a new disk. Insert the disk that has been dried into an empty jacket made by removing a new disk. The water damaged disk, which has been placed in the new jacket, is inserted into a disk drive. Copy and verify that the information has transferred, then discard the damaged disk. You need only prepare one new jacket for each five to ten disks since the same jacket can be reused several times. Most diskettes can be salvaged unless the diskette itself if magnetically damaged or warped. If copying is not successful, consult a computer recovery service.

Magnetic Media: Video and Audio Cassettes

Priority

Air dry within seventy-two hours.

Handling Precautions

Pack cassettes vertically into plastic crates or cardboard boxes.

Preparation for Drying

Often the casings will keep tape clean and dry. If the tape is damaged, disassemble the case and remove tape. Rinse dirty tapes, still wound on reel, in clean deionized or distilled water.

Drying Methods

Air dry by supporting the reels vertically or by laying the reels on sheets of clean blotter. Leave tapes next to their original cases. Use fans to keep air moving without blowing directly on the items.

Use dehumidifiers as needed to maintain humidity at or below 50 percent RH.

Additional Steps

Once dry, the tapes can be assessed for further cleaning and duplication by a specialized recovery service.

Magnetic Media: Reel-To-Reel Tapes

Priority

Air dry within seventy-two hours.

Handling Precautions

Pack vertically into plastic crates or cardboard cartons. Don't put heavy weight or pressure on the sides of the reels.

Preparation for Drying

Often contamination by water and other substances is mainly confined to the outermost layers of tape. Do not unwind tapes or remove from the reel. In these cases, wash the exposed edges with deionized water or with distilled water.

Drying Methods

Air dry by supporting the reels vertically or by laying the reels on sheets of clean blotter. Leave the tapes to dry next to their original boxes. Use fans to keep air moving without blowing directly on the items.

Use portable dehumidifiers to slowly remove moisture from the area/objects. Bring relative humidity down to 50 percent.

Additional Steps

Once dry, the tapes can be assessed for further cleaning and duplication. This procedure is done by specialized professional vendors.

Compact Discs and CD-ROMs

Priority

Immediately air dry discs. Dry paper enclosures within forty-eight hours.

Handling Precautions

Do not scratch surfaces.

Preparations for Drying

Remove discs from cases. Rinse discs with distilled water. Do not rub the discs because dirt could scratch. If necessary, blot, do not rub, with a soft lint-free cloth.

Drying Methods

Case and paper enclosures may be freeze dried. Do not freeze dry the discs. Air dry vertically in a rack.

Record Albums (Vinyl, Shellac, and Acetate Disks)

Priority

Dry within forty-eight hours. Freezing is untested; if there are not options, freeze at above 0°F.

Handling Precautions

Hold disks by their edges. Avoid shocks.

Packing Methods

Pack vertically in padded plastic crates.

Preparation for Drying

Remove the disks from their sleeves and jackets. If labels have separated, mark label information on the center of the disk with a grease pencil and keep track of the label.

Separate shellac, acetate, and vinyl disks. If dirt has been deposited on the disks, they may be washed in a 1 percent solution of Kodak Photo Flo in distilled water. Each disk media should be washed in its own container (i.e., do not wash shellac disks with vinyl disks). Rinse each disk thoroughly with distilled water.

Drying Methods

Jackets, sleeves, and labels may be air dried like other paper materials. See sections *Paper: Coated* and *Paper: Uncoated*, as appropriate.

Air dry disks vertically in a rack that allows for the free circulation of air. Dry slowly at ambient temperature away from direct heat and sources of dust.

Photographs and Transparencies

Priority

Salvage priorities. Within twenty-four hours: 1) ambrotypes, daguerreotypes, tintypes, silver gelatin glass plate negatives, wet collodion glass plate negatives; *Within forty-eight hours*: 2) color prints and film, silver gelatin prints and negatives; 3) albumen prints and salted paper prints. Cyanotypes in alkaline water must be dried as soon as possible; in acidic water they drop to priority 3.

Handling Precautions

Do not touch emulsion, hold by the edges or margins. Always lay with emulsion side up.

Preparations for Drying

Secure a clean area to work, free from particulates. Keep the photos and/or negatives in containers of fresh cold water until they are either air dried or frozen. *If allowed to partially dry in contact with each other, they will stick together.* To maintain wetness until the drying process can take place, pack photos inside plastic garbage pails or boxes lined with garbage bags.

Equipment and materials needed: plastic trays, cold water, clothesline, clothespins and/or photo clips, soft bristle brushes, Kodak Photo Flo Solution, Holytex and clean photographic blotter paper, Falcon squeegee and drying racks for resin-coated prints; and Salthill dryer for recent fiver-based prints.

Carefully remove prints and film positives and negatives from the enclosures. Keep the enclosure or the file number with each film item as it contains vital information to maintain intellectual control.

Daguerreotypes, glass, and metal-based collodion emulsions, such as ambrotypes, tintypes, wet collodion glass plates (which include some negatives, lantern slides, and stereo graphs on glass):

Cased photographs—Carefully open the case and place the photograph face up on blotters. Do not attempt to disassemble the components, remove debris, or wash the photograph. If the affected photo has water or debris trapped within the assemblage, contact a conservator for proper disassembly.

Uncased images—Air dry side up on clean absorbent blotters. Remove and retain cover slips from glass lantern slides if present. Do not attempt to clean debris or wash these images. These procedures should only be performed by a conservator.

Black and white prints—Place the prints in a tray and fill with cold water. Agitate the tray and change the water several times. After fifteen minutes, drain the water and air dry. Reduce washing time for deteriorated and card mounted prints.

Color prints—Use the same procedure as for black and white prints but with decreased washing time: ten minutes. Reduce washing time further for deteriorated prints.

Negatives (glass and film)–silver gelatin—Soak the films in clean, cold water for thirty minutes. If there are particulates on the film, rinse for ten to fifteen minutes while gently brushing surfaces under water with a soft bristle brush, then continue washing for an additional fifteen minutes. Rinse with Kodak Photo Flo Solution.

Glass plate negatives: collodion—Do not wash or expose plates to further moisture; if any image remains, air dry immediately, emulsion side up.

Kodachrome transparencies—Wash as described above for negatives C silver gelatin.

Ektachrome transparencies—Wash as described above for negatives C silver gelatin, omitting the Photo Flo, then dry. Consult a photo conservator after transparencies have dried, as some may require stabilization.

Color negatives—Wash as described above for negatives C silver gelatin, omitting Photo Flo, then dry. Consult a photo conservator after negatives have dried, as some may require stabilization.

Drying Method

Order of preference: 1) air dry, 2) freeze/thaw and air dry, 3) vacuum freeze dry. *Do not vacuum thermal dry or freeze dry.*

Prints and films—Dry film by hanging on a clothesline at room temperature in a dust free area. Lay glass plates and prints emulsion side up on a clean absorbent blotter.

Photo Albums—To air dry, place sheets of blotter covered with Holytex between each leaf. Change the blotter paper as it becomes damp or wet. If the binding structure is no longer intact or the album can be dismantled, separate the leaves and air dry on clean blotters covered with Holytex; periodically turn from recto to verso to promote even drying. If drying cannot proceed immediately, wrap the volume in plastic and freeze. The volume can then be thawed and air dried at a later date.

Keep the air moving at all times using fans. Direct fans into the air and away from the drying records. Use dehumidifiers as needed to maintain humidity at or below 50 percent RH.

If air drying is not possible due to media solubility or unacceptable disruption to the structural integrity of the volume, vacuum freeze-drying is recommended.

If difficulty is encountered, consult a conservator for assistance.

Scrapbooks

Priority

Freeze immediately.

Handling Precautions

Do not move items until a place has been prepared to receive them. Large scrapbooks should be supported with boards.

Preparation for Drying

If the scrapbook is not boxed and the binding is no longer intact, wrap in freezer paper. Freeze as quickly as possible, using a blast freezer if available.

    Freezing—Equipment needed: milk crates; cardboard boxes for large items; large flat supports such as bread trays or pieces of plywood; freezer, waxed, or silicone release paper, or polyester non-woven fabric.

    Air drying—Secure a clean, dry environment where the temperature and humidity are as low as possible. Equipment needed: flat surfaces for drying; fans and extension cords; dehumidifier; moisture meter; sheets of polyester film; nonstick interleaving materials, such as freezer, waxed, or silicone release paper; or polyester nonwoven fabric.

Drying Methods

Vacuum freeze-drying is the preferred method, although this should not be used for photographs. See section *Photographs and Transparencies*. If the book is to be vacuum freeze-dried, the photographs should first be removed. Wrapped scrapbooks should be packed laying flat in shallow boxes or trays lined with freezer paper.

    Air drying may be used for small quantities which are only damp or water-damaged around the edges. The books should not have large amounts of coated paper or soluble adhesives.

    Pages should be interleaved with uninked newsprint or blotter and the books placed on tables. The interleaving and page opening should be changes regularly and often to speed the drying. If the binding has failed, it may be advisable to separate the pages and lay them out individually to dry. Care must be taken to maintain page order.

    Keep the air moving at all times using fans. Direct fans into the air and away from the items. Use dehumidifiers as needed to maintain humidity at or below 50 percent RH.

Vellum and Parchment: Bindings and Documents

Priority

If the text block of the book is wet, priority should be placed on getting it dry over saving the binding, unless the binding has been assigned the higher priority by a curator. If the item has gotten wet, successful salvage will probably not be possible, so other high priority items should be treated first.

Handling Precautions

Do not move items until a place has been prepared to received them.

Drying Procedures

Drying must take place slowly and be carefully controlled. The item needs to be restrained as it dries for it to retain its shape.

Documents that have only been exposed to high humidity should be interleaved with dry blotters and placed under weights. Blotters should be checked after about a half hour to see if they need to be exchanged for drier ones.

For drying of slightly damp documents, the edges should be clipped and pinned or at least weighted. As the item dries, it should be checked at least every fifteen minutes and the tension adjusted as necessary. Once the item is almost dry, the clips or weights can be removed and the item should be placed between blotters and weighted overall to complete drying.

Vellum bindings need to be watched carefully. Blotters should be placed between the covers and text, and on the outside of the cover. The book should then be weighted or put in a press. As the binding dries, it may shrink and cause damage to the text block, in which case it should be carefully removed before more damage is caused.

Freeze-drying can be used as a last resort for drying vellum and parchment, but the limited experience with these procedures shows there will be much distortion and change in the object.

Leather and Rawhide

Priority

Begin drying within forty-eight hours to prevent mold growth. Leather with the condition known as "red rot" will be irreversibly stiffened and darkened by exposure to water if not treated quickly.

Handling Precautions

Wet leather may be fragile; leather with red rot, or which is torn, will require support to transport safely. Move items only after a place has been prepared to receive them.

Packing Method

Wrap items with freezer paper or plastic sheeting to prevent red-rotted leather from coming in contact with and soiling adjacent items and to keep it from drying before it can be treated. Support complex-shaped objects with uninked newsprint or other absorbent material.

Preparation for Drying

Rinse or sponge with clear water to remove mud or dirt before drying. Be careful in rinsing red-rotted or painted / gilded surfaces. Keep red-rotted leather damp if it is still in that condition, until proper consolidation can be done.

Drying Procedure

Some leather was intended to be flexible (e.g., much native tanned "buckskin," harness leather, and some rawhide) and will need to be manipulated during drying in order to retain its flexibility. Other leather was either not intended to flex (e.g., shields, fire buckets) or no longer needs to be flexible and may be padded out and allowed to dry slowly.

Sponges, clean towels, paper towels, or uninked newsprint may be used to absorb excess moisture. Pad out to correct shape using uninked newsprint or other absorbent material. Change padding material as it becomes saturated.

Air dry, using fans to keep air moving without blowing directly on the pieces. Raise items off the floor on trestles, 2 × 4 lumber, or screens to allow air to circulate on all sides.

Use portable dehumidifiers to slowly remove moisture from the area and objects. Bring the relative humidity down to as close to 50 percent as is practical. Check daily for mold.

Paintings: On Canvas

Priority

Begin drying within forty-eight hours to prevent mold growth.

Handling Precautions

Move items only after a place has been prepared to receive them. If the frame is unstable, remove from painting, pad corners with corrugated cardboard, bubble wrap, or unused newsprint and transport to area dealing with wood objects.

Packing Method

Pad corners of frame or painting with corrugated cardboard, bubble wrap, or newsprint. Transport paintings vertically; stand upright with corrugated cardboard between paintings so painted surfaces do not touch another painted or any rough surface.

Preparation for Drying

Remove painting from frame. Contact a paintings conservator to discuss. See section *Paper: Framed or Matted, Preparation for Drying*.

Drying Procedure

Prepare a horizontal bed of blotter paper and unused newsprint, equal in thickness to the paint layer, with top-most layer of strong clean tissue. Lay painting, still on stretcher/strainer, face down on this surface. Remove any remaining backing or labels from the painting to expose wet canvas. Retain and tag all associated labels, parts and/or components that are removed or detached from the painting or frame.

Place cut-to-fit blotters or unused newsprint against this back and apply a slight amount of pressure so the blotter makes good contact with the entire exposed canvas surface. Repeatedly change backing blotter, being careful not to create impressions in the canvas. *Do not change facing materials*.

When dry to the touch, remove backing blotter and pick up painting. If front facing tissue is still attached to painting front, do not attempt to remove it, since it will hold the painting surface together until it can be consolidated by a conservator.

Consult with a paintings conservator for any questions or problems and all circumstances not adequately covered by the above instructions.

Use fans to keep air moving in the room without blowing directly on the paintings. Use portable dehumidifiers to *slowly* remove moisture from the area/objects. Bring relative humidity down to 50 percent.

Wood

Priority

Begin drying within forty-eight hours to prevent mold growth. Polychromed objects require immediate attention; notify a conservator.

Handling Precautions

Move items only after a place has been prepared to receive them. Lift from the bottom of an object; tables from the apron; chairs by the seat rails, not by the arms, stretchers, slats, headpiece, or crest rails; trunks from the bottom; and so forth.

Packing Methods

Partially wetted objects can be packed with dry blotting materials such as uninked newsprint or acid free blotters to remove as much moisture as possible. Thoroughly wetted, unpainted objects should be wrapped with blotting materials, then wrapped in polyethylene sheeting to retain as much moisture as possible, since fast drying will cause irreversible damage.

Preparation for Drying

Rinse or sponge with clear water to remove mud or dirt before drying. Be careful not to wipe or scour as grit will damage remaining finish. Use a soft bristle brush to clean carvings and crevices. If mud has dried, dampen with a sponge and remove with a wooded spatula; rinse. Remove wet contents and paper liners from drawers and shelves.

Drying Procedure

Absorb excess moisture with sponges, clean towels, paper towels, or uninked newsprint. Blot, do not wipe, to avoid scratching the surface.

Air dry, using fans to keep air moving without blowing directly on the pieces. Tent the objects with polyethylene sheeting to slow the drying. Raise items off the floor on trestle or 2 × 4 lumber to allow air to circulate on all sides. Open doors and drawers *slightly* to allow air to circulate inside the items.

Use portable dehumidifiers to slowly remove moisture from the area and objects. Drying quickly will cause warping and cracking. Bring relative humidity down to 50–55 percent.

Inorganics: Ceramics, Glass, Metals, Stone (Decorative/Historic)

Priority

These materials can be dealt with last since they generally will suffer little damage from short term exposure to water.

Handling Precautions

Move items only after a place has been prepared to receive them.

Packing Method

Varies with the fragility of the material; water/wetness has no bearing.

Preparation for Drying

Rinse or sponge with clear water to remove mud or dirt before drying.

Drying Procedure

Sponges, clean towels, paper towels, or unused newsprint may be used to absorb excess moisture. Exchange wet for dry blotting material at least daily until items are dry. Check daily for mold growth.

Air dry, using fans to keep air moving without blowing directly on the pieces. Raise items off the floor on trestles or 2 × 4 lumber to allow air to circulate underneath.

Metal objects can be dried with moderate heat (90–100°F in an oven or using a heater or hair dryer).

Use portable dehumidifiers to *slowly* remove moisture from the area/objects. Bring relative humidity down to 50 percent.

Salvage Glossary

AIR DRYING—Use a cool, low-humidity area with good air circulation. Place absorbent material (see interleaving) under objects; replace as it becomes wet. If possible, air-dry materials on plastic racks (e.g., commercial bread trays or rust-proof screens) to allow more evaporation. Exposure to light may reduce the threat of mold. Bright sunlight can cause fading.

INTERLEAVING—Interleaving will keep items from sticking together and prevent dye transfer. Blotter paper, uninked newsprint, or paper towels may be used, except in cases when waxed paper, pellon or freezer paper is called for.

FREEZING—If objects cannot be dried within forty-eight hours, freeze them until action can be taken. Freezing is an effective way to stabilize collections for days or even months; it stops mold growth, ink running, dye transfer, and swelling. If possible, use a commercial freezer that provides sub-zero freezing or a home freezer. A refrigerated truck may at least keep materials cool enough to prevent mold growth.

ON-SITE DEHUMIDIFICATION—A useful technique for drying damp library and archival collections without the need to move them. Available from several companies in the United States. Super-dry air is pumped into the building and moist air drawn out.

RINSING—Mud or dirt; rinse items under a gentle stream of clean running water or gently agitate them in containers filled with water, before drying. Never scrub items in a way that might drive dirt in deeper. Use a sponge/soft cloth to blot off mud and debris. Hold books and file folders closed while rinsing.

VACUUM DRYING—Also called "thermal drying." Available from many companies in the U.S. Items are dried in a vacuum chamber, often at temperatures above 100°F. Slower than vacuum freeze-drying, but generally less expensive. Because high temperatures accelerate aging, *this method should not be used for library and archival materials.*

VACUUM FREEZE-DRYING—Frozen items are placed in a vacuum chamber and dried at below-freezing temperatures to minimize swelling and distortion. Generally provides the most satisfactory results and is recommended for library and archival materials. This service is available throughout the United States.

Emergency History

In the space below, describe emergencies that have occurred. Include the date, the location within the building, the number of materials affected, recovery procedures, and the resources (time, money, personnel, etc.) needed for complete recovery from the emergency. Also note any vendors or suppliers used in recovery actions and evaluate their performance for future reference. This section should be updated after any emergency occurrence. Use extra copies of this form as necessary.

_____

_____

_____

_____

_____

_____

_____

_____

_____

_____

_____

_____

_____

_____

_____

_____

_____

_____

_____

_____

_____

_____

_____

_____

Locations Where This Plan Is on File

Location	Responsible for Updates

In-House:

_____

_____

_____

_____

Off-Site:

_____

_____

_____

_____

Acknowledgements

This *Library Disaster Plan* template was prepared by the California Preservation Program and supported by the U.S. Institute of Museum and Library Services under the provisions of the Library Services and Technology Act, administered by the California State Library.

Elements of the plan were developed by Sheryl Davis, (UC Riverside), Julie Page, (UC San Diego), and the Amigos Preservation Service (APS), with information gathered from the following sources:

John P. Barton and Johanna G. Wellheiser, eds. *An Ounce of Prevention: A Handbook on Disaster Contingency Planning for Archives, Libraries and Record Centers.* Toronto: Toronto Area Archivists Group Education Foundation, 1985.

Minnesota Historical Society. *Disaster Preparedness Plan: Recovery Procedures for the Minnesota History Center* (revised for outside distribution). Saint Paul: Minnesota Historical Society, January 1, 1994.

Heritage Preservation. *Emergency Response.*

Appendix U

Sample Reference Policy: River Hills Archives

Information for Researchers

The River Hills Archives acquires and preserves records created by, for, and about the community of River Hills. These records include official records of the local government, manuscripts, books, campus newspapers, photographs, maps, sound recordings, and moving images concerned with the history of the community.

Hours

The archives is open to researchers on Mondays and Thursdays from 1 p.m. to 5 p.m. Access at other times may be arranged with the archivist.

Registration

All researchers are requested to register, providing their name, address, signature, student or other identification number, and their research topic.

Regulations

1. Coats, briefcases, parcels, and personal books are not permitted in the research area. Please leave them at the registration desk.
2. No ink of any kind may be used in the research area; use pencils only. Typewriters, computers, scanners, cameras or other devices may be brought into the archives and used in the typing room at the discretion of the archivist.
3. Smoking, eating, and drinking are prohibited in the archives.
4. All archival materials must be handled carefully: use only one folder at a time and keep the papers in their existing order. Do not place books or volumes face down. Do not lean or press on archival materials. Do not trace maps or other records.
5. No material in the archives may be removed from the research area.
6. Persons requesting access to restricted materials must contact the person or agency imposing the restrictions. The archives cannot permit access to these materials without written authority.
7. Researchers are advised that it is their responsibility, not the archives, to obtain copyright clearance to publish or otherwise reproduce or distribute archival material. Whenever possible, the archivist will provide the names and addresses of copyright holders.
8. If publishing material from the archives, please credit the archives: River Hills Archives, accession or record group number, volume number, file number, title of document or names of correspondents, and date, as follows:

River Hills Community Archives, Acc. 986.87, vol. 6, file 3, Report of the Mayor's Office, June 12, 1956.

Photocopying

Unless restricted or protected by copyright conditions, photocopies of material will be supplied for research purposes at the rate of 10 cents per page. Although there is no precise limit on the number of pages, it may not be possible to fill an order on the day requested, and the Archives reserves the right to carry out the work over a period of time.

Users requiring copies of photographs, maps, sound recordings, or moving image materials are requested to consult the archivist about conditions and charges. Researchers are not allowed to copy archival materials using their own cameras or other equipment.

Appendix V

Sample Researcher Registration Form

Researcher Registration

A valid form of identification must accompany this form.

Name _____

Address _____

City _____ State _____ Zip _____

Phone number _____ E-mail _____

Regulations

1. Coats, briefcases, parcels, and personal books are not permitted in the research area. Please leave them at the registration desk.
2. No ink of any kind may be used in the research area; use pencils only. Typewriters, computers, scanners, cameras, or other devices may be brought into the archives and used at the discretion of the archivist.
3. Smoking, eating, and drinking are prohibited in the archives.
4. All archival materials must be handled carefully: use only one folder at a time and keep the papers in their existing order. Do not place books or volumes face down. Do not lean or press on archival materials. Do not trace maps or other records.
5. No material in the archives may be removed from the research area.
6. Persons requesting access to restricted materials must contact the person or agency imposing the restrictions. The archives cannot permit access to these materials without written authority.
7. Researchers are advised that it is their responsibility, not the archives, to obtain copyright clearance to publish or otherwise reproduce or distribute archival material. Whenever possible, the archivist will provide the names and addresses of copyright holders.

I agree to the above listed regulations.

_____

Signature   Date

Appendix W

Photocopying policy of the Eva G. Farris Special Collections and Schlachter University Archives, W. Frank Steely Library, Northern Kentucky University
https://steelyarchives.nku.edu/aboutus/policiesandguidelines/copyingpolicy.html

Photocopying Policy

- All photocopying will be done by Special Collections and University Archives Department staff.
- Some archival paper records, photographs and books are in poor or fragile condition. The Archives reserves the right to refuse to copy such items if the staff member determines that copying will damage the material.
- The Archives reserves the right to refuse to copy material which in our judgment would violate copyright law. Copies of entire books, manuscript collections, or archival record groups will not be made.
- Every effort will be made to complete photocopying requests before a researcher departs, but in case of large volume requests, the Archives reserves the right to complete requests by the end of the following business day.
- Please refer to the most current fee schedule for photocopying costs. Cash payment only please. Our photocopying machine does not have an Allcard reader.

Appendix X
Mount Holyoke Reproduction Services Policy

Reproduction Services

Researchers can request scans and paper copies for personal use. These reproductions will be made by Archives and Special Collections staff after it is determined by the staff that the copying or scanning process will not damage the materials in question. The Archives and Special Collections staff reserves the right not to accept a copy order if, in the staff's judgement, fulfilling the order will involve violation of United States Copyright Law (Title 17, U.S.C.). For further information please see our copyright statement.

To Request Scans or Paper Copies

1. Complete the Photocopy and Scan Request Form [includes link to form] for photocopies and reference-quality scans; or complete the High-Resolution Digital Image Request Form [includes link to form] for publication-quality digital images.
2. Email the form to Archives and Special Collections [includes email address].

Permission to Publish

Reproductions (physical or digital) may be published or made publicly available with the prior permission of the Mount Holyoke College Archives and Special Collections.

Mount Holyoke Copyright Statement

The Mount Holyoke College Archives and Special Collections offers access to its collections in order to support education and scholarship. Some materials in these collections may be protected by the U.S. Copyright Law (Title 17, U.S.C. [link included]). Additionally, the use or reproduction of some materials may be restricted by terms of gift or purchase agreements, donor restrictions, privacy and publicity rights, and college policy.

Transmission or reproduction of protected items beyond that allowed by fair use requires the written permission of the copyright owners.

Whenever possible, the Archives and Special Collections will provide information about copyright owners and other restrictions in the catalog records and finding aids. The Mount Holyoke College Archives and Special Collections may not own rights to material in its collections. It is the researcher's obligation to determine and satisfy copyright or other use restrictions when publishing or otherwise distributing materials found in the Archives' collections.

Appendix Y

University of Illinois Archives Use and Reproduction Policy

Use and Reproduction Policy

As a cultural research repository at a public university, the University of Illinois Archives encourages the use of its materials by students, scholars, faculty staff, and members of the public. To protect the integrity of archival material and allow staff to meet user needs equitably, we have developed the following policies.

Services for Local and Remote Users

1. University departments and offices: Telephone and email reference service will be provided free of charge within reasonable limits. In the case of complicated and/or lengthy requests, Archives staff will provide advice and assistance in identifying appropriate sources and request that departmental staff visit the Archives.
2. Individuals affiliated with the University who are engaged in classroom instruction or scholarly/personal research are encouraged to visit the archives. Limited telephone reference service may be available, but all users are encouraged to place their requests in the form of an e-mail or letter. Archival staff are available to meet with students, faculty, and staff regarding research projects, assistance in identifying sources, or general classroom instruction.
3. Individuals outside the University who are unable to visit campus will receive up to twenty minutes of reference service free of charge after they have placed their requests in the form of an email or letter. Additional remote services are available for the rates shown on the fee schedule.

Use and Reproduction

1. All materials are for in-room use only. Archival materials and other items may NOT BE CHARGED OUT except to authorized representatives of the University department which created or donated the item(s), and ONLY for a period not to exceed twenty-four hours. Materials from faculty papers and other manuscript collections may be charged out ONLY to the item's donor. All charge-outs made according to these exceptions also require the permission of an archivist. Temporary loans of artifacts and documents for exhibitions and special performance programs may be requested by cultural institutions and organizations at least one month in advance of the event. These requests will be fulfilled only with approval of the Archives professional staff, and managed by the completion of all forms in compliance with the "Management of Library Materials in Transit" policy.
2. Users may photocopy items that are in good condition on the public coin/card-operated photocopier in the reference room, provided that care is exercised in handling the originals. Archival staff should be consulted prior to photocopying any item to ensure that brittle or large items are not damaged. Staff reserve the right to disallow photocopying of any item. In lieu of photocopying, researchers may use their own hand-held camera to make "fair use"/study copies. Tripods and scanning of images is not allowed except by Archives staff according to the fee schedule.
3. Fees for photocopying completed by archival staff are shown in the attached schedule. All users ordering photocopies are required to read and sign the *Agreement on*

Duplicating Textual Archival and Manuscript Materials and to pay in advance. Limits may be placed on orders based on staff availability.

4. Reproduction of photographs, audio, and audiovisual materials are governed by the separate *Agreement to Conditions for Use of Photographic, Musical, Motion Picture, and Audiovisual Works.*

5. Where publication, web presentation, public performance, or broadcast of the items is anticipated, a separate usage fee may apply under the Library's policy on use fees for publication. Archives' staff may refuse to provide copies of an item until appropriate use fees for publication are paid. All images provided for orders of materials for web presentation, broadcast, or filming/videotaping will be delivered with an in-image credit line and file reference number.

6. It is the user's responsibility to obtain the University's and/or other copyright holder's permission before using the material for any purpose other than private study, scholarship, or research.

Payment

Orders will not be completed until payment is received. The University Archives accepts checks and major credit cards. Checks should be payable to the University Archives in U.S. currency and mailed to University of Illinois Archives, 19 Library 1408 W. Gregory Dr., Urbana, IL 61801. Please include a copy of correspondence relating to your order. Credit card information may be faxed or phoned to the archives. Please do not send via email.

Appendix Z

Reference Policy Template

[Name of Program]

Information for Researchers

[This section provides background information for users about your mission and what you collect. It should be based on your mission statement.]

Hours

[Clearly state the hours that your facility is open and, if you accommodate users "by appointment" at other times, you should state how the users can make these alternative arrangements.]

Registration

[Explain briefly the registration process and the information users will be required to provide, including whether or not you require them to present valid identification.]

Regulations

[What follows are boilerplate regulations for using historical collections. You will need to review each of them carefully and make appropriate revisions for your own situation; delete any that don't apply; and add any specific rules that aren't included here.]

1. Coats, briefcases, parcels, and personal books are not permitted in the research area. Please leave them at the registration desk.
2. No ink of any kind may be used in the research area; use pencils only. Computers may be brought into the archives and used at the discretion of the archivist.
3. Smoking, eating, and drinking are prohibited in the archives.
4. All archival materials must be handled carefully: use only one folder at a time and keep the papers in their existing order. Do not place books or volumes face down. Do not lean or press on archival materials. Do not trace maps or other records.
5. No material in the archives may be removed from the research area.
6. Persons requesting access to restricted materials must contact the person or agency imposing the restrictions. The archives cannot permit access to these materials without written authority.
7. Researchers are advised that it is their responsibility, not the archives, to obtain copyright clearance to publish or otherwise reproduce or distribute archival material. Whenever possible, the archivist will provide the names and addresses of copyright holders.
8. If publishing material from the archives, please credit the archives: [citation format and sample citation should be included]

Copying

Unless restricted or protected by copyright conditions, copies of material will be supplied for research purposes at the rate of [amount here] cents per page. Although there is no precise limit on the number of pages, it may not be possible to fill an order on the day requested, and the archives reserves the right to carry out the work over a period of time.

Users requiring copies of photographs, maps, sound recordings, or moving image materials are requested to consult the archivist about conditions and charges. Researchers are not allowed to copy archival materials using their own cameras, scanners, or other equipment.

Appendix AA

Call Slip Example

ABC Archives
123 Main St., Any Town, OH 44444

Call Slip–Number XXX

Collection title or author/creator:
Collection or series number:
Box number:
Researcher's name:
Table number:
Date/time:
Reference staff member providing access to and inspecting the collection:
Condition of collection:
Notes:

Appendix AB

Press Release Template

[Note: Press releases are generally sent out on organizational letterhead; for second sheets use a quality bond paper. Press releases *do not* include cover letters and they are *not* signed.]

PRESS RELEASE   **FOR IMMEDIATE RELEASE**

For more information, contact: [DATE], 20XX
[Name of internal contact]
[Name of organization]
[Phone number] (   ) (voice)
[Phone number] (   ) (fax)
[Email address]

[Headline Goes Here, Initial Cap, Bold]
[CITY, STATE].—[Date], 20XX—[Text goes here, double spaced, indented paragraphs].

[Lead paragraph: The first paragraph needs to grab the reader's attention and should contain the relevant information to your message such as the five W's (who, what, when, where, why).]

[Text: The main body of your press release where your message should fully develop.]

If the press release is more than one page long, use the word:

—more—

centered at the bottom of the page, then continue the page on the next page with a brief description of the headline, and page number like this:

[*Shortened headline*]–Page 2

[Your last paragraph should be an organizational boilerplate, which is a brief description of the organization, and any information you want readers to know about it, such as what type of organization it is, its mission, etc.]

[At the end of the release, put the three pound signs centered at the bottom. This lets your reader know they've come to the end.]

# # #

Appendix AC

Sample Loan of Documents for Exhibition Policy

Loan Agreement

Applicants for loans must meet the conditions set out below and sign the accompanying loan form.

General Loan Procedures

1. A request for loan of material must be received not less than six months prior to the opening date of the exhibition. This is to allow sufficient time for appropriate conditions, checks, paperwork, and exhibit preparation to be completed.
2. The normal loan period is three months.
3. In cases where a document is unable to be lent, due to its condition, size, format, original photographic material, and so forth, a good-quality facsimile will be suggested as an alternative.
4. The loaned materials will be transported to and from the exhibit site via a method agreed upon by both parties. The preferred method is for a staff member to accompany the materials to and from the exhibit.
5. The borrower will be responsible for all expenses incurred by both parties in making the loan. These will include the following:
   a. Standard charges for conservation treatment (if necessary), mounting, and packing
   b. Standard charges for the cost of facsimile copies
   c. Insurance, when required
   d. An estimate of these costs will be provided before the loan agreement is finalized
6. Documents are lent for the purpose of public exhibition only and may not be made available for study or other purposes without the consent of the lending institution. Once documents have been mounted in the exhibit area they must be left undisturbed, except in case of emergency, until the exhibit is dismantled.
7. Documents are lent to a single organization. No traveling exhibits are permitted.
8. No mark in pencil, ink, paint, or any other material may be made on any document lent, nor may any such existing mark be obliterated. No adhesives of any kind may be applied to the documents. All materials used within the cases, with which the documents may come in contact, must be acid free.
9. Any caption used for display purposes and any description given in publications must state that the document(s) is on loan from the loaning institution.
10. Irrespective of the terms of the loan, the borrowing organization shall return any or all of the exhibited material at the written request of the lending organization.

Security

1. Exhibition premises shall in all respects be safe and secure and adequate safeguards must be available before any items are borrowed.
2. First time applications for a loan may be subject to an evaluation by the security advisor and/or preservation officer.
3. All documents must be displayed in locked showcases. Any other method of display, particularly wall mounted, must be discussed with the preservation officer.

4. No conservation measures of any description may be carried out by the borrowing organization.

Environment

1. Written assurance must be provided that the environmental conditions are suitable for the exhibits and will stipulate any necessary changes. The temperature in the exhibition should not exceed 70 F, the relative humidity should be 55% +/- 5%, and the lighting should not exceed 50 lux.
2. No food, drink, or smoking can be allowed in the exhibition area.

Insurance against Damage

1. The lending organization will create a report detailing the condition of the item being loaned including images prior to the loan period.
2. The lending organization will determine the insurance value required in all cases. The organization hosting the exhibit is required to insure the items during the loan period including transportation to and from the exhibit space. Proof of such insurance will be required before the loan is made.

Packing and Display

1. The lending organization will pack all items for transport to and from the exhibition. Such packaging must be stored safely by the borrower during the course of the exhibition to enable it to be used for the return of the exhibits.
2. Techniques for mounting the display will be agreed upon and outlined in the loan agreement. Wherever possible the items will travel ready mounted.
3. A condition report will accompany each item on loan and must be agreed with the borrower before display. It must be checked and agreed at the end of the exhibition.

Answers to Quizzes

Chapter 1 Quiz Answers

1. B	3. D	5. D	7. B	9. E
2. D	4. D	6. A	8. C	10. B

Chapter 5 Quiz Answers

1. A	3. A	5. B	7. C	9. C
2. B	4. B	6. B	8. B	10. B

Chapter 6 Quiz Answers

1. This is almost a trick question; if you do not preserve an archival collection you have nothing to provide access to, at the same time there is no reason to preserve an archival collection if you are not going to provide access to it. It is a fine line but preservation comes first.
2. C

3. C
4. B
5. C
6. A
7. C
8. B
9. A
10. B

Chapter 8 Quiz Answers

1. Storing archival records in archival quality acid-free, lignin-free, buffered folders and boxes
2. A) drastic climate change   B) leaks from roof   C) Low humidity   D) Fire hazard
3. A) Moisture—high humidity   B) Pest friendly environment
   C) Trickle-down effect—water problems end up in the basement
4. A) Store collections 4 to 6 inches off the ground   B) Put plastic sheeting over boxes
   C) Monitor for pests   D) Install dehumidifier   E) Install water monitors
   F) Monitor electrical equipment
5. Thirty percent to 50 percent
6. The goal is to reduce both intensity and amount of exposure to light—turn off lights when possible, use curtains or shades, expose collections to light only when needed

Chapter 10 Quiz Answers

1. Access is a privilege, not a right. Access is granted provided the individual agrees to follow your reference policies and use rules. Access to governmental records may be a right defined in public records law, but researchers still have to follow reference policies and use rules to access records.
2. Preservation is more important than access. If you do not preserve the historical records in your care, you will have nothing to provide access to.
3. Research on demand is not required. It is often something that is needed, but it is not a necessity.
4. False—there is no reason for an archive to exist if it does not provide reference services to the collections it holds. Some collections may be closed (restricted) for a period of time for various reasons, but an archive acquires and preserves such collections based on providing reference to them in the future.
5. To listen carefully and know your collections.
6. To make sure that all the items are present and to make sure the physical condition of the collection is such that it can be used without further harm.
7. No—it is too easy for them to harm a collection when making copies.
8. A—the historic records program should make it clear that it is the researchers responsibility to determine the copyright holder and to obtain clearance to publish copyrighted materials.

Chapter 11 Quiz Answers

1. Check your call slips or other collection usage records
2. Making sure researchers have a good experience using your archives
3. To be your programs representative—its ambassador
4. A key method of spreading your news and making announcements to your community
5. A record that follows the Machine Readable Cataloging standard
6. Records describing collections from many organizations that are made available to a wide community via searchable databases
7. Security and preservation issues
8. What you need, why you need it, and how much it is going to cost—a needs statement
9. Fun and interesting
10. The grant funders requirements

Chapter 12 Quiz Answers

1. This is kind of a trick question. The simple answer is no, a record is a record; it doesn't matter what format the record is in. However, they are many differences between digital records and nondigital records including the media the digital record is imprinted on, the temporal nature of digital media, and the need for the correct software and hardware to record the digital record.
2. Native or born digital records and converted or re-formatted digital records.
3. Data about data—information about an information resource.
4. The selection, preservation, maintenance, collection, and archiving of digital assets—an ongoing set of actions taken to ensure continued access to digital records.

5. That you get started doing it. Maintenance is the heart of digital curation, but the most important thing is that you get started doing digital curation.
6. Reliability—is the record what it purports to be? Can I have faith in the record, is it real, can I believe it? Was it created as it claims it was? Will the record be accepted as evidence in court?
7. Authenticity—proven reliability over time.
8. Context, content, and structure. Context—the circumstances surrounding the creation of the record. Content—the imprint of the record. Structure—the arrangement of the content.
9. A fixity check defines the number and arrangement of the digital record's bits and bytes.
10. Keeping a second complete copy of all your digital holdings (records and metadata) for preservation purposes. Access to this copy of your digital holdings should be very strictly controlled—it is your last safeguard, your protection from all evil. Be vigilant in protecting it.

Chapter 13 Quiz Answers

1. Digitization is an access tool with preservation implications
2. True
3. False
4. Optical character recognition
5. Dots per inch
6. True
7. False
8. Preservation always trumps access; it is more important to preserve archival materials than it is to provide access to them
9. Derivative copies are digital use copies created from the master digital image
10. False

Index

About the Author

Charlie Arp has a BA and an MA in history from Ohio University, where he specialized in archival studies. From 1991 to 2003, he worked at the Ohio Historical Society, where he held a variety of positions including head of reference, assistant state archivist, and state archivist. In 2003, Charlie was hired by the Battelle Memorial Institute as enterprise content manager. In 2015, he tested and validated the use of an electronic management program to enable Battelle to use electronic records as part of submissions to the FDA. In early 2016, Charlie started an archival and records management consulting firm.

Made in the USA
Columbia, SC
24 August 2020

16990037R00193